In an effort to **go green**, Oxford University Press is providing a **Sampler Edition** of *Of the People: A History of the United States*, Fourth Edition. This **Sampler includes** chapters 15–20, the full table of contents and front matter, and the index. By using less paper in this Sampler, we're saving more trees. By providing the full text in a digital format, we lessen carbon emissions with reduced shipping. The cost savings from these green initiatives will help fund our mission to support Oxford University's objective of excellence in research, scholarship, and education.

If you are considering the text for adoption and would like to see more, you can view the complete text via eBook or receive a full printed copy of the text. Simply contact your Oxford University representative or call 800.280.0280 to request a copy.

Less paper = more trees saved

eBook = no carbon emission from shipping

Cost savings = more money to fund OUP's mission

What's New to the

AMERICAN PORTRAIT

John Turchinetz

In January 1946, John Turchinetz finally headed home to Boston, Massachusetts, from World War II. Just out of high school, this son of a Romanian-born father and Ukrainian-born mother had joined the Navy three years earlier at the age of 18. Serving as a seaman aboard the cruiser named for his home city, John had manned an antiaircraft gun, suffered a disabling injury, and won medals in the Pacific. After the Japanese surrender, he and some of his shipmates from the *Boston* toured the city of Hiroshima, devastated by the first atomic bomb. "It was unbelievable," the seaman recalled. Like other Americans, John and his shipmates had had enough of war. "We were glad that it was over," he said. "We wanted peace."

At first, they found it. Back in Boston, John had a joyful reunion with his family. The mayor threw a big party for the crew of the *Boston*. Living with his parents again, John went to work at the federal Navy Yard in the harbor. The government needed the veteran, but not his beloved ship, in the new era of peace: the *Boston* was taken out of service—"mothballed," they called it. Although John, like many veterans, "felt a little different," his neighborhood and his country seemed the same. After the experience of war, people were friendly and united. "We were trying to help each other," John remembered. "We were trying to be normal."

The sense of normality—the feeling of friendliness, unity, and peace—did not last long at all. Before the end of 1946, the cold war, a tense confrontation with the Soviet Union, began to disrupt American life. Soviet influence quickly spread in Eastern Europe. The USSR absorbed Ukraine, the homeland of John Turchinetz's father, and took territory from Romania, his mother's homeland, which then became a Soviet ally. Convinced the Soviets would keep trying to expand their power and spread communism across Europe, US leaders challenged their former allies. While the cold war developed, Americans also faced the task of maintaining prosperity in peacetime. Laborers, women, and African Americans struggled to preserve and extend their rights and opportunities. President Harry Truman and the Democratic Party struggled as well to preserve their power and implement a liberal agenda.

The cold war quickly became the dominant fact of national life in the late 1940s. To contain Soviet and communist expansion, the US government took unprecedented peacetime actions. But massive foreign aid, new alliances, and a military buildup did not prevent the cold

AMERICAN LANDSCAPE

"Gitmo"

From the camera eye of a satellite miles above, Guantánamo Bay stood out from the rest of eastern Cuba. The inlet was a horseshoe of brown and gray amid the lush green of the island and the bright blue of the Atlantic. To the administration of George W. Bush, Guantánamo Bay was a gray area, too: one of the few places on earth that was American and yet not American, a drab anomaly perfect for one of the most controversial phases of the war on terror.

Guantánamo Bay, 520 miles from Miami, Florida, had been an anomaly for more than a century. After the Spanish-American War of 1898, the US government had taken the spot for a well-protected naval base. The Cuban-American Treaty of 1903 effectively gave America perpetual control over the base. For less than $4,000 a year, the United States could keep the facility until both Washington and Cuba agreed to end

base and the only one in a Communist country.

Gitmo became less and less valuable over the years. As the cold war ended and the United States closed down military bases, there was no real need for a naval installation so close to the US mainland. Then the war on terror began. The Bush administration needed to put captured Taliban fighters and other "enemy combatants" somewhere safe. It was too risky to leave detainees in unstable Afghanistan or Iraq, but it was also too risky to bring them to the United States, where courts, Congress, and public opinion could interfere in their imprisonment. So the Bush administration looked, in the words of Secretary of Defense Donald Rumsfeld, for "the least worst place" to hold those captured in the war on terror.

They found it at Guantánamo Bay. The US military controlled the base, but US

AMERICA AND THE WORLD

American Tourists in Cold War Europe

"THIS IS YOUR YEAR FOR EUROPE," an American Airlines magazine ad proclaimed in 1948. "Anyone with only a week or two—or even a few days—can enjoy a fascinating trip to the 'Old World,' traveling by time-saving American Flagship. Don't put off that dreamed-of-journey abroad. Make this your year—your family's year—for Europe!"

Hundreds of thousands of Americans were eager to follow the airline's advice. The Great Depression and then World War II had reduced overseas tourism to almost nothing. But now, Americans were prosperous again and war-torn Europe was at peace and eager for dollars. Technological advances made steam-powered ships and propeller-driven airplanes, such as American Airlines' Flagship, faster and more affordable than ever. In 1949, over half a million Americans traveled overseas; in 1955, that number soared past a million. With the advent of jet-powered air travel, that figure would reach over 2 million by 1961.

Various impulses spurred American tourists. Americans wanted to relax, enjoy themselves, and explore exotic places. A nation of immigrants, Americans wanted

For the US government, American tourism represented something else altogether: a weapon in the cold war. In a letter to recipients of new passports, President Eisenhower explained that "you represent us all in bringing assurance to the people you meet that the United States is a friendly nation and one dedicated to the promotion of the well-being and security of the community of nations." Echoing that sentiment, Americans and foreigners alike spoke of US tourists as "unofficial ambassadors" abroad.

Those ambassadors did a mixed job. In Europe, an unflattering stereotype of the American tourist emerged. "He is a mobile human armed with cameras and broad-rimmed sunglasses, dressed-up in many-colored shirts and multi-colored neckties, who chewing-gums his way across an old and alien continent," wrote a European tour guide. American travelers were stereotyped as too loud, too critical, too unsophisticated, and too demanding: they actually wanted cold beer and private bathrooms!

Americans pushed back. Some of the criticism, they suggested, was the product of envy and insecurity: Europeans, their nations' wealth and power diminishing

on such a trip becomes magnified and is finally blamed on the United States as a whole."

American travelers developed another image, one rooted in the 1950s ideal of a democratic United States without social classes. "What the Italians like most about Americans is their free and easy manner," a journalist reported in 1957. "They consider Americans truly democratic, since they show not the slightest trace of class consciousness, and deal considerately and politely with one and all." Despite the reputation of some, the mass of travelers seemed to promote a positive understanding of their country, as US officials hoped. "Americans who are traveling abroad this Summer," said a Swiss teen in 1948, "are good ambassadors."

Travel also helped Americans get past some of their own stereotypes and prejudices. For instance, Americans who traveled to Moscow were in for a surprise. "Many American tourists here profess astonishment . . . that the Russians are people, that they smile and laugh and talk like people, that there are automobiles here. . . ," a writer noted in 1959. "Almost invariably, the Russians a tourist bumps into and talks with are friendly, helpful, deeply curious about the United States."

The encounters appeared to ease some of the cold war tensions and fears of the Soviets, too. "Some Russians who have

Fourth Edition?

STRUGGLES FOR DEMOCRACY

The Russian Attack on Democracy

It was a strange, almost paradoxical aspect of democracy: the simple, even boring act of standing in line and then checking a box or pulling a lever could have a dramatic impact on the future of the richest, most powerful country in the world. For all the attention given to who had the right to vote, Americans seldom devoted much thought to the mechanism of casting a ballot. After states and localities took firm control of the voting process from political parties around the turn of the twentieth century, fears of fraud decreased. With increased federal oversight of elections during and after the civil rights movement, those fears largely vanished.

Then, during the 2016 presidential election, strange, unsettling events occurred. In June, some voters turned up at the polls for California's primary only to find that they were mysteriously no longer registered. Hackers had gotten into the official computer system and altered their voting records. Similar break-ins happened in at least 20 more places around the country before the end of voting in November.

Meanwhile, US intelligence agencies revealed that the Russian government was behind the hacking and release of the emails of Hillary Clinton's campaign manager and the Democratic National Committee. The agencies also disclosed that Russia had used social media to spread false stories in another effort to affect the election. Despite these revelations, President Obama avoided public retaliation against Russia: he did not want to seem to be helping Clinton, who looked likely to win anyway. Instead, the president privately warned Russia's president, Vladimir Putin, not to interfere further.

After Donald Trump's surprising victory, Obama finally took public action. Late in 2016, the United States sanctioned Russian

individuals and groups, seized two Russian compounds in the United States, and ordered 35 Russian diplomatic personnel to leave the country. "Russia's cyber activities were intended to influence the election, erode faith in US democratic institutions, sow doubt about the integrity of our electoral process, and undermine confidence in the institutions of the US government," the White House explained. "These actions are unacceptable and will not be tolerated."

Even so, it was unclear how the United States could stop further Russian activity. It was unclear, too, how to protect the sprawling machinery of elections, much of it computer based, controlled by so many states and communities.

Moreover, Americans were divided about Russian hacking, as they were about so many things in the 2010s. Putin had not only wanted to make Americans lose faith that elections were genuine. The Russian president, who loathed Hillary Clinton for her strong opposition to his country's foreign policy, had also wanted to elect Donald Trump. For Trump and his supporters, stories of Russian hacking and manipulation of social media seemed like an attempt by Democratic sore losers to undermine his legitimacy. But other Americans believed the government should aggressively pursue the Russian campaign. Suspicious of Trump's refusal to criticize Putin or fully acknowledge the Russian hacking, some people believed that the Trump campaign had colluded with Russians to get him elected.

As the nation awaited reports by Congress and the special counsel, information about Russian activity continued to emerge. Facebook admitted that starting the month Trump announced his candidacy in 2015, the company had unknowingly let Russian "troll farms" run fake, divisive advertisements, sometimes pro-Trump, on the social media site. Another Russian source bought ads on Google's Gmail and YouTube platforms.

Americans were left wondering about a distinctively twenty-first century problem: whether a foreign government could use technology to influence voters, keep some from casting ballots, elect a president, and undermine confidence in democracy itself.

■ More than thirty new primary sources

30.6 DONALD TRUMP, EXTRACT OF REMARKS AT A "MAKE AMERICA GREAT AGAIN" RALLY IN HARRISBURG, PENNSYLVANIA (2017)

After his election as president, Donald Trump continued holding campaign-style rallies for his supporters around the country. Feeding off the energy of the crowd, Trump articulated his right-wing populist message in the Rustbelt community of Harrisburg, Pennsylvania. Whom does he blame for the condition of the country?

As you may know, there's another big gathering taking place tonight in Washington, D.C. Did you hear about it?

AUDIENCE: Booo—
THE PRESIDENT: A large group of Hollywood actors and Washington media are consoling each other in a hotel ballroom in our nation's capital right now. (Applause.) They are gathered together for the White House Correspondents Dinner—without the President. (Applause.) And I could not possibly be more thrilled than to be more than 100 miles away from Washington Swamp—(applause)—spending my evening with all of you, and with a much, much larger crowd and much better people. Right? (Applause.) Right?
AUDIENCE: U-S-A! U-S-A!
THE PRESIDENT: And look at the media back there. . . .
AUDIENCE: Booo—
THE PRESIDENT: That's right.
AUDIENCE: CNN Sucks! CNN Sucks!
THE PRESIDENT: Media outlets like CNN and MSNBC are fake news. Fake news . . .
The truth is, there is no place I'd rather be than right here in Pennsylvania to celebrate our 100-day milestone to reflect on an incredible journey together, and to get ready for the great, great battles to come, and that we will win in every case, okay? We will win. (Applause.) Because make no mistake, we are just beginning in our fight to make America great again. (Applause.)
Now, before we talk about my first 100 days, which has been very exciting and very productive, let's rate the media's 100 days. Should we do that? Should we do it? Because, as you know, they are a disgrace. . . .
So just as an example of media, take the totally failing New York Times.
AUDIENCE: Booo—
THE PRESIDENT: But that's what we have. They're incompetent, dishonest people. . .
So here's the story. If the media's job is to be honest and tell the truth, then I think we would all agree the media deserves a very, very, big fat failing grade.
AUDIENCE: Booo—

- To improve narrative flow and to better align with syllabi, the number of Gilded Age chapters has been reduced from three to two

- New and revised coverage throughout (see pp. xxxii-xxxv in the Preface for details)

Economic Change and a Divided Nation

As so often in American history, anxieties about religion, race, and gender partly reflected anxieties about economic change. In the twenty-first century, the implications of deindustrialization, digitization, and globalization became increasingly clear. Despite the recovery from the Great Recession, the economy seemed to divide Americans into unequal groups: the rich and everyone else; men and women; old and young; urban and rural.

Jobs and Growth

By the 2010s, some optimistic forecasts about the information revolution and globalization were not coming true. New technologies and freer trade turned out to be more disruptive than expected. While observers anticipated that globalization would threaten some American manufacturing, they were unprepared for the sharp decline in the twenty-first century. Instead of increasing, jobs in manufacturing dropped 20 percent

- A revised and significantly expanded Chapter 30: "A Nation Transformed," The Twenty-First Century (formerly the Epilogue), that covers the span of years since 2001

"Make America Great Again" Donald Trump rallies his supporters during the 2016 presidential campaign.

- Numerous new photos

Praise for *Of the People*

"This is an excellent book. It covers topics and ideas well, branches into subjects that other books gloss over, appeals to many different groups of students, and can be used not only to teach, but to spur discussion."

—Michael Frawley, *University of Texas of the Permian Basin*

"This is a great book that will bring students into deep discussion about the American story. It is accessible to students and comprehensible enough to make instructors happy."

—Matthew Campbell, *Lone Star College–Cypress Fairbanks*

"*Of the People* is the complete package. Its engaging narrative captures the grand sweep of U.S. history and animates the diverse lives that populate the past. The book is interesting and accessible, and the price is right. The volume also comes with many add-ons that can be useful in the classroom or online."

—Matthew Oyos, *Radford University*

"*Of the People* has some strong themes. In addition, the special features are intriguing and can be effectively woven into classroom discussions, and the selection of primary documents is good."

—Brenden Rensink, *Brigham Young University*

Learning Resources

- **INSTRUCTOR'S RESOURCE MANUAL**
  Includes, for each chapter, a detailed chapter outline, suggested lecture topics, learning objectives, and approximately forty multiple-choice, short-answer, true-or-false, fill-in-the-blank, and essay questions for each chapter

- **POWERPOINTS AND COMPUTERIZED TEST BANK**
  Includes PowerPoint slides and JPEG files for all the maps and photos in the text. The Computerized Test Bank includes all of the test items from the Instructor's Resource Manual.

- **THE US HISTORY VIDEO LIBRARY**
  Produced by Oxford University Press, each 3–5 minute video covers a key topic in U.S. history, from Squanto to John Brown and from Mother Jones to the "disco wars" of the late 1970s/early 1980s. Combining motion pictures, stills, audio clips, and narration, these videos are ideal for both classroom discussion or as online assignments.

- **THE US HISTORY IMAGE LIBRARY**
  Includes more than 2,000 images organized by period, topic, and region.

To view a demo video from the **US History Video Library** or sample images from the **US History Image Library**, go to: **https://oup-arc.com/access/us-history**.

- **OXFORD FIRST SOURCE**
This database includes hundreds of primary source documents in world history. The documents cover a broad variety of political, economic, social, and cultural topics and represent a cross section of American voices. Special effort was made to include as many previously disenfranchised voices as possible. The documents are indexed by date, author, title, and subject. Short documents (one or two pages) are presented in their entirety while longer documents have been carefully edited to highlight significant content. Each document is introduced with a short explanatory paragraph and accompanied by study questions.

A complete **Course Management cartridge** is also available to qualified adopters.

Student Companion Website at www.oup.com/us/oakes-mcgerr: The open-access Online Study Center helps students to review what they have learned from the textbook and explore other resources online. Practice quizzes allow them to assess their knowledge of a topic before a test.

Enhanced Study Resources

Students who purchase a new copy of *Of the People*, Fourth Edition, can redeem an access code to access these additional study resources, at no extra charge:

- Twenty-five quizzes per chapter that offer an explanation and page reference for each question

- A study guide that provides note-taking worksheets and chapter summaries for each chapter

- Animated maps that deepen understanding of key developments in American history. Each animation is accompanied by quiz questions.

- Video quizzes that assess comprehension of key topics in American history

- Students can also purchase access to these enhanced study resources at the Ancillary Resource Center: **www.oup.com/us/oakes-mcgerr**.

Please visit **www.oup.com/us/oakes-mcgerr** for a demo of the enhanced study resources.

- **PRIMARY SOURCE COMPANION AND RESEARCH GUIDE**, a brief online Research Primer with a library of annotated links to primary and secondary sources in U.S. history

- **INTERACTIVE FLASHCARDS**, using key terms and people listed at the end of each chapter; these multimedia cards help students remember who's who and what's what

Of the People:
A History of the
United States,
Fourth Edition,
is available in
these volumes:

VOL. I: TO 1877 (CHAPTERS 1–15)
EBOOK: 978-0-19-093211-4
LOOSE-LEAF: 978-0-19-091062-4
STUDENT EDITION: 978-0-19-091020-4

VOL. II: SINCE 1865 (CHAPTERS 15–30)
EBOOK: 978-0-19-093212-1
LOOSE-LEAF: 978-0-19-091063-1
STUDENT EDITION: 978-0-19-091021-1

WITH SOURCES

VOL. I: TO 1877 *WITH SOURCES*
EBOOK: 978-0-19-093209-1
LOOSE-LEAF: 978-0-19-091012-9
STUDENT EDITION: 978-0-19-090996-3

VOL. II: SINCE 1865 *WITH SOURCES*
EBOOK: 978-0-19-093210-7
LOOSE-LEAF: 978-0-19-091013-6
STUDENT EDITION: 978-0-19-090997-0

Package and Save!

Sources for Of the People (978-0-19-091015-0): Edited by Maxwell Johnson, this two-volume companion sourcebook includes approximately eighty primary sources, both textual and visual. Chapter introductions, document headnotes, and study questions provide learning support. The sourcebook is only **$5.00 per volume** when bundled with *Of the People*.

Of the People V1 + Sourcebook V1 = Pkg ISBN 978-0-19-094139-0
Of the People V2 + Sourcebook V2 = Pkg ISBN 978-0-19-094141-3
Of the People V1 w/ Sources + Sourcebook V1 = Pkg ISBN 978-0-19-094140-6
Of the People V2 w/ Sources + Sourcebook V2 = Pkg ISBN 978-0-19-094142-0

Mapping United States History: A Coloring and Exercise Book (978-0-19-092166-8): Providing both full-color reference maps and eighty outline maps, this two-volume coloring and exercise book offers students opportunities to strengthen their geographical and spatial-learning skills. *Mapping United States History* is **FREE** when bundled with *Of the People*.

Of the People V1 + Mapping V1 = Pkg ISBN 978-0-19-094184-0
Of the People V2 + Mapping V2 = Pkg ISBN 978-0-19-094183-3
Of the People V1 w/ Sources + Mapping V1 =
Pkg ISBN 978-0-19-094185-7
Of the People V2 w/ Sources + Mapping V2 =
Pkg 978-0-19-094186-4

Save your students **20%** when you package *Of the People* with any other Oxford book!

Suggested titles:

Writing History: A Guide for Students, Fifth Edition, by William Kelleher Storey

The Information-Literate Historian: A Guide to Research for History Students, Third Edition, by Jenny Presnell

Of the People

Of the People

A HISTORY OF THE UNITED STATES   *Fourth Edition*
WITH SOURCES

VOLUME I to 1877

Michael McGerr

Jan Ellen Lewis

James Oakes

Nick Cullather

Mark Summers

Camilla Townsend

Karen M. Dunak

New York   Oxford
Oxford University Press

Oxford University Press is a department of the University of Oxford.
It furthers the University's objective of excellence in research, scholarship,
and education by publishing worldwide. Oxford is a registered trademark of
Oxford University Press in the UK and certain other countries.

Published in the United States of America by Oxford University Press
198 Madison Avenue, New York, NY 10016, United States of America.

For titles covered by Section 112 of the US Higher Education
Opportunity Act, please visit www.oup.com/us/he for the latest
information about pricing and alternate formats.

ISBN: 978-0-19-090996-3

9 8 7 6 5 4 3 2 1
Printed by LSC Communications, United States of America

Jeanne Boydston
1944–2008
Historian, Teacher, Friend

Brief Contents

Contents

CHAPTER 2 Colonial Outposts, 1550–1650   32

CHAPTER 3 The English Come to Stay, 1600–1660   60

CHAPTER **4** Continental Empires, **1660–1720**   88

CHAPTER 5 The Eighteenth-Century World, 1700–1775   124

CHAPTER 6 Conflict in the Empire, 1713–1774   156

CHAPTER 7 Creating a New Nation, 1775–1788   188

CHAPTER 8 Contested Republic, 1789–1800   224

CHAPTER 9   A Republic in Transition, 1800–1819   256

CHAPTER 10 Jacksonian Democracy, **1820–1840**   **288**

CHAPTER 11   Reform and Conflict, 1820–1848   330

CHAPTER 12 Manifest Destiny, 1836–1848   360

CHAPTER 13 The Politics of Slavery, 1848–1860   388

CHAPTER 14   A War for Union and Emancipation, 1861–1865   420

CHAPTER 15 Reconstructing a Nation, 1865–1877   458

Appendices

Maps

Features

Paying for War (Chapter 6)

Mercenaries in Global Perspective (Chapter 7)

Frederick Douglass Tours the British Isles (Chapter 11)

John Riley and the Mexican War (Chapter 12)

Slavery as a Foreign Policy (Chapter 13)

Reconstructing America's Foreign Policy (Chapter 15)

STRUGGLES FOR DEMOCRACY

Native Americans Debate the Question of the Europeans (Chapter 1)

The French and the Indians Learn to Compromise (Chapter 2)

The First African Arrivals Exercise Some Rights (Chapter 3)

Maryland's Colonists Demand a New Government (Chapter 4)

Books Become More Accessible (Chapter 5)

The Boston Massacre (Chapter 6)

The Ratification of the Constitution (Chapter 7)

Sedition and the Limits of Dissent (Chapter 8)

The Gabriel Revolt (Chapter 9)

The Federal Government Responds to Abolitionism (Chapter 10)

The Seneca Falls Convention (Chapter 11)

Mexicans in California Lose Their Rights (Chapter 12)

The Settling and Unsettling of Kansas (Chapter 13)

The Citizen Soldier Learns a Profession (Chapter 14)

An Incident at Coushatta, August 1874 (Chapter 15)

Preface

At Gettysburg, Pennsylvania, on November 19, 1863, President Abraham Lincoln dedicated a memorial to the more than 3,000 Union soldiers who had died turning back a Confederate invasion in the first days of July. There were at least a few ways that the president could have justified the sad loss of life in the third year of a brutal war dividing North and South. He could have said it was necessary to destroy the Confederacy's cherished institution of slavery, to punish southerners for seceding from the United States, or to preserve the nation intact. Instead, at this crucial moment in American history, Lincoln gave a short, stunning speech about democracy. The president did not use the word, but he offered its essence. The term *democracy* came from the ancient Greek word *demos*—for "the people." To honor the dead of Gettysburg, Lincoln called on northerners to ensure "that government of the people, by the people, for the people, shall not perish from the earth."

With these words, Lincoln put democracy at the center of the Civil War and at the center of American history. The authors of this book share his belief in the centrality of democracy; his words, "of the people," give our book its title and its main theme. We see American history as a story "of the people," of their struggles to shape their lives and their land.

Our choice of theme does not mean we believe that America has always been a democracy. Clearly, it has not. As Lincoln gave the Gettysburg Address, most African Americans still lived in slavery. American women, North and South, lacked rights that many men enjoyed; for all their disagreements, white southerners and northerners viewed Native Americans as enemies. Neither do we believe that there is only a single definition of democracy, either in the narrow sense of a particular form of government or in the larger one of a society whose members participate equally in its creation. Although Lincoln defined the northern cause as a struggle for democracy, southerners believed it was anything but democratic to force them to remain in the Union at gunpoint. As bloody draft riots in New York City in July 1863 made clear, many northern men thought it was anything but democratic to force them to fight in Lincoln's armies. Such disagreements have been typical of American history. For more than 500 years, people have struggled over whose vision of life in the New World would prevail.

It is precisely such struggles that offer the best angle of vision for seeing and understanding the most important developments in the nation's history. In particular, the democratic theme concentrates attention on the most fundamental concerns of history: people and power.

Lincoln's words serve as a reminder of the basic truth that history is about people. Across the 30 chapters of this book, we write extensively about complex events. But we also write in the awareness that these developments are only abstractions unless they are grounded in the lives of people. The test of a historical narrative, we believe, is whether its characters are fully rounded, believable human beings.

The choice of Lincoln's words also reflects our belief that history is about power. To ask whether America was democratic at some point in the past is to ask how much power various groups of people had to make their lives and their nation. Such questions of power necessarily take us to political processes, to the ways in which people work separately and collectively to enforce their will. We define politics quite broadly in this book. With the feminists of the 1960s, we believe that "the personal is the political," that power relations shape people's lives in private as well as in public. *Of the People* looks for democracy in the living room as well as the legislature, and in the bedroom as well as the business office.

Focusing on democracy, people, and power, we have necessarily written as wide-ranging a history as possible. In the features and in the main text, *Of the People* conveys both the unity and the great diversity of the American people across time and place. We chronicle the racial and ethnic groups who have shaped America, differences of religious and regional identity, the changing nature of social classes, and the different ways that gender identities have been constructed over the centuries.

While treating different groups in their distinctiveness, we have integrated them into the broader narrative as much as possible. A true history "of the people" means not only acknowledging their individuality and diversity but also showing their inter-relationships and their roles in the larger narrative. More integrated coverage of Native Americans, African Americans, Latinos, and other minority groups appears throughout the fourth edition.

Of the People also offers comprehensive coverage of the different spheres of human life—cultural as well as governmental, social as well as economic, environmental as well as military. This commitment to comprehensiveness is a reflection of our belief that all aspects of human existence are the stuff of history. It is also an expression of the fundamental theme of the book: the focus on democracy leads naturally to the study of people's struggles for power in every dimension of their lives. Moreover, the democratic approach emphasizes the interconnections between the different aspects of Americans' lives; we cannot understand politics and government without tracing their connection to economics, religion, culture, art, sexuality, and so on.

The economic connection is especially important. *Of the People* devotes much attention to economic life, to the ways in which Americans have worked and saved and spent. Economic power, the authors believe, is basic to democracy. Americans' power to shape their lives and their country has been greatly affected by whether they were farmers or hunters, plantation owners or slaves, wage workers or capitalists, domestic servants or bureaucrats. The authors do not see economics as an impersonal, all-conquering force; instead, we try to show how the values and actions of ordinary people, as well as the laws and regulations of government, have made economic life.

We have also tried especially to place America in a global context. The history of America, or any nation, cannot be adequately explained without understanding its relationship to transnational events and global developments. That is true for the first chapter of the book, which shows how America began to emerge from the collision of Native Americans, West Africans, and Europeans in the fifteenth and sixteenth centuries. It is just as true for the last chapters of the book, which demonstrate how globalization and the war on terror transformed the United States at the turn of the twenty-first century. In the chapters in between, we detail how the world has changed America and how America has changed the world. Reflecting the concerns of the rest of the book, we focus particularly on the movement of people, the evolution of power, and the attempt to spread democracy abroad.

Abraham Lincoln wanted to sell a war, of course. But he also truly believed that his audience would see democracy as quintessentially American. Whether he was right is the burden of this book.

New to the Fourth Edition

We are grateful that the first, second, and third editions of *Of the People* have been welcomed by instructors and students as a useful instructional aid. In preparing the fourth edition, our primary goal has been to maintain the text's overarching focus on the evolution of American democracy, people, and power; its strong portrayal of political and social history; and its clear, compelling narrative voice. To that end, the broad representation of Native Americans, African Americans, and other minority groups in this text shows the full diversity of the American people. One of the text's strengths is its critical-thinking pedagogy because the study of history entails careful analysis, not mere memorization of names and dates.

History continues, and the writing of history is never finished. For the fourth edition, we have updated the following elements based on the most recent scholarship:

Number of Chapters

The book has been condensed from 30 chapters and an epilogue to 30 chapters: the number of Gilded Age chapters has been reduced from three (formerly Chapters 16, 17, and 18 in the third edition) to two (Chapters 16 and 17 in the fourth edition) to stream-line the narrative flow and more evenly balance the distribution of chapters to allow for more coverage of recent history. The chapter content has been redistributed as follows to accommodate this restructuring.

Chapter 15: Reconstructing a Nation, 1865–1877
- Includes a new section titled "A Reconstructed West," which is comprised of the following sections from the third edition's Chapter 16:
  - The Overland Trail
  - The Origins of Indian Reservations
  - The Destruction of Indian Subsistence
- The chapter-ending section "The End of Reconstruction" now concludes with "Sharecropping Becomes Wage Labor" from the third edition's Chapter 16.

Chapter 16: The Triumph of Industrial Capitalism, 1850–1890
- Includes the section "Social Darwinism and the Growth of Scientific Racism" from the third edition's Chapter 17
- Includes "Struggles for Democracy: 'The Chinese Must Go'" from the third edition's Chapter 17
- Includes the section "The Knights of Labor and the Haymarket Disaster" from the third edition's Chapter 18

Chapter 17: The Culture and Politics of Industrial America, 1870–1892
- Formerly Chapter 18 in the third edition
- Includes the section "The Elusive Boundaries of Male and Female," which is comprised of the following sections from the third edition's Chapter 17:
  - The Victorian Construction of Male and Female
  - Victorians Who Questioned Traditional Sexual Boundaries

- Content from the third edition's Chapter 17 "American Portrait: Anthony Comstock's Crusade Against Vice" is incorporated into the discussion "The Victorian Crusade for Morality."
- Includes the section "The Varieties of Urban Culture" from the third edition's Chapter 17, now simply titled "Urban Culture."
- Includes the section "A New Cultural Order: New Americans Stir Old Fears," which is comprised of the following sections from the third edition's Chapter 17:
  - Josiah Strong Attacks Immigration
  - From Immigrants to Ethnic Americans
  - The Catholic Church and Its Limits in Immigrant Culture
  - Immigrant Cultures
- Includes the section "The Rise and Fall of the National Labor Union" from the third edition's Chapter 15

Chapter 30: "A Nation Transformed," The Twenty-First Century

Formerly the Epilogue, this chapter has been revised and significantly expanded to cover the span of years since 2001.

- Revised discussion of Obama's second term in office
- New discussions on:
  - Climate change
  - The rise of the Islamic State
  - Diversity, division, and discrimination in the United States, with emphasis on the justice system's treatment of African Americans and Deferred Action for Childhood Arrivals (DACA)
  - Expanded discussion of LGBTQ rights
  - Shifting religious beliefs and practices in the United States
  - The implications of deindustrialization, digitization, and globalization on jobs and growth
  - The growing income inequality gap
  - How economic change has impacted the status of women, men, baby boomers, and millennials, as well as increased the divide between urban and rural areas
  - How growing wealth inequality has intensified the problem of money in politics
  - The emergence of four contending political approaches
  - The Presidential Election of 2016

New Additions to American Portrait, American Landscape, America and the World, and Struggles for Democracy Features

These popular features from the third edition have been updated with eight new American Portraits, four new American Landscapes, eight new America and the World features, and three new Struggles for Democracy.

Photos

Approximately one-third of the photos have been revised throughout the chapters and sources.

Primary Sources

A version of the text is available with end-of-chapter primary source documents, both textual and visual, designed to reinforce students' understanding of the material by drawing connections among topics and thinking critically. Nearly all chapters include at least one new source document:

- Source 2.3 Father Pierre Cholonec, Life of Kateri (1715)
- Source 3.1 Edward Waterhouse's Report on the Uprising of 1622
- Source 5.4 George Whitefield, Account of a Visit to Georgia (1738)
- Source 6.5 The Stamp Act Riots: The Destruction of Thomas Hutchinson's House (1765)
- Source 7.2 Alexander Hamilton Recommends Arming Slaves and George Washington Rejects the Idea (1779)
- Source 8.2 Thomas Jefferson's Letter to Philip Mazzei (1796)
- Source 9.5 Elder David Purviance's Description of the Cane Ridge Revival (1801)
- Source 10.5 Frances Kemble's Journal (1838–1839)
- Source 11.2 Angelina Grimké, Excerpt from *An Appeal to the Women of the Nominally Free States* (1838)
- Source 12.5 María Amparo Ruiz, *The Squatter and the Don* (1885)
- Source 13.4 Abraham Lincoln, Speech at Springfield, Illinois (1857)
- Source 14.1 John Sherman, A Letter on the Crisis to Philadelphians (1860)
- Source 14.3 Cornelia Hancock, Letter to Her Sister (1863)
- Source 14.4 John Beauchamp Jones Observes the Deterioration on the Confederate Home Front (1863–1864)
- Source 15.5 A Southern Unionist Judge's Daughter Writes the President for Help (1874)
- Source 15.6 Red Cloud Pleads the Plains Indians' Point of View at Cooper Union (1870)
- Source 16.6 James Baird Weaver, *A Call to Action* (1892)
- Source 17.5 Visual Documents: "Gift for the Grangers" (1873) and the Jorns Family of Dry Valley, Custer County, Nebraska (1886)
- Source 18.1 Frederick Winslow Taylor, Excerpts from *The Principles of Scientific Management* (1911)
- Source 20.1 World War I–Era Music: "I Didn't Raise My Boy to Be a Solider" (1915) and "Over There" (1917)
- Source 21.1 Hiram Wesley Evans, Excerpts from "The Klan: Defender of Americanism" (1925)
- Source 22.4 Remembering the Great Depression, Excerpts from Studs Terkel's *Hard Times* (1970)
- Source 23.2 Charles Lindbergh, America First Committee Address (1941)
- Source 24.2 High School and College Graduates in the Cold War (1948–1950)
- Source 25.1 Gael Greene, "The Battle of Levittown" (1957)
- Source 25.3 Visual Documents: Automobile Advertisements (1953–1955)
- Source 26.5 John Wilcock, "The Human Be-In" and "San Francisco" (1967)
- Source 27.2 Nixon Decides on the Christmas Bombing (1972)
- Source 28.1 Visual Document: US Centers for Disease Control, AIDS Awareness Poster (1980s)
- Source 29.3 Visual Document: Aziz + Cucher, "Man with Computer" (1992)
- Source 30.2 Barack Obama, Keynote Address, Democratic Party Convention (2004)

- Source 30.3 Debate in the House of Representatives on a Resolution "That Symbols and Traditions of Christmas Should Be Protected" (2005)
- Source 30.4 Harry M. Reid, "The Koch Brothers" (2015)
- Source 30.5 Steve A. King, "Illegal Immigration," House of Representatives (2007)
- Source 30.6 Donald Trump, Extract of Remarks at a "Make America Great Again" Rally in Harrisburg, Pennsylvania (2017)

Hallmark Features

- Each chapter opens with an **American Portrait** feature, a story of someone whose life in one way or another embodies the basic theme of the pages to follow.
- Select chapters include an **American Landscape** feature, a particular place in time where issues of power appeared in especially sharp relief.
- To underscore the fundamental importance of global relationships, select chapters include a feature on **America and the World**.
- Each chapter includes a **Struggles for Democracy** feature, focusing on moments of debate and public conversation surrounding events that have contributed to the changing ideas of democracy, as well as the sometimes constricting but overall gradually widening opportunities that evolved for the American people as a result.
- **Common Threads** focus questions at chapter openings.
- **Time Lines** in every chapter.
- A list of chapter-ending key terms, **Who, What, Where**, helps students recall the important people, events, and places of that chapter.
- All chapters end with both **Review Questions**, which test students' memory and understanding of chapter content, and **Critical-Thinking Questions**, which ask students to analyze and interpret chapter content.

Learning Resources for *Of the People*

Oxford University Press offers instructors and students a comprehensive ancillary package for qualified adopters.

Ancillary Resource Center (ARC)

This online resource center, available to adopters of *Of the People*, includes the following:

- Instructor's Resource Manual: Includes, for each chapter, a detailed chapter outline, suggested lecture topics, and learning objectives, as well as approximately 40 multiple-choice, short-answer, true-or-false, fill-in-the-blank, and 10 essay questions for each chapter
- A Computerized Test Bank that includes all of the test items from the Instructor's Resource Manual
- PowerPoints and Computerized Test Bank: Includes PowerPoint slides and JPEG and PDF files for all the maps and photos in the text, and approximately 1,000 additional PowerPoint-based slides from OUP's US History Image Library, organized by themes and periods in American history.

- The US History Video Library, Produced by Oxford University Press: Each 3- to 5-minute video covers a key topic in US history, from Squanto to John Brown, from Mother Jones to the "disco wars" of the late 1970s/early 1980s. Combining motion pictures, stills, audio clips, and narration, these videos are ideal for both classroom discussion or as online assignments.

Oxford First Source

This database includes hundreds of primary source documents in US history. The documents cover a broad variety of political, economic, social, and cultural topics and represent a cross section of American voices. Special effort was made to include as many previously disenfranchised voices as possible. The documents are indexed by date, author, title, and subject. Short documents (one or two pages) are presented in their entirety while longer documents have been carefully edited to highlight significant content. Each document is introduced with a short explanatory paragraph and accompanied with study questions.

A complete **Course Management cartridge** is also available to qualified adopters. Instructor's resources are also available for download directly to your computer through a secure connection via the instructor's side of the companion website. Contact your Oxford University Press sales representative for more information.

Student Companion Website at www.oup.com/us/oakes-mcgerr

The open-access Online Study Center designed for *Of the People: A History of the United States*, Fourth Edition helps students to review what they have learned from the textbook as well as explore other resources online.

Sources for *Of the People: A History of the United States, Volume I to 1877* (ISBN 978019091014) and *Of the People: A History of the United States, Volume II Since 1865* (ISBN 9780190910150)

Edited by Maxwell Johnson, and organized to match the table of contents of *Of the People*, this two-volume sourcebook includes five to six primary sources per chapter, both textual and visual. Chapter introductions, document headnotes, and study questions provide learning support. Each volume of the sourcebook is only $5.00 when bundled with *Of the People*.

Mapping and Coloring Book of US History

This two-volume workbook includes approximately 80 outline maps that provide opportunities for students to deepen their understanding of geography through quizzes, coloring exercises, and other activities. *The Mapping and Coloring Book of US History* is free when bundled with *Of the People*.

E-Books

Digital versions of *Of the People* are available at many popular distributors, including Chegg, RedShelf, and VitalSource.

Other Oxford Titles of Interest for the US History Classroom

Oxford University Press publishes a vast array of titles in American history. The following list is just a small selection of books that pair particularly well with *Of the People: A History of the United States*, Fourth Edition. Any of these books can be packaged with *Of the People* at a significant discount to students. Please contact your Oxford University Press sales representative for specific pricing information or for additional packaging suggestions. Please visit www.oup.com/us for a full listing of Oxford titles.

Writing History: A Guide for Students, Fifth Edition, by William Kelleher Storey, Professor of History at Millsaps College

Bringing together practical methods from both history and composition, *Writing History* provides a wealth of tips and advice to help students research and write essays for history classes. The book covers all aspects of writing about history, including **finding topics and researching** them, **interpreting source materials, drawing inferences from sources, and constructing arguments.** It concludes with three chapters that discuss writing effective sentences, using precise wording, and revising. Using numerous examples from the works of cultural, political, and social historians, *Writing History* serves as an ideal supplement to history courses that require students to conduct research. The fifth edition includes expanded sections on peer editing and topic selection, as well as new sections on searching and using the Internet. *Writing History* can be packaged with *Of the People: A History of the United States*, Fourth Edition. Contact your Oxford University Press sales representative for more information.

The Information-Literate Historian: A Guide to Research for History Students, Third Edition, by Jenny Presnell, Information Services Library and History, American Studies, and Women's Studies Bibliographer, Miami University of Ohio

This is the only book specifically designed to teach today's history student how to most successfully select and use sources—primary, secondary, and electronic—to carry out and present their research. Written by a college librarian, *The Information-Literate Historian* is an indispensable reference for historians, students, and other readers doing history research. *The Information-Literate Historian* can be packaged with *Of the People: A History of the United States*, Fourth Edition. Contact your Oxford University Press sales representative for more information.

Acknowledgments

We are grateful to our families, friends, and colleagues who encouraged us during the planning and writing of this book. We would like once again to thank Bruce Nichols for helping launch this book years ago. We are grateful to the editors and staff at Oxford University Press, especially our acquisitions editor, Charles Cavaliere, and our development editor, Maegan Sherlock. Charles's commitment made this text possible and Maegan deftly guided the development of the fourth edition. Thanks also to our talented production team, Barbara Mathieu, senior production editor, and Michele Laseau, art director, who helped to fulfill the book's vision. And special thanks go to Leslie Anglin, our copyeditor; to Rowan Wixted, assistant editor; and to the many other people behind the scenes at Oxford for helping this complex project happen.

The authors and editors would also like to thank the following people, whose time and insights have contributed to the first, second, third, and fourth editions.

Expert Reviewers of the Fourth Edition

Daniel Anderson
Cincinnati State University

Tramaine Anderson
Tarrant County College

Matthew Campbell
Lone Star College–Cypress Fairbanks

Gregg S. Clemmer
Carroll Community College

John Patrick Daly
College at Brockport, State University of New York

Maureen Elgersman Lee
Hampton University

Michael Frawley
University of Texas of the Permian Basin

Robert Genter
Nassau Community College

Sakina M. Hughes
University of Southern Indiana

Katrina Lacher
University of Central Oklahoma

Robert Lee
St. Louis Community College–Meramec

Matthew Oyos
Radford University

Stephen Todd Pfeffer
Columbus State Community College

Brenden Rensink
Brigham Young University

Marie Stango
California State University, Bakersfield

Expert Reviewers of the Third Edition

Greg Hall
Western Illinois University

Ross A. Kennedy
Illinois State University

Randall M. Miller
Saint Joseph's University

David W. Morris
Santa Barbara City College

Adam Pratt
University of Scranton

Judith Ridner
Mississippi State University

Robert A. Smith
Pittsburg State University

Timothy B. Smith
University of Tennessee at Martin

Linda D. Tomlinson
Fayetteville State University

Gerald Wilson
Eastern Washington University

Expert Reviewers of the Second Edition

Marjorie Berman
Red Rocks Community College–Lakewood

Will Carter
South Texas Community College

Jonathan Chu
University of Massachusetts, Boston

Sara Combs
Virginia Highlands Community College

Mark Elliott
University of North Carolina–Greensboro

David Hamilton
University of Kentucky

James Harvey
Houston Community College

Courtney Joiner
East Georgia College

Timothy Mahoney
University of Nebraska–Lincoln

Abigail Markwyn
Carroll University

Brian Maxson
Eastern Tennessee State University

Matthew Oyos
Radford University

John Pinheiro
Aquinas College

James Pula
Purdue University–North Central

John Rosinbum
Arizona State University

Christopher Thrasher
Texas Tech University

Jeffrey Trask
University of Massachusetts–Amherst

Michael Ward
California State University–Northridge

Bridgette Williams-Searle
The College of Saint Rose

Expert Reviewers of the First Edition

Thomas L. Altherr
Metropolitan State College of Denver

Luis Alvarez
University of California–San Diego

Adam Arenson
University of Texas–El Paso

Melissa Estes Blair
University of Georgia

Lawrence Bowdish
Ohio State University

Susan Roth Breitzer
Fayetteville State University

Margaret Lynn Brown
Brevard College

W. Fitzhugh Brundage
University of North Carolina–Chapel Hill

Gregory Bush
University of Miami

Brian Casserly
University of Washington

Ann Chirhart
Indiana State University

Bradley R. Clampitt
East Central University

William W. Cobb Jr.
Utah Valley University

Cheryll Ann Cody
Houston Community College

Sondra Cosgrove
College of Southern Nevada

Thomas H. Cox
Sam Houston State University

Carl Creasman
Valencia Community College

Christine Daniels
Michigan State University

Brian J. Daugherity
Virginia Commonwealth University

Mark Elliott
University of North Carolina–Greensboro

Katherine Carté Enge
Texas A&M University

Michael Faubion
University of Texas–Pan American

John Fea
Messiah College

Anne L. Foster
Indiana State University

Matthew Garrett
Arizona State University

Tim Garvin
California State University–Long Beach

Suzanne Cooper Guasco
Queens University of Charlotte

Lloyd Ray Gunn
University of Utah

Richard Hall
Columbus State University

Marsha Hamilton
University of South Alabama

Mark Hanna
University of California–San Diego

Joseph M. Hawes
University of Memphis

Melissa Hovsepian
University of Houston–Downtown

Jorge Iber
Texas Tech University

David K. Johnson
University of South Florida

Lloyd Johnson
Campbell University

Catherine O'Donnell Kaplan
Arizona State University

Rebecca M. Kluchin
California State University–Sacramento

Michael Kramer
Northwestern University

Louis M. Kyriakoudes
University of Southern Mississippi

Jason S. Lantzer
Butler University

Shelly Lemons
St. Louis Community College

Charlie Levine
Mesa Community College

Denise Lynn
University of Southern Indiana

Lillian Marrujo-Duck
City College of San Francisco

Michael McCoy
Orange County Community College

Noeleen McIlvenna
Wright State University

Elizabeth Brand Monroe
*Indiana University–Purdue
University Indianapolis*

Kevin C. Motl
Ouachita Baptist University

Todd Moye
University of North Texas

Charlotte Negrete
Mt. San Antonio College

Julie Nicoletta
University of Washington–Tacoma

David M. Parker
California State University–Northridge

Jason Parker
Texas A&M University

Burton W. Peretti
Western Connecticut State University

Jim Piecuch
Kennesaw State University

John Putman
San Diego State University

R. J. Rockefeller
Loyola College of Maryland

Herbert Sloan
Barnard College, Columbia University

Vincent L. Toscano
Nova Southeastern University

William E. Weeks
San Diego State University

Timothy L. Wood
Southwest Baptist University

Jason Young
SUNY–Buffalo

Expert Reviewers of the Concise Second Edition

Hedrick Alixopulos
Santa Rosa Junior College

Guy Alain Aronoff
Humboldt State University

Melissa Estes Blair
Warren Wilson College

Amanda Bruce
Nassau Community College

Jonathan Chu
University of Massachusetts–Boston

Paul G. E. Clemens
Rutgers University

Martha Anne Fielder
Cedar Valley College

Tim Hacsi
University of Massachusetts–Boston

Matthew Isham
Pennsylvania State University

Ross A. Kennedy
Illinois State University

Eve Kornfeld
San Diego State University

Peggy Lambert
Lone Star College–Kingwood

Shelly L. Lemons
St. Louis Community College

Carolyn Herbst Lewis
Louisiana State University

Catherine M. Lewis
Kennesaw State University

Daniel K. Lewis
California State Polytechnic University

Scott P. Marler
University of Memphis

Laura McCall
Metropolitan State College of Denver

Stephen P. McGrath
Central Connecticut State University

Vincent P. Mikkelsen
Florida State University

Julie Nicoletta
University of Washington Tacoma

Caitlin Stewart
Eastern Connecticut State University

Thomas Summerhill
Michigan State University

David Tegeder
Santa Fe College

Eric H. Walther
University of Houston

William E. Weeks
University of San Diego

Kenneth B. White
Modesto Junior College

Julie Winch
University of Massachusetts–Boston

Mary Montgomery Wolf
University of Georgia

Kyle F. Zelner
University of Southern Mississippi

Expert Reviewers of the Concise First Edition

Hedrick Alixopulos
Santa Rosa Junior College

Guy Alain Aronoff
Humboldt State University

Melissa Estes Blair
Warren Wilson College

Amanda Bruce
Nassau Community College

Jonathan Chu
University of Massachusetts–Boston

Paul G. E. Clemens
Rutgers University

Martha Anne Fielder
Cedar Valley College

Tim Hacsi
University of Massachusetts–Boston

Matthew Isham
Pennsylvania State University

Ross A. Kennedy
Illinois State University

Eve Kornfeld
San Diego State University

Peggy Lambert
Lone Star College–Kingwood

Shelly L. Lemons
St. Louis Community College

Carolyn Herbst Lewis
Louisiana State University

Catherine M. Lewis
Kennesaw State University

Daniel K. Lewis
California State Polytechnic University

Scott P. Marler
University of Memphis

Laura McCall
Metropolitan State College of Denver

Stephen P. McGrath
Central Connecticut State University

Vincent P. Mikkelsen
Florida State University

Julie Nicoletta
University of Washington Tacoma

Caitlin Stewart
Eastern Connecticut State University

Thomas Summerhill
Michigan State University

David Tegeder
Santa Fe College

Eric H. Walther
University of Houston

William E. Weeks
University of San Diego

Kenneth B. White
Modesto Junior College

Julie Winch
University of Massachusetts–Boston

Mary Montgomery Wolf
University of Georgia

Kyle F. Zelner
University of Southern Mississippi

About the Authors

Michael McGerr is the Paul V. McNutt Professor of History at Indiana University–Bloomington. He is the author of *The Decline of Popular Politics: The American North, 1865–1928* (1986) and *A Fierce Discontent: The Rise and Fall of the Progressive Movement, 1870–1920* (2003), both from Oxford University Press. He is writing *"The Public Be Damned": The Kingdom and the Dream of the Vanderbilts*. The recipient of a fellowship from the National Endowment for the Humanities, Professor McGerr has won numerous teaching awards at Indiana, where his courses include the US Survey; War in Modern American History; Rock, Hip Hop, and Revolution; Big Business; The Sixties; and American Pleasure. He has previously taught at Yale University and the Massachusetts Institute of Technology. He received his BA, MA, and PhD from Yale.

Jan Ellen Lewis is Professor of History and Dean of the Faculty of Arts and Sciences, Rutgers University–Newark. She also teaches in the history PhD program at Rutgers, New Brunswick, and was a visiting professor of history at Princeton. A specialist in colonial and early national history, she is the author of *The Pursuit of Happiness: Family and Values in Jefferson's Virginia* (1983) as well as numerous articles and reviews. She has coedited *An Emotional History of the United States* (1998), *Sally Hemings and Thomas Jefferson: History, Memory, and Civic Culture* (1999), and *The Revolution of 1800: Democracy, Race, and the New Republic* (2002). She has served as president of the Society of Historians of the Early American Republic, as chair of the New Jersey Historical Commission, and on the editorial board of the *American Historical Review*. She is an elected member of the Society of American Historians and the American Antiquarian Society. She received her AB from Bryn Mawr College and MAs and PhD from the University of Michigan.

James Oakes has published several books and numerous articles on slavery and antislavery in the nineteenth century, including *The Radical and the Republican: Frederick Douglass, Abraham Lincoln, and the Triumph of Antislavery Politics* (2007), winner of the Lincoln Prize in 2008. Professor Oakes is Distinguished Professor of History and Graduate School Humanities Professor at the City University of New York Graduate Center. In 2008, he was a fellow at the Cullman Center at the New York Public Library. His new book is *Freedom National: The Destruction of Slavery in the United States* (February 2013).

Nick Cullather is a historian of US foreign relations at Indiana University–Bloomington. He is author of three books on nation building: *The Hungry World* (2010), a story of foreign aid, development, and science; *Illusions of Influence* (1994), on US–Philippines relations; and *Secret History* (1999 and 2006), a history of the CIA's overthrow of the Guatemalan government in 1954. He received his PhD from the University of Virginia.

Mark Summers is the Thomas D. Clark Professor of History at the University of Kentucky–Lexington. In addition to various articles, he has written *Railroads, Reconstruction, and the Gospel of Prosperity* (1984), *The Plundering Generation* (1988), *The Era of Good Stealings*

(1993), *The Press Gang* (1994), *The Gilded Age; or, The Hazard of New Functions* (1997), *Rum, Romanism and Rebellion* (2000), *Party Games* (2004), and *A Dangerous Stir* (2009). At present, he has just completed a book about a Tammany politician, *Big Tim and the Tiger*. He is now writing a survey of Reconstruction and a book about 1868. He teaches the American history survey (both halves), the Gilded Age, the Progressive Era, the Age of Jackson, Civil War and Reconstruction, the British Empire (both halves), the Old West (both halves), a history of political cartooning, and various graduate courses. He earned his BA from Yale and his PhD from the University of California–Berkeley.

Camilla Townsend is Professor of History at Rutgers University–New Brunswick. She is the author of five books, among them *Annals of Native America* (2016), *Malintzin's Choices: An Indian Woman in the Conquest of Mexico* (2006), and *Pocahontas and the Powhatan Dilemma* (2004), and she is the editor of *American Indian History: A Documentary Reader* (2010). The recipient of fellowships from the National Endowment for the Humanities and the John Simon Guggenheim Memorial Foundation, she has also won awards at Rutgers and at Colgate, where she used to teach. Her courses at the graduate and undergraduate level cover the colonial history of the Americas, as well as Native American history, early and modern. She received her BA from Bryn Mawr and her PhD from Rutgers.

Karen M. Dunak is Associate Professor of History at Muskingum University in New Concord, Ohio. She is the author of *As Long as We Both Shall Love: The White Wedding in Postwar America* (2013), published by New York University Press. She currently is working on a book about media representations of and responses to Jacqueline Kennedy Onassis. Her courses include the US Survey, Women in US History, Gender and Sexuality in US History, and various topics related to modern US history. She earned her BA from American University and her PhD from Indiana University.

Jeanne Boydston was Robinson-Edwards Professor of American History at the University of Wisconsin–Madison. A specialist in the histories of gender and labor, she was the author of *Home and Work: Housework, Wages, and the Ideology of Labor in the Early American Republic* (1990); coauthor of *The Limits of Sisterhood: The Beecher Sisters on Women's Rights and Woman's Sphere* (1988); and coeditor of *Root of Bitterness: Documents in the Social History of American Women*, second edition (1996). The recipient of numerous teaching awards, she gave courses in women's and gender history, the United States before the Civil War, and global and comparative history. Her BA and MA were from the University of Tennessee, and her PhD was from Yale University.

Of the People

Worlds in Motion

1450-1550

< Moctezuma's Tribute Rolls

AMERICAN PORTRAIT

Malinche, Cultural Translator

When the Native American woman who would later be known as La Malinche was a little girl, she listened to the poems and histories of her people on starlit evenings. Her father was a nobleman from Coatzacoalcos, on the Gulf of Mexico; his people had lived there for generations in adobe houses built around communal courtyards. Her mother, though, was lowborn, maybe even a captive concubine, and this made the child vulnerable. Trouble came when she was still young. The powerful Aztecs from the Central Valley of Mexico were expanding their dominion, and she was either taken in battle or, more likely, given away as a preemptive peace offering to the invaders. Then the Aztecs sold her to the Mayas, and she lived with them for years as a slave.

When strangers from across the sea came on huge canoes with cloth sails, the Mayas attacked them—and lost the battle. Once again the girl was given away as a peace offering. This time, she found herself among the newly arrived Spaniards, who baptized her "Marina." The Indians heard the name as "Malina" (as they had no "r") and called her "Malintzin" to convey respect. The Spaniards heard "Malinchi" or "Malinche" (as they had no "tz" sound), and so we still call her today. We will never know what her mother had once named her. She had become someone different, and she soon discovered her potential importance to her new captors. Her native language was Nahuatl, the same tongue spoken by the Aztecs, and by now she also spoke the coastal Mayan dialect. The Spaniards had with them one Jerónimo de Aguilar, who had lived for years among the Mayas as a shipwreck victim and also spoke their language. In a perfect translation chain, Hernando Cortés spoke to Aguilar, who spoke to Malinche, who in turn spoke to the Aztecs. She was a gifted young woman and learned Spanish quickly, soon becoming the only translator needed.

Malinche told the Spaniards about the Aztec capital where Moctezuma ruled, and she helped to guide them there. She had no reason to protect the Aztec people; after all, they had threatened her own family and caused her enslavement. And she had every reason to work cooperatively with the newcomers. If she did, they would treat her well. If not, they would use her as a sexual slave. She also soon saw that the Spanish were brutal on the battlefield and learned that there were many thousands more of them ready to come. Often she advised indigenous villages that they passed to make peace with the strangers rather than fight them. She said, quite rightly, that they could be useful friends but would make dangerous enemies. When they reached the Aztec capital, she translated adroitly between Cortés and Moctezuma, refusing to be intimidated, and helped Cortés determine what to do at each stage.

Hernando Cortés probably would not have been able to bring down the Aztecs without the help of Malinche. And yet if he had failed, some other Spaniard almost certainly would eventually have found some other captive woman to act as translator and mediator, for the domineering Aztecs had many enemies.

Like many people who have been forced to become cultural mediators, Malinche survived as best she could. She bore a son by Cortés, and when, after the conquest, she demanded a Spanish husband for her own protection, he saw her married to one of his lieutenants. She later bore her husband a daughter. Malinche died when she was about 30 of one of the diseases brought by the Europeans, but not before she had helped her children enter the Spanish world on a firm footing, with wealth and position. She knew by then that the New World she had helped to create was proving dangerous to indigenous people, even those who befriended the Spaniards. She may have had fears for the future, but she could not have had any real regrets about the past, for at the time, she had had very few options. She had done the best she could in an extraordinarily difficult situation.

The Worlds of Indian Peoples

For most of human history, there were no people in the Americas. Archaeologists have found that modern humankind (*Homo sapiens*) originated in Africa about 400,000 years ago. In a sense, all people alive today are ultimately African, as we are all descended from those early humans. Some of them migrated northward and eventually populated Europe and Asia. Mutations occurred along the way, yielding populations who looked different but still had almost all of their genetic material—and their natures and abilities—in common.

Great Migrations

In the last Ice Age, arctic glaciers expanded so extensively that the world's sea level dropped, perhaps by as much as 350 feet. This phenomenon created a land bridge (called "Beringia") between Siberia in Asia and Alaska in America. Humans hunting mammoths and other big game traveled along the new corridor into America. Linguistic evidence indicates that there were three great waves of migration. Archaeologists argue fiercely about when the first one occurred. Most agree it was about 12,000 BCE, but there are a few sites that may suggest otherwise. The Monte Verde site in Chile—where a child's footprint next to a hearth has been forever preserved—seems to have been inhabited a thousand years earlier, for example. Eventually, about 9000 BCE, the ice melted, the sea level rose, and the land bridge disappeared, closing off the Old World from what would later be called the New. The people living in the Americas, known now as Paleo-Indians, at first remained what they had been—hunter-gatherers who moved in small groups of no more than about 25, generally choosing their spouses from other bands whom they met in passing.

Because of the end of the Ice Age, the climate began to shift, yielding distinct changes in lifestyle. At the start of the Archaic period (approximately 8000 BCE), most of the large mammals that were hunted for food went extinct. Overhunting may have contributed to their disappearance, but climactic shifts probably explain the demise of species like the woolly mammoth. The men learned to hunt and trap smaller species, and the women foraged more determinedly for edible and useful plants. They moved through their environment in seasonal cycles, making satisfying and productive lives for themselves for many generations. By the time of Columbus's voyage, there were hundreds of indigenous groups in the Americas.

The Emergence of Farming

As temperatures rose and more species of plants appeared, people around the world began to experiment with planting the seeds of their favorite types. They continued to follow the game as they always had, but then returned to the same place months later to harvest what they had planted. In some places, the available plants proved so rich in protein—containing the amino acids necessary to support life—that human populations gradually ceased to be nomadic hunter-gatherers and became full-time farmers instead. In other places, the available plants were not nutritious enough to enable a major change in lifestyle. In Southwest Asia, for example, in the area traditionally known as "the Fertile Crescent," located between the Tigris and the Euphrates Rivers, wheat, barley, and peas were all native to the region, and all were protein-rich. Not surprisingly, humans' early efforts to domesticate plants in this part of the world led relatively rapidly to the adoption of farming as a full-time occupation by about 8000 BCE. In New Guinea, to take a contrary example, the native plants included bananas and sugarcane, both delicious but not rich in protein. People planted them occasionally, but they continued their hunting-and-gathering lifestyle.

In the Americas, there were also very few plant species rich in the amino acids needed to synthesize protein. The ancestor of today's corn, which first appeared in what is today Mexico, was an exception to some extent, but the kernels at that time were extremely tiny, and they were missing some key amino acids. During the Archaic period (8000 BCE–2000 BCE), a number of groups did experiment with growing it (as well as squash and other plants). However, it took many generations of selective planting to create the ears of corn we know today. It took people even longer to discover that if they ate corn together with beans, they were left as well-nourished as if they had eaten meat. (The beans provided the amino acids missing from corn: together, they form a complete protein.) Once these breakthroughs had occurred, more societies adopted full-time agriculture.

The Cradle of the Americas

Mesoamerica, the area stretching from the Rio Grande to today's Panama, has been called "the Cradle of the Americas" because it was here that the hemisphere's first technologically advanced civilizations emerged. They appeared wherever corn became the centerpiece of a farming culture, beginning in about 2000 BCE. In every part of the ancient world, numerous technological innovations followed the advent of full-time farming. A sedentary lifestyle in which only a portion of the population was engaged in full-time food production enabled the emergence of such things as complex architecture, large ceramics, forges, irrigation techniques, and detailed recordkeeping. Mesoamerica was no exception.

By about 200 CE, two distinct zones of Mesoamerican culture had emerged. In the Yucatan Peninsula, the Classic Mayan civilizations flourished. The central basin of Mexico saw a succession of prominent states, beginning with the city of Teotihuacan—the breathtaking ruins of which still stand—and ending with the Aztec Empire, dominant when the Europeans arrived. We know a great deal about the Mayas and Aztecs because they had

AMERICAN LANDSCAPE

Xicallanco

The ancient Mesoamerican world was inhabited by states that were often at war with one another. This raised a complex issue: for kingdoms to grow, their long-distance merchants needed to be able to trade without constant risk of capture and death. To handle this problem, the ancient Mesoamericans established neutral trade towns, where merchants from various nations lived and worked together in peace. Among the greatest of these was Xicallanco, on the north coast of the isthmus of Mexico, between Nahua (Aztec) territory to the west, and Maya territory to the east.

Heavily laden merchant canoes entered at what appeared to be a little inlet but turned out to be a protected inland sea. From above, the gods could see that two great arms of land, like the front claws of a crab, reached out and around a huge lagoon, and between them lay a long, thin strip of an island that almost touched the tips of the two arms. Within the lagoon, the clear blue waters were peaceful and allowed a town to grow on the shore, free from great waves.

Xicallanco literally meant "place near the gourds," but far more than carved gourd cups and canteens were sold here. The Nahua-speaking peoples brought beautiful obsidian crafts and other artisanal products made in the Aztec capital, as well as food crops from their mountainous territories, and prisoners of war (children and very young women) to be sold as slaves. The coastal Maya-speaking peoples brought enormous quantities of rough cotton, yarn, and woven cloth, as well as pearls, shells, ceramics, and jewelry. Rivers that stretched inland connected the city to people in the

Model of a Coastal Home in Ancient Mexico
Models like this one were not toys, but rather funerary objects. Still, they allow us to catch a glimpse of people's daily lives.

hinterland who had raw materials to sell, including the plumage of tropical birds or, sometimes, the birds themselves. At least four languages were spoken in the city's streets, although Nahuatl, the Aztec language, was the lingua franca that merchants had to know if they wanted to be able to do business with everybody.

Xicallanco was a crowded, practical, businesslike place—a warren of low, adobe buildings and stalls, with no monumental architecture intended to withstand the centuries. This was simply a place for merchants to trade. Mostly, they bartered, but this was not always effective, and agreed-upon currency was sometimes needed. *Cacao* beans, used to make chocolate, became a form of specie, as did bolts of cotton.

continued

What do we make of an ancient town with polyglot outdoor cafes surrounded by stalls selling songbirds and beautiful jewelry—knowing that children were also for sale? There is no question that those young people suffered. But they were not destined to toil in agricultural fields or face the lash and other forms of torture; rather, they became domestic servants, and their own children would be free. They faced the type of slavery found in the ancient world on all the inhabited continents. The Mesoamericans were no different from other peoples in this regard.

their own pictoglyphic writing traditions, and they wrote down more about their culture when they learned the Roman alphabet from Spanish priests in the sixteenth century. In reading these individuals' writings, sometimes we stumble eerily into a moment from the past. One day in about the year 800, for example, a skilled Mayan artisan crafted a cup for drinking hot chocolate as a gift for a young prince. In the midst of the complicated paintings on the cup, which had religious and astronomical significance, he composed a poem in glyphic writing. He ended it by connecting the earthly world to the divine world, honoring both a powerful prince and a creator god: "He who gave the open space its place/who gave Jaguar Night his place/was the Black-Faced Lord, the Star-Faced Lord."

Scholars studying the writings and other remains of ancient Mesoamerican peoples have helped dispel some of the myths about them. Like people everywhere, they could be gentle and had senses of humor, but they were also competitive and often fought for dominance. They sometimes sacrificed prisoners of war to the gods, but they were not inherently more violent than other humans; they did *not* routinely sacrifice thousands of people at a time, as was once believed. In general, victors in political power struggles preferred that outsiders choose to ally with them rather than be destroyed. The more scholars learn about individual ethnic groups in the pre-Columbian period, the clearer it becomes that they were nearly all based on alliances formed between disparate groups in a more remote past. As bands grew to become chiefdoms—and in some cases, actual states—they governed themselves successfully by allowing the different subunits to have a voice in the increasingly complex polity. Constituent groups negotiated with each other and rotated between them the duties of going to war, for example, or working on a temple. In some regards, Mesoamerican native cultures thus constituted the hemisphere's first democracies although they were ruled by chiefs.

The Northern World Takes Shape

In the pre-Columbian period, North America was peripheral to Mesoamerica. Due to the centrality of farming in Mesoamerica, the population there was many millions strong (scholars debate the exact number), while the population of all of North America was about 1 million. Because a desert covered northern Mexico, the culture centered on corn did not travel northward as easily as comparable crops had once traveled from the Fertile Crescent throughout Europe and Asia. But ancient Mesoamerican migrants and traders did eventually spread their valuable commodities, largely through canoe travel along the coasts and eventually even across the Gulf of Mexico.

Beginning as early as 100 CE, small villages began to be established in what we call the American Southwest following the Mexican model. The Anasazi, the Mogollon, and the Hohokam cultures all experimented with agriculture and built houses around courtyards. Later, the climate and their nomadic enemies caused most of them to return to hunting and gathering for a time. The Anasazi, however, persistently circled back to planting corn and eventually built their remarkable cliff dwellings and the towns of Chaco Canyon, among them the 800-room complex at Pueblo Bonito. This extraordinary architectural wonder seems to have been built largely for ceremonial purposes; thousands of people working over generations were dedicated to its construction.

Meanwhile, the Mississippi River had long functioned as a great highway for the exchange of goods and ideas. Once corn reached the mouth of the river, it was not long before it spread northward. We call the style of culture that traveled up the artery of the river "Mississippian." Mississippian sites, ranging from about 800 CE to 1500 CE, included the region's more ancient funerary mounds, as well as Mexican-style ball courts next to grand pyramids, central courtyards, and, of course, corn farming. Cahokia, a city-state located near the point where the Missouri River runs into the Mississippi, rose to become the greatest power in the region for a time, exacting tribute from surrounding villages. In the eleventh century, the town boasted about 10,000 people. After that, its power declined and its people abandoned the site; perhaps the powerful lords had made too many enemies, or perhaps a terrible drought struck, or both.

Even as Cahokia saw its demise, however, Mississippian culture spread into the American Southeast, and corn also traveled up the Ohio River to the Great Lakes, to the ancestors of the Iroquoian peoples. By the time the Europeans met the cultures of the Eastern Woodlands, many of them had been part-time farmers for a few hundred years, although they also continued to rely on hunting deer and gathering wild plants. Those groups

Image of Community of Cahokia The community at Cahokia, at eye level, as envisioned by a modern-day graphic artist. The town was surrounded by a stockade, which enclosed the mounds, plazas, temples, and homes.

who farmed most successfully saw their populations rise relative to their neighbors. The Iroquoian peoples in particular translated this into political power by resolving their internal differences through democratic discussion and presenting a united face to the world. It seems that at least a century before the Europeans arrived, the leader Deganawidah helped them found the entity later known as the League of Five Nations. Women, whose work in agriculture was deemed highly important, had a voice in the selection of chiefs.

Some parts of North America were not subject to the influence of Mexican culture and corn. The peoples of the far north, relatively few in number, survived through expert hunting. The Great Plains were largely uninhabited, for in a world without horses, their vastness and aridity seemed impenetrable, except for a few people who piled their goods onto a chamois pulled by dogs. A few corn farmers nestled around the edges of the prairies, and sometimes enterprising men drove roaming herds of buffalo over cliffs to harvest the meat. Many of these people lived in villages of earthen lodges. Farther west, along the coast of California and in the Pacific Northwest, large numbers of people lived by fishing and processing acorns. They built lodges and totem poles out of wood and painted them with bright colors. On the Columbia Plateau, a great annual trade fair centered on the buying and selling of dried salmon. Even here, although the people had not become farmers, some Mexican influence was felt. Travelers brought luxury goods to trade, like turquoise jewelry, which had come from the lands to the south.

These northwestern fisher peoples would be among the last to come face-to-face with Europeans. The newcomers were approaching from the south and east.

The Worlds of Christopher Columbus

In the world into which Christopher Columbus was born, Europe was peripheral. Great overland trade caravans and the sea routes of the Indian Ocean connected the known world. The Middle Eastern merchants at the center formed the hub (see Map 1–1). The goods of China were in greatest demand. Europeans constituted the least powerful element of the world's trade system. Princes and merchants there longed to be able to compete with other players on the world stage, and some desperately sought ways of doing so.

The *Reconquista*

Middle Eastern economic power had spurred the spread of the Islamic faith after its inception in the seventh century. By the year 711, most of the Iberian Peninsula (today's Spain and Portugal) had fallen to Muslim conquerors of Arab and Berber descent (called "Moors" by Christians). The new authorities were generally tolerant of those they had vanquished and allowed Christian and Jewish subjects to coexist peacefully alongside Muslims. Toward the end of the eleventh century, however, dissatisfied descendants of the ousted ruling families began a concerted effort toward reconquest, or *reconquista*. In 1085, Alfonso VI of Castile retook Toledo. "Inspired by God's grace," he wrote triumphantly, "I moved an army against this city, where my ancestors once reigned in power and wealth, deeming it acceptable in the sight of the Lord." Over the course of the next four centuries, other Christian princes followed Alfonso's lead. In these years, warfare shaped all aspects of Iberian society. The priests who proclaimed the *reconquista* a holy struggle against the Moorish infidel and the soldiers who waged such wars were elevated to positions of prestige. The surest path to wealth and honor lay in plunder and conquest.

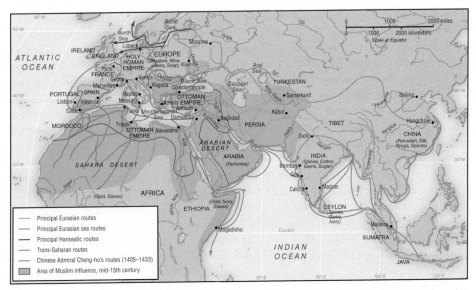

Map 1-1   World Trade on the Eve of Discovery For a thousand years, world trade centered on the Mediterranean. European, Arab, and Asian traders crisscrossed much of the Eastern Hemisphere, carrying spices, silks, and cottons from Asia; linens, woolens, and wine from Europe; and gold and slaves from Africa.

By the time the Italian-born Christopher Columbus arrived in Spain in 1485, the Muslim rulers had been ejected from the entire peninsula, except Granada. The 1469 marriage of Isabel, princess of Castile, and her cousin Ferdinand, prince of Aragon, had unified the heart of what would soon be the nation of Spain. Although Isabel was only 18 when she married (and her husband a year younger), she had already shown herself to be a woman of boldness and determination, and because Castile was more powerful than Aragon, she was able to dictate the terms of the marriage contract. Together, she and Ferdinand launched a final campaign against the Moors. In 1492, Isabel and Ferdinand defeated the Muslim ruler at Granada. Muslims who chose to remain in Spain had to convert to Christianity. The noblemen surrounding Ferdinand and Isabel then insisted that the monarchs banish the roughly 150,000 Jews living in Spain. Jews could depart, convert, or face public execution.

The Age of Exploration

The same energy that fueled the *reconquista* animated many Europeans in this era to attempt to expand their power. Some organized the Crusades; some expanded militarily into Ireland and others into the region around the Baltic Sea. Merchants and ambitious princes dreamed of finding a way to circumvent the Muslim traders who were the middlemen in a thriving trade with the Far East. Europe's nobility and prosperous urban peoples desired the East's sugar, spices, fabrics, jewels, and precious metals. They were dazzled by the Italian Marco Polo's accounts of his journeys between 1275 and 1292 to the cities of China. So it was that European explorers set off in search of new routes to Asia.

In the fifteenth century, for the first time, Europeans had the necessary technology to be able to travel far from home in numbers. While Norsemen had briefly established a settlement in Newfoundland in about the year 1000, it had remained an isolated event. Now times had changed. The printing press, invented by Johannes Gutenberg in the middle of the century, allowed the rapid spread of information—like Marco Polo's text, as well as valuable maps. Through the traditional international trade routes, Europeans had gleaned gunpowder (originally from China) and navigational tools such as the compass (from the Arabs). They took the cannons they had originally learned of in the East and mounted them on ships so that they might make demands of people they encountered. The seafaring Portuguese absorbed all they had seen of other people's boats and designed the caravel, a ship that could sail faster than any previous vessel, making it possible to go farther with limited food and water.

Indeed, throughout the fifteenth century, having expelled the Muslims from their territory more rapidly than the Spaniards, the Portuguese had been gradually exploring the hitherto unknown coast of Africa. Prince Henry the Navigator encouraged many of these expeditions. By the 1470s, the Portuguese had discovered the kingdom of Benin (where Nigeria now is), and by the 1480s, they had rounded the southern tip of Africa at a point they named the Cape of Good Hope. This left them prepared to sail on to Asia and establish trading posts.

New Ideas Take Root

Because of the existence of the Sahara Desert, Europeans had previously known very little about Africa. Myths and stories had abounded, coming to Europe through the trade networks. Muslim merchants had established caravan routes across the desert and influenced the establishment of such states as the Mali and then the Songhay Empires (home of the fabled Timbuktu). But educated Europeans had learned from the works of the ancient Greeks that people could not live below the "burnt" zone and thus imagined that cities like Timbuktu were literally at the edge of the habitable world. It was therefore quite surprising to them to learn of such places as the densely populated, agricultural Benin as the Portuguese traveled farther down the African coast. And they were impressed to find that craftsmen in the neighboring Yoruba city-states produced stunningly beautiful items of bronze and ivory, including weapons (see Map 1–2).

However, even these kingdoms were no match, technologically speaking, for the Europeans. It would not have been possible, for example, for them to have come to explore Portugal. Because of a lack of protein-rich plants and domesticable animals, sub-Saharan Africans had turned to full-time farming significantly later than Eurasians and North Africans. When the Europeans found them in the fifteenth century, their technological power was roughly on a par with that of the ancient Sumerians of the Fertile Crescent, when they, too, had been relatively new to farming. The Portuguese thus found that the Africans were eager to trade desirable natural resources like gold, ivory, and also human slaves in exchange for textiles, metal goods like guns, and other items from the workshops of the North.

In these early years, the Portuguese sailors brought back only a few hundred Africans annually from their exploratory voyages and sold them in Mediterranean markets as household servants. They did not immediately imagine that the trade would grow, not associating slavery with Africans in particular. (The Latin root of the word "slave" referred to Slavic peoples taken in war.) In Africa, as almost everywhere on earth, there existed an ancient practice of selling prisoners of war into slavery. These slaves were mostly women

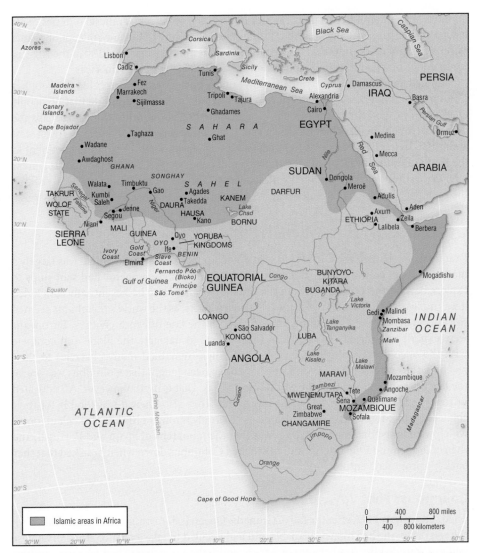

Map 1-2   Africa in the Age of Discovery   Before 1450, Europeans knew little of Africa. Until that time, trade between Africa and Europe was controlled by Islamic traders whose empire extended across North Africa. In the middle of the fifteenth century, the Portuguese reached the western coast of Africa and began importing both trade goods and a small number of slaves.
Source: Mark Kishlansky et al., *Societies and Culture in World History* (New York: HarperCollins, 1995), p. 414.

and children who worked as domestics in other people's households. Theirs was not an enviable fate, but they generally were not treated cruelly, and their children were not usually considered slaves.

However, after Portugal gained control of the island of Madeira, off the coast of Africa, in the 1420s, and Spain seized the Canary Islands at the end of the century, businessmen conceived the idea of large-scale sugar cultivation based on slave labor. Enslaved Africans on the islands did not live in their captors' households or become enmeshed in ties of affection; and if they had any children, they became slaves, too. The new concept of chattel slavery was emerging. In the coming centuries, plantation slavery would strip the African continent of much of its population and bring new suffering to the Americas.

In the late fifteenth century, the findings of the Portuguese explorers led Christopher Columbus to think that if the experts had been wrong in their assumption that no people lived south of the Sahara, they might have been wrong about other things. Perhaps the globe was much smaller than they believed. It might be possible for a ship to travel west and arrive in the East before its food and water supplies ran out. And if the continent to the south of Europe was full of seemingly conquerable peoples, perhaps there was similar territory to the south of Asia. Such lands could be taken and used as a foothold in seeking the riches of the East. Columbus set about attempting to convince others of his theories.

Collision in the Caribbean

Exactly which part of the Old World would encounter the New, and when, was largely a matter of chance. In the early fifteenth century, the Chinese emperor had sent ships to explore beyond their usual routes in the Indian Ocean, but he had eventually concluded it was not worth the cost of investing in expensive fleets, as the world's merchants seemed so bent on coming to his country in any case. In the late fifteenth century, Europeans were experiencing heady successes in their efforts to navigate the globe and compete with the once-dominant Muslim states. Still, there remained many obstacles to their reaching the unknown New World. We have often been taught that Columbus was one of the few who understood that the world was not flat. That is myth, however. All educated Europeans in his era knew the world was round. They also knew it was too big for their small ships to circumnavigate. Columbus was simply wrong in his hopeful calculations, which were based on ignorance. So it was that the monarchs of Spain and Portugal, and then of France and England, all initially turned Columbus down when he asked that they back his proposed venture.

Columbus's First Voyage

Then suddenly in 1492, after the fall of Granada, Queen Isabel summoned Columbus. With the wars over, she had money available and had decided to take a chance. The Portuguese had just rounded the southern tip of Africa, and Italian merchants had far more positive relations with Muslim merchants than Spanish ones did at present. She was desperate to prevent her newly unified country from falling into economic dependence on others.

In the accord that both sides signed, it is evident that Columbus was being sent on more than a trade mission. The monarchs were also clearly interested in the possibility that he might conquer a foothold in the East. He was to sail not due west, but southwest, toward Asian lands they hoped would be weaker than China. Columbus was also granted the position of governor-general of all the lands that he might conquer. Needless to say, he was also to conduct trade with China, and after deducting for expenses, he could keep one-tenth of the income from the enterprise, with the monarchy retaining the rest. The amount spent on the voyages, though larger than any individual merchant could afford, was relatively small in the context of Spain's budget; it would prove to be one of the shrewdest investments in the history of nations.

Christopher Columbus There are no surviving images of Christopher Columbus taken from life, but this painting was completed while people who remembered him well still lived.

By his calculations, Columbus was sure his tiny fleet would be at sea no more than a few weeks. After nearly six weeks, with supplies dwindling, the men grew dangerously restless. They occasionally saw seagulls and tufts of grass in the water, but no land. Then, at two hours after midnight on October 12, 1492, a lookout spotted land. It was an island, and they named it San Salvador, after Jesus Christ the savior.

Columbus believed they were off the coast of China, Japan, or India. Not understanding that he had found an unknown continent, he called the people they met "Indians." He conducted a ceremony to take possession of the island in the name of Ferdinand and Isabel. When the Indians came to see the newly arrived strangers, he presented gifts to initiate trade. The people responded with alacrity, bringing cotton and parrots to exchange for what the Spaniards offered. Columbus wrote in his journal, "They should be good and intelligent servants, for I see that they say very quickly everything that is said to them; and I believe that they would become Christians very easily, for it seemed to me that they had no religion. Our Lord pleasing, at the time of my departure, I will take six of them from here to Your Highnesses in order that they may learn to speak." Modern readers often stop at this point, chagrined but not surprised by Columbus's evident condescension and the Native Americans' apparent innocence. Reading further in the journal, however, the picture becomes more complicated. The Indians did, of course, have a religion, a language, and a set of diplomatic understandings of their own, and they did not respond positively to everything the newcomers did. In frustration, Columbus seized a number of them with brutal violence.

Columbus and his men visited the islands in the area over the next three months. The Arawak (or Taino) people who lived there had been farmers for a few hundred years. They grew corn and beans, lived in settled villages, and had begun to weave cotton into cloth. They had no metal weapons of any kind, and their towns could not withstand concerted attacks by the Spaniards. Other Indians, relative newcomers coming up from today's Venezuela, were in the process of conquering some of the smaller islands for themselves. These were the Caribs who later gave the Caribbean its name. They were much vilified by the Spaniards due to the effectiveness of their guerilla warfare tactics. After a futile search for China, hampered not only by geographic realities but also by an absolute inability to communicate, Columbus decided to return to Spain. He traded for as much gold jewelry and wild cotton, and as many exotic birds as he could. Then he set sail for home, bearing the cargo, the kidnapped Indians, and his exciting news to an eager Spanish court.

The Origins of a New World Political and Economic Order

Columbus was treated like a hero upon his return. Large investments were readily forth-coming, and within a year he embarked again. (He would sail two more times before he died.) Over a thousand people accompanied him this time. They were to settle the islands and from there continue to seek the fabulous wealth of China and Japan. This time, they would even be able to gather information from the indigenous people, as some of those they had brought back to Europe had learned to speak Spanish.

It soon became clear that the vast treasures Columbus had anticipated were not ac-tually at hand. The people who had accompanied him, however, expected to be rewarded, and the queen and king who had financed his expedition awaited profits. Therefore, Columbus packed off more than 500 Indians to be sold as slaves in Europe and distributed another 600 or so among the Spanish settlers of Hispaniola for them to use to establish plantations and gold mines. The level of violence increased considerably. One man wrote home with relish about a young Indian woman whom he had brought on board a ship and brutally raped.

Yet as the monarch who had driven the Muslims and then the Jews out of Spain, Isabel took seriously her responsibilities to evangelize and care for her Indian subjects. Isabel and her successors also had political and economic goals, all of which they at-tempted to reconcile by insisting that the Indians who inhabited the islands seized by the Spanish were her vassals, subjects of the Spanish Crown. Like other vassals in Spain and its growing empire, the Indians were to be technically free, although they could be required to both work and pay tribute to the Crown. Isabel instructed the governor to impose European-style civilization and Christianity on them. They were to be "made to serve us through work, and be paid a just salary," and in order to assure their salvation, "they must live in villages, each in a house with a wife, family and possessions, as do the people of our kingdoms, and dress and behave like reasonable beings." Humane treatment and freedom from slavery would thus depend on the Indians' willingness to abandon their religion and customs and adopt those of the Spanish.

With the Spanish monarchy refusing to sanction the enslavement of friendly Indians, settlers had to devise an alternate means of getting labor from them. Out of this struggle a New World political economy emerged. For the first several years, the Spanish simply demanded a certain amount of tribute from the Tainos as a whole. Individual Spaniards found this arrangement insufficiently lucrative, and across the island of Hispaniola, they began subduing individual *caciques* (chiefs) and demanding that they compel their people to work for whomever the governor named. The settlers received neither land—which had to be obtained from Spanish royal officials through grant or purchase—nor actual ownership of the Indians. They possessed only the right to compel the Indians they held in *encomienda* (as the system was called) to work for them. In exchange, each *encomendero*, or holder of an *encomienda*, was to ensure that the Indians received Christian instruction and lived in godly villages. Theoretically, the colonists thus complied with Isabel's insis-tence that friendly Indians be made vassals of the Crown rather than slaves. But although the system appeared to give due regard to the rights and spiritual requirements of the native people, they were in fact subjected to overwork and abuse even if they could not legally be bought and sold as slaves. This form of exploitation, though akin to European serfdom, was unique to the New World.

The Division of the World

Meanwhile, in Europe, the report of Christopher Columbus had touched off a veritable frenzy of international competition. In 1493, at the request of the Spanish monarchs, Pope Alexander VI confirmed Spanish dominion over all the lands that Columbus had explored and commanded the Spanish "to lead the peoples dwelling in those islands and countries to embrace the Christian religion." The Portuguese feared that they might lose control of Madeira and the nearby Azores and other current or future settlements on islands off the coast of Africa, so they complained to the pope. In 1494, the office of the pope arranged for both parties to sign the Treaty of Tordesillas, giving Spain all lands to be discovered to the west of an imaginary line 270 leagues west of the Azores, and Portugal all lands east of it. The treaty later formed the basis for Portugal's claim to Brazil, which her explorers accidentally reached in 1500. In the same period, in 1497, Henry VII of England, who deeply regretted having rejected Columbus's overture, sent off John Cabot to sail past Greenland and seek a "Northwest Passage" to the East. Cabot came to Newfoundland, concluded it must be part of Asia, and claimed it for England.

An Italian merchant named Amerigo Vespucci joined some of the expeditions sailing off to explore these new lands. In 1499, he saw the northeast coast of what we now know is South America. He still believed he was seeing some part of the Asian world, but he and his companions were increasingly convinced that these were significant southern territories—either an extensive peninsula or even a severed southern landmass—not previously heard of, as Columbus had predicted. A few years later, an embellished version of his letters was published. At the time, many intellectuals questioned whether the newly discovered lands actually fell within the Asian world or constituted an entire, previously unknown continent separating the great ocean into two. In 1507, a German cartographer concluded that the latter must be true. He published a map that circulated widely because it was the first to assert the geographic truth so unmistakably. He named the new landmass after Amerigo Vespucci, whom he wrongly believed to have been the first European to see it, and the unlikely label stuck.

Onto the Mainland

Even after the Europeans had become convinced that they were nowhere near the mainland of Asia, they continued their exploratory missions with zeal. In a little more than a quarter of a century, the population of the Caribbean islands had collapsed. The Spaniards who had arrived first divided its arable lands among themselves. Therefore, newly arriving European settlers, seeking both land and slaves, continued to sail beyond charted territories. In 1513, the Crown issued the *Requerimiento*, or "Requirement," a document drafted by legal scholars and theologians. It promised all Indians that if they accepted Christianity, including the authority of the pope and the Spanish monarch, the conquerors would leave them in peace; but if they resisted, the conquerors would have the right to make war on them and capture and enslave prisoners. Some evidence suggests that explorers read the document in Latin to uncomprehending Indians and then proceeded to wage what could now be defined as a "just war" against them. The Indians learned to tantalize the Spaniards with accounts of glittering empires a little farther west, just far enough away to get the dangerous strangers out of their territory. It was not long before the Spaniards were convinced that there was a large continent to be found. Eventually, they discovered the Aztec Empire in Mexico and the Inca Empire in Peru, each of which rivaled the most fantastic images from literature and legend.

The First Florida Ventures

Ambitious Spaniards set off on their exploratory missions in all directions (see Map 1–3). They crossed Central America at one point and saw the Pacific, and they touched on the northern coasts of South America. Juan Ponce de León was the first European explorer to reach the mainland that would later be called the United States. In March 1513 he reached the Atlantic shore of the land he named Florida, which he mistakenly thought was another island. He and his men sailed around Florida to the Gulf Coast, encountering hostile Indians who probably had already heard about the Spanish slave traders. On the west coast of Florida, he met the Calusas, the most powerful ethnic group in the region. When

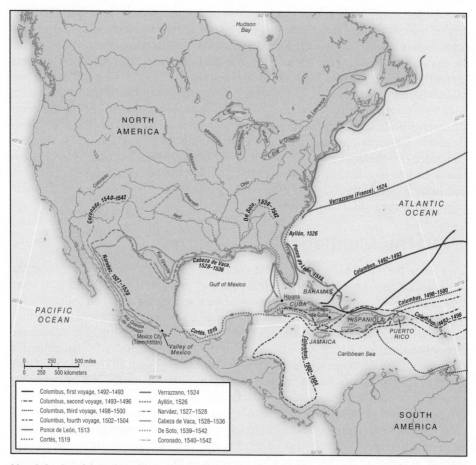

Map 1-3 Spanish Exploration In the 50 years after Columbus's first voyage, Spanish explorers traveled across most of the southern half of the United States.

Ponce de León returned with another expedition in 1521, they were ready for him. The Calusas attacked. Ponce de León was wounded by an arrow and returned to Cuba to die.

In Florida, the diseases the Spaniards brought with them struck the densely settled agricultural population particularly hard, and explorers routinely pillaged local villages and enslaved those whom they captured. Of the hundreds of small tribes, each with its own history, politics, economy, and culture, all that remains today are the names that the Spaniards recorded.

The Conquest of Mexico

For almost 30 years, the fabled cities of gold sought by the Spaniards proved elusive. However, the capital of a great empire really was nearby, and its ruler, through his network of spies, soon learned of the coming of the strangers. His name was Moctezuma II (later renamed "Montezuma" by the English), and he was the sixth in a line of powerful Aztec kings. The Mayan states in the Yucatan had long ago declined from their former glory and now existed as relatively small, separate chiefdoms. But the star of the central basin of Mexico had risen. Waves of nomadic invaders from the north (that is, the southwestern part of the future United States) had regularly brought new blood and new ideas to the famed farming regions of central Mexico, and there they had been incorporated (as Europe sometimes incorporated the Vikings, or China the Mongolian hordes). Moctezuma's people, the Mexica (pronounced Me-SHEE-ka), arriving 200 years previously, had constituted the last wave of invaders. After several generations of jockeying for power with other local chiefs, through strategic alliances and extraordinary military bravado, they had launched the most powerful state yet known in the Americas.

Moctezuma's power was still growing. At the start of his reign, he had led the invasion of areas including the Coatzacoalcos region, the home of Malinche. Other ethnic groups were always offered the prospect of joining the empire voluntarily at first by paying an annual tribute. They were then left alone as largely self-governing entities. Only if they resisted did the Aztec lord bring his military might and that of his subject states and allies to bear. Great resistance was punished harshly: prisoners were taken as sacrifices for the gods, who in exchange for all they did for humankind demanded the greatest gift of all, that of human life.

In 1517 and 1518, two different Spanish expeditions rounded the Yucatan Peninsula and touched on the coast of central Mexico in Mayan territory. Aztec merchants lived in the area, and through them, Moctezuma would have heard of the events. In 1519, Hernando Cortés followed the paths they had charted. He was both luckier and bolder than his predecessors. After a skirmish with the Mayas, he was given 20 women as a peace offering, and among them was the young woman, Malinche. With her at his side translating, explaining, and bargaining for food, Cortés was able to learn the whereabouts of the Aztec capital and begin to make his way upward into the mountains along the paths that led to the city. Messengers from the outskirts of his territories brought Moctezuma the news.

As Cortés and his entourage of about 500 made their way toward the city of Tenochtitlan (on the site of present-day Mexico City), they worked to form alliances with Moctezuma's avowed enemies, or with people recently conquered by him and still smarting from their defeat. When the Spaniards were occasionally attacked, they attacked back, sending mounted and armored men galloping through villages with long spears and torches, wreaking destruction, until the people sued for peace and declared themselves willing to join the Spanish.

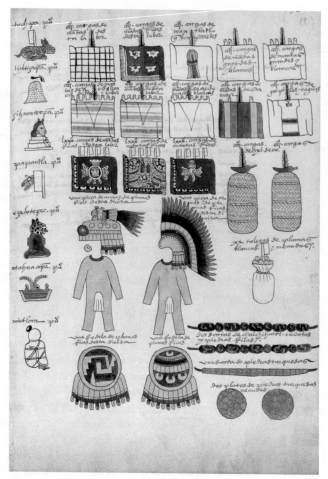

Moctezuma's Tribute Rolls After the conquest, Moctezuma's former subjects made charts for the Spaniards showing what they had once paid in tribute.

Moctezuma himself probably ordered some of the attacks as he tested the strangers' military capabilities. He then sent messengers offering to pay the Spaniards an annual tribute if they would stay away (essentially what those whom he could defeat offered him). This, however, was not what the Spaniards wanted. They pressed forward, and Moctezuma decided to let them and their new indigenous allies enter the city. Politically, he could not afford a battle with major casualties close to home, and if he let them enter, he might be able to work out an arrangement satisfactory to both parties. In November 1519, Hernando Cortés and Moctezuma II met formally and exchanged ostentatious greetings on a grand causeway leading over the lake that surrounded the beautiful island city of Tenochtitlan.

For the next few months, the Spaniards were the unwelcome yet honored guests of Moctezuma. They visited all parts of the city and asked for and were given large quantities of gold. Both sides schemed to learn more of each other and gain control of the situation. Eventually, Cortés had his men seize Moctezuma and hold him prisoner. He then proceeded to issue orders to the populace through his new hostage. Not long after, some jumpy Spaniards panicked at the sight of a religious dance put on by warriors in full regalia and slaughtered all the performers. This was enough for the Mexica people. They decided to disregard the words of their king. Surrounding the building where their hated guests were staying, they moved in to kill. The terrified Spaniards broke out, but only about a third escaped. An unknown number of the Spaniards' indigenous allies were also killed, as well as Moctezuma himself.

Cortés gathered his shattered forces in Tlaxcala, home of the Aztecs' greatest enemies. While the Tlaxcalans publicly debated whether or not to continue the alliance—eventually deciding that they should—Cortés penned a letter to the king of Spain. He made little of his present plight and also made the claim that Moctezuma had voluntarily turned his kingdom over to him on the day they met and had been in Cortés's custody ever since. If that were true, then the warriors who had just driven him out could be defined as rebels, and he would be justified in bringing them to heel, which he fully intended to do. Interestingly, he made no claim at all that the Aztecs had taken him for a god. That was a flattering story invented by Spaniards many years later, a fiction that certainly took hold of the European imagination, but for which there was never any real evidence.

Cortés waited for more men, horses, and supplies from Europe and the Caribbean, and he worked actively to persuade other indigenous groups to join him. Many of these groups did so when they saw additional European ships arrive. One of the newly arrived boats also brought the smallpox virus to Mexico for the first time. Most of the Spaniards were immune, but the disease decimated the Tlaxcalans as well as the Mexica.

Eventually, in April 1521, Cortés was ready to launch a great assault on Tenochtitlan. For over two months, the Aztecs and their allies fought him street by street. Cortés used his cannons to level the city, leaving open areas in which mounted and armored Spaniards with long lances could fight with impunity against their adversaries. "Bit by bit they came pressing us back against the [city] wall," an Aztec warrior later remembered. When there were almost no warriors left to fight, and the starving women and children in the city were reduced to eating insects, Moctezuma's successor sought peace. The mighty Aztec state had been defeated.

The Establishment of a Spanish Empire

In many ways, the Aztecs' experiences were similar to those of most Native Americans in their early dealings with Europeans. An early period of tentative, even fumbling European exploration was followed by a formal, ceremonial exchange. Then came a brief time of mutual curiosity and trade, before European intentions became fully clear to the indigenous and a crisis erupted in which they violently rejected the outsiders. After a setback of greater or lesser extent, however, the Europeans always collected themselves and ultimately asserted their authority. The Indians strategized creatively and fought bravely, but they could not compete with European technology. The problem was that people who had only recently become farmers (or in some cases were still hunter-gatherers) were pitted against people who were the cultural heirs of 10,000 years of sedentary living. One side had such things as horses, protective metal armor, far-shooting crossbows, and ships constantly bringing new men and supplies, while the other side did not. The people of the central basin of Mexico had been farming longer than anyone else in the Americas, and not surprisingly, they were able to put up the most dramatic fight against the Europeans. However, even they could win only a battle, not a long, drawn-out war.

After defeating the Aztecs, the Spaniards continued to wage war against other ethnic groups, but it did not take many years to subdue most of Mexico, leaving only the most

Native Americans Debate the Question of the Europeans

Before a great pyramid temple, surrounded by sunbaked adobe buildings, the nobles of Tlaxcala (Tlash-KA-la) met to discuss the fate of the Spaniards. It was July 1520 (in the European calendar), and the invading Spaniards under Hernando Cortés had just been driven from the Aztec capital of Tenochtitlan; about two-thirds of them had been killed. Dying at their sides had been hundreds of Tlaxcalans who chose to ally with the Europeans. Now the Tlaxcalan council had to decide if they should protect the Spaniards who had fled back to them or turn on their former allies.

When the newcomers first appeared from the east more than a year before, the Tlaxcalans met them in battle, but they soon learned that they could not defeat the metal-clad warriors mounted on large beasts, wielding long spears and shooting

fire arrows from a distance. The Indians' stone arrows shattered when they hit their enemies' armor, and the Spaniards could storm into their villages on horseback, skewer people, set fire to buildings, and then escape unhurt themselves. Within days the Tlaxcalans had made peace, offering to help the Spaniards move against the Aztecs, who were the Tlaxcalans' longtime enemies. They sent hundreds, perhaps thousands of warriors to Tenochtitlan. The Spaniards, however, were ejected from the powerful Aztec capital a few months later, and many of the Tlaxcalan allies died.

The exhausted and impatient Spanish survivors waited for two weeks while the Tlaxcalans' democratic process unfolded. Many people were allowed to have a say in the public forum in order for consensus to emerge. Tlaxcala consisted of four

remote areas still independent and unconquered. Meanwhile, the Europeans built ships on the Pacific coast and began to make their way down the side of the continent. In the 1530s, they discovered and conquered the astounding Inca Empire (centered in today's Peru), another farming kingdom, whose network of roads had covered much of the Andes. Now the Spaniards had at least nominal control of the lands stretching from the tip of South America to halfway up what is now the United States, excepting only the Portuguese colony of Brazil.

Both Mexico and Peru were found to contain vast deposits of silver, and Colombia contained a significant amount of gold. This yielded extraordinary profits for both Spanish investors and the Crown (as collector of the tax called the King's fifth). The Indians everywhere were given out in *encomienda* to work on the plantations of the Spaniards.

The plantations produced widely varying crops, but the most profitable one was sugar. As its cultivation spread, so did the demand for labor, as producing sugar was extremely labor intensive at certain seasons. The *encomienda* system could not meet the demand. By the second half of the sixteenth century, Indian laborers in sugar had been replaced by enslaved Africans. Brazil and some of the Caribbean colonies were largely dedicated to its subkingdoms, each ruled by its own chief, or *tlatoani*, meaning "he who speaks on behalf of others." Sometimes the four units worked together on internal, domestic tasks, such as the building of roads; they always operated in tandem in their diplomatic dealings with outsiders and the making of war. Regarding the present occasion, it was not merely a question of allowing each of the four chiefs to speak. Each chief was supported by the heads of the noble lineages within his domain; to retain power, the chief needed to be sure that each man felt he was heard and respected. The four subunits took turns allowing men to step forward and voice their thoughts. Sometimes the highest nobles interjected a summary or underscored a central point to keep the group moving gradually toward a resolution.

Some of the nobles believed they had learned enough about Spanish capability to be sure they would win in the end; they noted that they had it on good authority from Indians who were learning Spanish that more Europeans, horses, and weapons were on their way. Others believed the power of the Spanish was exaggerated, that the Aztecs' recent victory demonstrated that the Europeans could be defeated, and that their present weakness provided the Tlaxcalans a perfect opportunity to destroy them. One young prince named Xicotencatl (SHEE-ko-ten-kat), the son of the chief of the second most powerful quadrant, had engaged in negotiations with the Aztecs: the Aztecs promised, he said, that if they turned on the Spanish now, the Aztecs would make the Tlaxcalans their closest allies. Having resisted Aztec authority themselves for so long, it was tempting to the Tlaxcalans to become the Aztecs' partners in ruling the land. Others, however, cautioned that the Aztecs could not be trusted.

The debate went back and forth until the vast majority had decided it was safer to hold fast to the Spaniards and help them survive until more Europeans arrived. Xicotencatl did not agree, but his father did, and he expressed willingness to abide by the community's decision. His people had taught him that governance was more effective when power was shared.

cultivation. For the first time, Africans became yet another commodity to be transported across the seas, robbing Africa of its population and adding to the wealth of the Old World.

The Return to North America

After the conquest of Mexico, the Spaniards resumed their exploration of Florida with heightened expectations. There were several ventures, the most significant ones led by Lucas Vázquez de Ayllón, Pánfilo de Narváez, and Hernando de Soto. In 1526, Ayllón explored the South Carolina coast and established a short-lived town on the coast of Georgia. Two years later, Narváez landed near modern-day Tampa with 400 men. Battles and shipwrecks, however, destroyed the expedition. Ultimately, only four men survived: three Spaniards and an enslaved North African. They washed up on the shores of Texas. By good luck, they came to be accepted as healers and, eight years later, walked down into Spanish Mexico from the north.

The Spaniard who left the greatest mark on the southeastern part of the future United States was Hernando de Soto. He had participated in the assault on the Inca Empire in

Peru, which provided him with a small fortune and the belief that more wealth could be found in exploring unknown territories. He and his forces landed near Tampa in 1539. His party of about 600 soldiers spent the next four years exploring the area, which was densely populated by Mississippian tribes, and eventually reached the Mississippi River.

De Soto took whatever food, treasure, and people he wanted in his journey. Some communities fought back fiercely, whereas others attempted to placate the invaders. The region never really recovered from the expedition's depredations: deaths from disease, the destruction of many chieftains, and losses incurred in battles made it impossible for ruling families to continue to command tribal members to produce food surpluses and build great towns. On the other hand, the resistance on the part of the Indians took its toll on the Spaniards as well. Only about 300 of them made it back to Mexico, and de Soto himself died en route in 1542.

In the Southeast, the Spanish never found the great sought-after cities of gold resembling the Aztec and Inca capitals. And because much of the land did not seem suitable for large-scale agriculture, and most of the peoples were still nomadic hunter-gatherers for part of each year—who therefore could not be given out in *encomienda*—Spain never colonized most of the territory de Soto saw. Instead, military outposts, such as St. Augustine, were established to protect the more valuable lands to the south. To prevent rival nations from claiming the northern reaches of its empire, Spain did not disclose the geographic information it had secured from expeditions like de Soto's. This secrecy ultimately weakened Spain's claim to the region, however, because such claims traditionally depended on the right of prior exploration.

In the meantime, another group of Spaniards was setting out northward from Mexico City, toward the southwestern part of the future United States. They had heard tales of the Seven Cities of Cíbola, supposedly filled with gold and gems. In May 1539, a party guided by Esteban the Moor—one of the four survivors of the Narváez expedition, who had survived because they had attained the status of healers—reached the Zuni Pueblo in today's New Mexico. The inhabitants of the town no longer interpreted Esteban to be a healer; they killed him when he approached. A year later, another aspiring conquistador, Francisco Vásquez de Coronado, arrived at Zuni with about 300 Spaniards, 1,000 Indian allies, and 1,500 horses and pack animals. They took the pueblo and several others by force and later traveled west to the Grand Canyon and east as far as Wichita, Kansas, coming within 300 miles of de Soto's expedition.

Unprepared for the cold winter of 1540–1541, Coronado's party depleted the food and supplies of the Indians near their camp at Bernalillo. When a Spaniard raped an Indian woman, the Pueblos rebelled. By the time they were put down, at least 100 Indians had been burned at the stake and about

Timucua Indians, 1591 Here, they celebrate the defeat of the enemy.

13 villages destroyed. To the relief of the local people, silver was shortly thereafter discovered in Mexico and became the focus of the settlers' attention for many years. The Southwest had proved disappointing to them; they left and did not return in numbers until the 1590s. A warning of the struggles to come, however, had been given to both sides.

The Consequences of Conquest

Some of the most important changes produced by contact between Europeans and Native Americans were wholly unintentional. Most indigenous communities needed the effort of all members to provide a food supply. Even those who demanded tribute from others were well aware of this. European demands often tipped a delicate social balance, though the newcomers did not realize it. The Europeans also unintentionally introduced new diseases that spread rapidly. If the biological effects of human contact were felt immediately, however, the consequences of plant and animal exchange took much longer. New breeds of animals were introduced into the Americas, and plants were exchanged between the Americas and Europe. The American landscape was forever changed, as domestic animals trampled grasslands and increasing acreage was turned over to the cultivation of Old World crops.

Demographic Disaster

The violent warfare that made conquest possible turned out to be only a small part of the problem faced by indigenous peoples. Although the *encomienda* system at first satisfied the Spanish settlers, it proved disastrous for the Indians. They could not produce the surplus necessary to support the Europeans in addition to feeding their own families. Besides facing the direct effects of malnutrition, the dislocation of their normal way of life was deeply disturbing, and the birthrate began to fall.

Within a few years after the appearance of Europeans, the Native American population began to decline, and the introduction of the smallpox virus to Hispaniola in 1518 hastened the process. Soon, no more than a thousand of the island's original half million inhabitants survived. Disease worked the same terrible destruction on the nearby islands of Cuba, Puerto Rico, and Jamaica. Sickness followed the Spanish and other Europeans wherever they went in the Americas, making conquest that much easier for them. Epidemics also spread to and decimated native populations that had not yet encountered Europeans.

Europeans did not set out to kill off the Native Americans, but the diseases they brought with them did just that. Isolation had protected the native peoples from the diseases of the Old World, whereas centuries of trade had caused Europeans, Africans, and Asians to become exposed to the microbes present in one another's environments and thus acquire some biological defenses. Without such immunities, Indians were overcome by wave after wave of European diseases, including smallpox, typhus, and influenza. Scholars debate the exact number of deaths, but it is clear that over the course of the first century, the indigenous population dropped by about 90 percent—in some places more, in some less. The psychological trauma inflicted by such events is almost impossible for those who have not experienced them to imagine. A Cakchiquel Indian remembered the spread of an epidemic in his native Guatemala in 1521 that killed a substantial proportion of his community. "After our fathers and grandfathers succumbed, half of the people fled to the fields. The dogs and the vultures devoured the bodies. . . . Your grandfathers died, and with them died the son of the king and his brothers and kinsmen. So it was that we became orphans, oh my sons! . . . We were born to die."

The Columbian Exchange

In what historians have called the Columbian Exchange, plants and animals, as well as human beings and their diseases, were shared between the two worlds connected in 1492, eventually transforming them both. Along with the 1,500 Spaniards who joined him on his second voyage, Columbus brought horses, pigs, cattle, sheep, and goats, as well as wheat, sugarcane, and seeds for fruits and vegetables (see Map 1–4). And he returned to Europe with a variety of plants hitherto unknown there.

The introduction of the new plants and animals had the negative effect of sometimes overrunning native farm fields and other ecosystems, but the new species also had some positive effects. Indians often adopted Old World life forms to their own purposes. American Southwestern and Plains Indians took to the horse, for example, which changed their way of life, making them more productive hunters and more dangerous enemies. Mounted Indians could easily kill more buffalo than they needed for their own subsistence, creating a surplus they could trade for European goods.

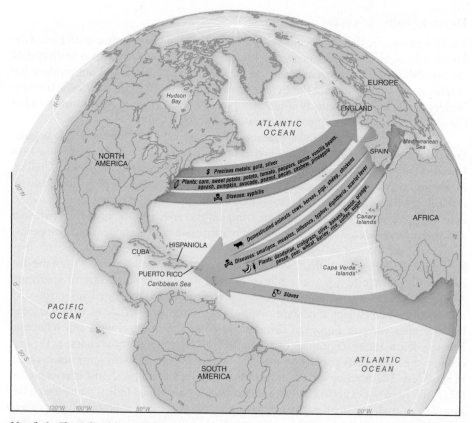

Map 1–4 The Columbian Exchange The exchanges of plants, animals, and diseases dramatically altered both the Old World and the New.

The Old World was also profoundly transformed by plants introduced from the Americas. Some plants that we associate with Europe came from the Americas. We might identify potatoes with Ireland, tomatoes with Italy, and fine chocolate with France, but none of these foods was produced in Europe before the sixteenth century. Moreover, the cultivation of American foods (particularly potatoes and corn) in the Old World, as well as of Old World foods (such as wheat) in the New, is often thought to have made possible the dramatic growth in world population that occurred in the ensuing centuries (see Figure 1–1).

Men's and Women's Lives

Every society has its own notion of the proper relationship between the sexes; this is one of the ways it establishes order. When one society conquers another, not only do different notions of gender come into conflict, but gender itself becomes one of the instruments of conquest. Conquerors often demonstrate dominance through rape, and the conquistadors wrote without self-consciousness of the ways in which they used native women whom they seized as commodities.

Yet not all encounters between European men and native women were violent. In many indigenous societies as well as in Europe, people were accustomed to using sexual relationships and marriage to cement alliances between prominent families—sometimes at great personal cost to the young women involved. Thus, for example, after Cortés defeated the Tlaxcalans, whose kingdom stood on the path to the Aztec capital, the Tlaxcalans presented a number of young women as part of the peace agreement. A page from a Tlaxcalan codex (a pictorial account painted on bark or paper) illustrates the ceremony. In the picture, Cortés sits on a chair, his officers behind him. In front of him is the Tlaxcalan leader, also backed up by his nobles. Malintzin stands addressing the Tlaxcalan women, who include elegantly dressed nobles, intended to be accepted as wives for Spanish leaders. The group also includes the daughters of lesser nobles, as well as some commoners intended as slaves.

Several decades later, the names and fates of some of the elite women were still remembered by both sides. Tlecuiluatzin, a daughter of Xicotencatl, an important Tlaxcalan chief, was renamed doña Luisa and became the mistress of Pedro de Alvarado, second in

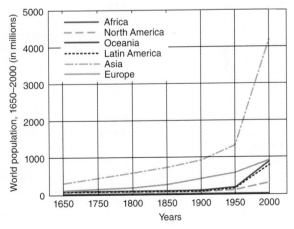

Figure 1-1 World Population, 1650-2000 These rough estimates of world population suggest the way that the colonization of the New World affected world population. The introduction of Old World disease led to population decline in the Americas, while the enslavement of millions of Africans led to population decline in Africa. At the same time, foods from the New World made possible the population increase of Europe and Asia.
Source: Based on Alfred W. Crosby Jr., *The Columbian Exchange: Biological and Cultural Consequences of 1492* (Westport, CT: Greenwood, 1972), p. 166.

Defeat of the Tlaxcalans Here, Malinche stands next to Cortés, receiving the Tlaxcalan women who have been presented to them as gifts from a defeated people.

command after Cortés. She accompanied him to Guatemala, and although they were not married, their children entered the higher ranks of Spanish society in the New World. Many of the first generation of elite *mestizo* (or mixed) sons, including Malinche's son by Cortés, were brought up in their fathers' households and even sent to Spain for their education, while the daughters generally found prominent husbands.

This state of affairs did not last, however. Indigenous women continued to bear children by European men, but once there were more Spanish women in the colonies, fewer such women ended up married, and fewer of the children received places of honor when

Time Line

▼**ca. 12,000 BCE**
Indian peoples arrive in North America

▼**711 CE**
Moors invade Iberian Peninsula

▼**1275–1292**
Marco Polo travels in Asia

▼**1434**
Portuguese arrive at West Coast of Africa

▼**1492**
Spanish complete the *reconquista*, evicting Moors from Spain
Jews expelled from Spain
Columbus's first voyage to America

▼**1493**
Columbus's second voyage

▼**1494**
Treaty of Tordesillas divides New World between Spain and Portugal

▼**1496**
Spanish complete conquest of Canary Islands

▼**1497**
John Cabot arrives in North America

▼**1498**
Columbus's third voyage to America, reaches South American coast

▼**1500**
Portuguese arrive in Brazil

they reached adulthood. Nevertheless, many of the relationships between the Spaniards and Native American women were consensual. The women had few options, given the devastation in their communities, and their cultures had instilled the idea that true strength lay in survival, rather than choosing death over compromise. The mestizo population grew larger every year.

Conclusion

Within a half century after Columbus's arrival in the New World, both the world he had come from and the one he had reached had been transformed into a new, global political economy (see Map 1–5). Thanks to the decision made by Queen Isabel, Spain dominated exploration, colonization, and exploitation of the New World. The wealth that Spain extracted from her colonies encouraged rival nations to enter into overseas ventures. Eventually France, England, the Netherlands, Sweden, and Russia all established New World colonies. Because Spain (along with Portugal, which claimed Brazil) had such a head start, rival nations would have to settle for the lands Spain left unclaimed.

In the wake of the unprecedented wealth gained in the Americas, a new global economy was established, linking the Old and New Worlds. Gold and silver extracted from its empire sustained Spain's rise to power, and the plantation crops of the New World made many Europeans wealthy. Thus, the divergence in the power of the two hemispheres grew wider, and Europe's power also grew relative to Asia's.

Native Americans faced enslavement or were given out in *encomienda*. As the native population was depleted and the morality of enslaving native populations was questioned, Europeans turned to the African slave trade. Suffering in the Americas was therefore intense, and yet at the same time, the people who survived learned to carry on with their lives. Ways of life stemming from multiple traditions unfolded, and cultures evolved in creative ways. The young girl named Malinche, it turned out, had been pointing the way.

▼**1504**
Columbus's fourth voyage to America ends

▼**1508**
Spanish conquer Puerto Rico

▼**1513**
Spanish *Requerimiento* promises freedom to all Indians who accept Spanish authority
Spanish conquer Cuba
Ponce de León reaches Florida
The Laws of Burgos attempt to regulate working conditions of Indians

▼**1518**
Spanish introduce smallpox to New World

▼**1519**
Cortés lands on Yucatan coast

▼**1519–1522**
Ferdinand Magellan's crew sails around the world

▼**1521**
Tenochtitlan falls to the Spanish
Ponce de León returns to Florida

▼**1526**
Ayllón explores South Carolina coast and establishes fort in Georgia

▼**1528**
Narváez explores Florida

▼**1539–1543**
De Soto and his party explore Southeast, arriving at Mississippi, devastating the Indians and their land

▼**1540–1542**
Coronado explores Southwest

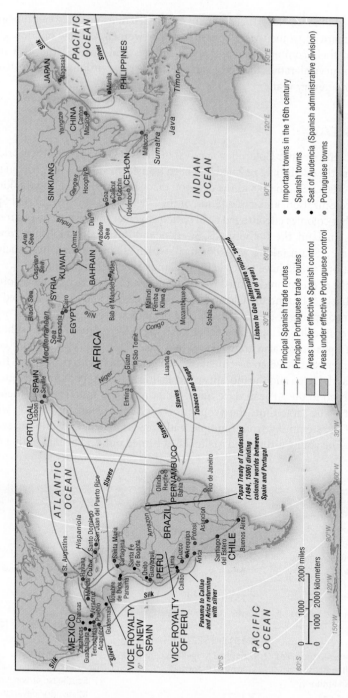

Map 1-5 A New Global Economy By 1600, both Spain and Portugal had established empires that reached from one end of the globe to the other.

Who, What, Where

Beringia 5

Brazil 17

Cahokia 9

Chaco Canyon 9

Coronado, Francisco Vásquez de 24

Cortés, Hernando 4

Encomienda 16

Hispaniola 16

Iberian Peninsula 10

Malinche (Malintzin, doña Marina) 4

Political economy 16

Ponce de León, Juan 18

The *Requerimiento* 17

Soto, Hernando de 23

Tenochtitlan 19

Tlaxcala 21

Xicallanco 7

Yucatan Peninsula 6

Review Questions

1. Describe the development of indigenous civilizations in Central and North America from Archaic times until 1500. What were the major forces of change within these early populations?

2. What were the forces that led European countries, and particularly Spain, to explore the New World?

3. What was the impact of European conquest on the population and environment of the New World?

Critical-Thinking Questions

1. Compare older ways of explaining the conquest (such as Moctezuma's supposed belief that Hernando Cortés was a god) with scholars' more recent explanations. What beliefs about Native Americans does each set of explanations reflect?

2. How would Native American men and women have experienced conquest differently?

3. Compare Spain's treatment of Muslims and Jews in Spain following the *reconquista* with the country's later treatment of conquered Native Americans in the New World. Do you think these groups received similar or different treatment? Why?

Suggested Readings

Diamond, Jared. *Guns, Germs and Steel: The Fates of Human Societies*. New York: Norton, 1997.

Lockhart, James, ed. *We People Here: Nahuatl Accounts of the Conquest of Mexico*. Los Angeles: University of California Press, 1993.

Richter, Daniel K. *Before the Revolution: America's Ancient Pasts*. Cambridge, MA: Harvard University Press, 2011.

Tedlock, Dennis. *2000 Years of Mayan Literature*. Los Angeles: University of California Press, 2011.

Wey-Gómez, Nicolas. *Tropics of Empire: Why Columbus Sailed South to the Indies*. Cambridge, MA: MIT Press, 2008.

For further review materials and resource information, please visit www.oup.com/us/oakes-mcgerr

CHAPTER 1: WORLDS IN MOTION, 1450–1550
Primary Sources

1.1 AZTEC MIDWIFE'S PRAYER

The Nahuas began to arrive in central Mexico in the 900s. They migrated from what is today Arizona and New Mexico and settled among people who had been farmers for at least two millennia. One of the last groups to arrive, the Mexica (Me-SHEE-ka), had risen to great power by the time the Spanish came, ruling over hundreds of other city states. We know them now as the Aztecs. They had a remarkable literary culture, including poetry, songs, histories, and prayers. However, it was an oral culture and would probably be lost to us today were it not for the efforts of Christian missionaries. In the 1560s, forty years after the Spanish conquest, a Franciscan named Bernardino de Sahagún orchestrated a project in which Nahuatl-speaking assistants interviewed Indian elders about their former lives. The work was eventually taken to Florence, Italy, and thus became known as the Florentine Codex.

Uncan mitoa: in quenin ticitl quitlatlauhtiaia, in piltzintli in ooallacat . . .
Auh in otlalticpac quiz piltzintli: niman tzatzi in ticitl, tlacaoatza, quitoznequi: ca ouel iaot in cioatzintli, ca onoquichtic, ca otlama, ca ocacic in piltzintli . . .

Here is told how the midwife exhorted the baby who had been born:

When the baby had arrived on earth, then the midwife shouted; she gave war cries, which meant that the woman had fought a good battle, had become a brave warrior, had taken a captive, had captured a baby.

Then the midwife spoke to it. . . . You have suffered exhaustion, you have suffered fatigue, my youngest one, my precious noble child, precious necklace, precious feather, precious one. You have arrived. Rest, find repose. Here are gathered your beloved grandfathers, your beloved grandmothers, who await you. Here into their hands you have arrived. Do not sigh! Do not be sad! Why have you come, why have you been brought here? Truly you will endure the sufferings of torment and fatigue, for our lord has ordered, has disposed that there will be pain, affliction, misery [in our lives on earth]. There will be work, labor for morning and evening sustenance. [But] there is sweat, weariness and labor so that there will be eating, drinking, and the wearing of raiment. Truly you will endure . . .

Source: Charles Dibble and Arthur J. O. Anderson, eds., *General History of the Things of New Spain*, Book 6: *Rhetoric and Moral Philosophy* (Salt Lake City: University of Utah Press, 1969), pp. 35–36, 167–168. (We have amended their translations.)

1.2 VISUAL DOCUMENTS: CHACO CULTURE NATIONAL HISTORICAL PARK, PUEBLO BONITO

The corn that sustained Mesoamerican civilization eventually spread outward through long-distance trade. For example, in the San Juan River basin and especially in Chaco Canyon in the northwestern corner of today's New Mexico, people experimented with agriculture from the ninth to the eleventh century, adopting it for a few generations and then, when times were tougher, breaking into small nomadic groups. They built impressive stone-and-wood villages organized around *kivas*, large communal ceremonial chambers. The largest of these sites is now called Pueblo Bonito. Archaeologists have confirmed that the people who lived there were well aware of their history. A small original construction

became the ceremonial heart of the large village, which was built around it several generations later. There the people concentrated their burials, reliquaries, and precious goods, which included products brought from as far away as Mexico. At the town's height, as many as a thousand people lived there.

Source: Getty Images/DEA/SIOEN/Contributor and Getty Images/Education Images/Contributor.

1.3 KING FERNANDO AND QUEEN ISABELLA OF SPAIN, "GRANADA CAPITULATIONS" (1492)

In 1492, King Fernando and Queen Isabella of Spain defeated the last Muslim kingdom on the Iberian Peninsula, freeing them to turn their attention to international trade. They signed a business contract with a Genoese explorer named Christopher Columbus, who believed he could reach Asia by sailing west. They promised him a percentage of all the profits, and later, at his request, they also agreed that he could govern any territories he might conquer. They were all imagining he might conquer territories on the outskirts of Asia. This document, called the "Granada Capitulations," was signed April 30, 1492.

Sir Fernando and Lady Isabel, by the grace of God king and queen of Castile, Leon, Aragon, Sicily, Granada, Toledo, Valencia, Galicia, the Balearics, Seville, Sardinia, Cordoba, Corsica, Murcia, Jaen, the Algarve, Algeziras, Gibraltar and the Canary Islands, count and countess of Barcelona, lords of Vizcaya and Molina, dukes of Athens and Neopatria, counts of Roussillon and Cerdagne, marquises of Oristano and Goceano.

Because you, Christopher Columbus, are going at our command with some of our ships and personnel to discover and acquire certain islands and mainland in the Ocean Sea, and it is hoped that, with the help of God, some of the islands and mainland in the Ocean Sea will be discovered and acquired by your command and expertise, it is just and reasonable that you should be remunerated for placing yourself in danger for our service.

Wanting to honor and bestow favor for these reasons, it is our grace and wish that you, Christopher Columbus, after having discovered and acquired these islands and mainland in the Ocean Sea, will be our admiral of the islands and mainland that you discover and acquire and will be our admiral, viceroy and governor of them. You will be empowered from that time forward to call yourself Sir Christopher Columbus, and thus your sons and successors in this office and post may entitle themselves sir, admiral, viceroy and governor of them.

You and your proxies will have the authority to exercise the office of admiral together with the offices of viceroy and governor of the islands and mainland that you discover and acquire. You will have the power to hear and dispose of all the lawsuits and case, civil and criminal, related to the offices of admiral, viceroy, and governor, as you determine according to the law, and as the admirals of our kingdoms are accustomed to administer it. You and your proxies will have the power to punish and penalize delinquents as well as exercising the offices of admiral, viceroy, and governor in all matters pertaining to these offices. You will enjoy and benefit from the fees and salaries attached, belonging and corresponding to these offices, just as your high admiral enjoys and is accustomed to them in the admiralty of our kingdoms. . . .

Source: Granada Capitulations, Granada, April 30, 1492, as translated in Geoffrey Symcox and Blair Sullivan, eds., *Christopher Columbus and the Enterprise of the Indies* (Boston: Bedford, 2005), pp. 60–61.

1.4 AZTEC PRIESTS, STATEMENT TO THE FRANCISCAN FRIARS (1520s)

In 1524, three years after the conquest of Tenochtitlan, a group of 12 Franciscan friars representing the 12 apostles arrived in Mexico. They orchestrated a series of official meetings with high-ranking Aztec political leaders and priests. On several of these occasions, the Europeans took notes. Years later, in the 1560s, another Franciscan rewrote these notes as though the exchange he was recording had occurred on a single occasion, though he was really creating a composite picture. Here is a direct translation from the Nahuatl of what he claimed the Aztec priests said after having listened for several hours to the messages of the Christians. Notice that what has truly angered them is not so much the idea of a new god as the demand that they abandon the old.

You say that we do not recognize the being who is everywhere, lord of heaven and earth. You say our gods are not true gods. The new words that you utter are what confuse us; due to them we feel foreboding. Our makers [our ancestors] who came to live on earth never uttered such words. They gave us *their* laws, their ways of doing things. They believed in the gods, served them and honored them. They are the ones who taught us everything, the gods' being served and respected. Before them we eat earth [kiss the ground]; we bleed; we pay our debts to the gods, offer incense, make sacrifice. . . . indeed, we live by the grace of those gods. They rightly made us out of the time, the place where it was still dark. . . . They give us what we go to sleep with, what we get up with [our daily sustenance], all that is drunk, all that is eaten, the produce, corn, beans, green maize, chia. We beg from them the water, the rain, so that things grow upon the earth.

The gods are happy in their prosperity, in what they have, always and forever. Everything sprouts and turns green in their home. What kind of place is the land of Tlaloc [the rain god]? Never is there any famine there, nor any illness, nor suffering. And they [the gods] give people virility, bravery, success in the hunt, [bejeweled] lip rings, blankets, breeches, cloaks, flowers, tobacco, jade, feathers and gold.

Since time immemorial they have been addressed, prayed to, taken as gods. It has been a very long time that they have been revered, since once upon a time in Tula, in Huapalcalco, Xochitlapan, Tlamohuanchan, in Teotihuacan, the home of the night. These gods are the ones who established the mats and thrones [that is, inherited chieftainships], who gave people nobility, and kingship, renown and respect.

Will we be the ones to destroy the ancient traditions of the Chichimeca, the Tolteca, the Colhuaca, the Tepaneca? [No!][1] It is our opinion that there is life, that people are born, people are nurtured, people grow up, [only] by the gods' being called upon, prayed to. Alas, o our lords, beware lest you make the common people do something bad. How will the poor old men, the poor old women, forget or erase their upbringing, their education? May the gods not be angry with us. Let us not move towards their anger. And let us not agitate the commoners, raise a riot, lest they rebel for this reason, because of our saying to them: address the gods no longer, pray to them no longer. Look quietly, calmly, o our lords, at what is needed. Our hearts cannot be at ease as long as we cannot understand each other. We do not admit as true [what

---

[1] Nahuatl texts are full of rhetorical questions, the answer to which is always meant to be a resounding "No!"

you say]. We will cause you pain. Here are the towns, the rulers and kings who carry the world. It is enough that we have lost political power, that it was taken from us, that we were made to abandon the mats and thrones. We will not budge; we will just end [this conversation]. Do to us whatever you want. This is all with which we return, we answer, your breath, your words, o our lords.

Source: Miguel León Portilla, ed., *Coloquios y doctrina cristiana* (Mexico City: UNAM, 1986). This edition provides a facsimile of the original document; we have translated from the original Nahuatl into English.

1.5 ALVAR NÚÑEZ CABEZA de VACA, DESCRIBING NORTH AMERICA (1535)

In 1528, a Spanish exploratory expedition wrecked off the coast of Florida. The survivors met with a hostile Indian population and eventually fled from them in rafts that they built. Ultimately, only four men survived—three Spaniards and one North African, who had been a slave. They lived for years along the coast of what is today Texas, where they gained a reputation as healers among the local people. In 1535, they wandered into Spanish settlements in northern Mexico and re-entered European society. One of them, Alvar Núñez Cabeza de Vaca, wrote a long narrative about his experiences among people who had never seen a white man—or a black man—before.

The Indians from the Island of Malhado . . . are warlike people, and they have as much cunning to protect themselves from their enemies as they would have if they had been raised in Italy and in continuous war. When they are in a place where their enemies can attack them, they set up their houses at the edge of the most rugged woods and of the greatest density they find there. And next to it they make a trench and sleep in it. All the warriors are covered with light brush, and they make their arrows. And they are so well covered and hidden that even if their heads are uncovered, they are not seen. And they make a very narrow path and enter into the middle of the woods. And there they make a place for their women and children to sleep. And when night comes, they light fires in their houses, so that if there should be spies, they would believe that they are in them. And before dawn, they again light the same fires, and if by chance their enemies come to attack the houses themselves, those who are in the trench surprise them and from the trenches do them much harm without those outside seeing them or being able to find them. . . . While I was with the ones of Aguenes, they not being warned, their enemies came at midnight and attacked them and killed three of them and wounded many others, with the result that they fled from their houses forward through the woods. And as soon as they perceived that the others had gone, they returned to them. And they gathered up all the arrows that the others had shot at them, and as secretly as they could, they followed them and were near their houses that night without being perceived. And in the early morning they attacked them and they killed five of them and injured many others, and made them flee and leave their houses and their bows with all their possessions . . .

The manner in which they fight is low to the ground. And while they are shooting their arrows, they go stalking and leaping about from place to place, avoiding the arrows of their enemies, so much so that in such places they manage to suffer very little harm. The Indians are more likely to make fun of crossbows and harquebuses [than to fear them] because these weapons are ineffective against them in the flat, open areas where they roam free. They are good for enclosed areas and wetlands, but in all other areas, horses are what must be used to defeat them, and are what the Indians universally fear. Whoever might have to fight against them should be advised to prevent them from perceiving weakness or greed for what the [Indians] have. And as long as war lasts, they must treat them very badly, because if they know that their enemy has fear or some sort of greed [that may affect their decisions] they are people who know how to recognize the times in which to . . . take advantage of the fear [or greed] of their enemies.

Source: Rolena Adorno and Patrick Charles Pautz, eds., *The Narrative of Cabeza de Vaca* (Lincoln: University of Nebraska Press, 2003), pp. 127–129.

Colonial Outposts

1550-1650

< John White's Watercolor of Indians Fishing

AMERICAN PORTRAIT

Paquiquineo Finds His Way Home

The son of a chieftain, Paquiquineo was a young man, perhaps still a teenager, when the Spanish picked him up in 1561 on one of their exploratory expeditions. The Europeans often abducted young Indians and took them back to their own nations so that they could serve as translators and guides. Sometimes the process worked the other way around, and Europeans who were members of expeditions were accidentally left behind. To survive, they learned the Native Americans' language and customs. If and when they were ever reunited with their countrymen, they were valuable as interpreters. In the early years of colonization, those who had learned the ways of another culture gained influence far out of proportion to their numbers.

Don Luis did not see his own people again for 10 years. First the Spanish took him to Spain, where King Philip II asked him to convert to Christianity. He refused and asked only that he be taken home. The king, recognizing him as a fellow prince, agreed and sent him off in the next convoy to Mexico with orders that he be returned to his homeland on the expedition's return to Spain, following the winds. In Mexico, while he was staying with the Dominican Order, Paquiquineo became dangerously ill and decided to accept baptism. He was renamed don Luis de Velasco after the viceroy, who became his godfather. Unfortunately for him, the head of the order decided that such an astute young man would be invaluable as an intermediary in conversion efforts in North America, and would not let him leave. Years later, don Luis managed to travel to Havana, from there back to Spain, and then back to Havana, where he persuaded some Jesuits that he would help them establish a Christian mission among his own people on the North American mainland.

In 1570, less than a week after the Jesuits and their Indian convert had settled in Virginia, don Luis returned to his own people and customs. He scandalized the Jesuits by taking several wives, a privilege of Indian men of high rank. The Jesuits had expected don Luis to act as an intermediary with his people, securing them supplies and favorable treatment, so they threatened to bring the wrath of Spain down upon him. Paquiquineo had learned too much about Europeans during his time among them to doubt their ability to do this. He knew that his people had to act quickly if they were to act at all.

The Powhatans killed eight of the nine people at the mission. According to Indian custom, a young boy named Alonso was spared, although don Luis apparently argued for his death also. Knowing that the Spanish would someday return, he wanted no witnesses. As don Luis predicted, the Spanish did come back. They retrieved Alonso, through him ordered don Luis to appear for an inquest, and began executing other Indians when he failed to appear. Don Luis never returned to the Spanish, and in frustration, they sailed home.

In 1607, the English planted their first permanent colony on the mainland at Jamestown among people who were kin to don Luis's people. Throughout the seventeenth century, the English heard rumors about a Powhatan Indian who had spent time in the Spanish colonies.

During this period of American history, no sharp geographic or cultural line separated the Indians and Europeans. Indians such as don Luis lived among the Europeans, and Europeans such as Alonso spent time with the Indians. Even before permanent colonies were established, each group thus knew the other moderately well. Although the customs and practices of the other group often seemed odd and even ungodly, they were never completely alien. By the time actual settlements were established, there were usually already people who could act as go-betweens.

Pursuing Wealth and Glory Along the North American Shore

The search for wealth and prestige soon propelled other European nations to cross the Atlantic. In the minds of European leaders, riches, glory, and power were almost inseparable. As the English explorer Sir Walter Raleigh explained, "Whosoever commands the sea commands the trade; whosoever commands the trade of the world commands the riches of the world, and consequently the world itself." Most of the North American colonies established by European nations in the first half of the seventeenth century were outposts in the global economy. Despite significant differences, these colonies all shared certain elements: First, they were intended to bring in the greatest amount of revenue to the mother country at the lowest cost. Second, success depended on harmonious relations with—or elimination of—local Indians. Third, colonial societies slowly developed their own distinctive patterns, depending on which route they followed to prosperity.

European Objectives

At first, Europeans believed that Columbus had reached Asia. By the time they understood that he had discovered a new land, the Spanish were well on their way to conquering native peoples and stripping them of their wealth. Their success inspired other European nations to search for new sources of gold and silver in the regions Spain had not yet claimed. They also continued to seek a path through the Americas to Asia. For northern Europeans, colonization was not a goal for almost a century, and even then their colonies were designed primarily to provide a quick return on investment, not to transplant Europeans onto foreign soil.

The nations of northern Europe were unwilling to invest in permanent settlements for good reason. A foreign colony was costly. It involved procuring and provisioning a ship, providing a settlement with food and equipment, and resupplying it until it could turn a profit. Spain had been lucky: Isabel and Ferdinand's risk paid off relatively quickly because they found a hospitable climate, deposits of precious metals, and, most important, sedentary farming peoples who were already accustomed to a political hierarchy and to paying tribute to others. The northern European nations could not afford expeditions comparable to that of Columbus when it became clear that the North American world was very different from New Spain in these key regards.

Northern European nations learned what they knew of the North American world by sponsoring small, economical expeditions designed to establish trade and seek a sea route to Asia. Would-be explorers sold their services to the highest bidder. John Cabot, who sailed for England, was, like Columbus, born in Genoa, Italy. (His real name was Giovanni Caboto.) Before coming to England, he had spent time in Muslim Arabia, Spain, and Portugal, apparently looking for sponsors for a voyage to Asia. He found them in the English port city of Bristol, from whence he sailed in 1497. He landed in Newfoundland and claimed the territory for England.

Soon both England and France sent fishing expeditions to the waters off Newfoundland (see Map 2–1). The population of northwestern Europe exploded in the sixteenth and seventeenth centuries, creating an increased demand for fish, and fishing expeditions to Newfoundland were relatively inexpensive to sustain.

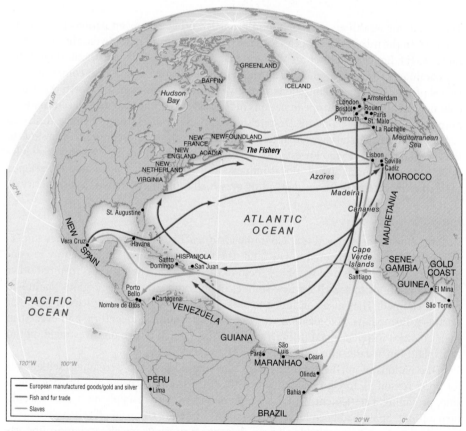

Map 2–1   North Atlantic Trade Routes at the End of the Sixteenth Century Hundreds of entrepreneurs from England, France, and Portugal sent ships to fish off the coast of Newfoundland to feed the growing population of Europe. The fur trade grew out of the Newfoundland fishing enterprise when fishermen who built winter shelters on the shore began trading with local Algonquian Indians (green lines). At the same time, European cities sent food, cloth, and manufactured goods to New Spain, in return for gold and silver (red lines). After 1580, the Portuguese began transporting slaves from Africa to sell in Brazil and New Spain (yellow lines). *Source:* D. W. Meinig, *The Shaping of America* (New Haven, CT: Yale University Press, 1986), vol. 1, p. 56.

The French colony of New France, planted in the St. Lawrence River region of Canada, grew out of the French fishing ventures off Newfoundland. Although early French explorers discovered neither gold nor a Northwest Passage to Asia, French fishermen found that the Indians were willing to trade beaver pelts at prices so low that a man could make a fortune in a few months' time.

The Huge Geographical Barrier

At first, North America seemed little more than an obstacle on the way to Asia. In 1522, Ferdinand Magellan's expedition had completed the first round-the-world voyage for Spain, proving finally that one could get to the East by heading west. Other nations then became interested in finding a way through, rather than around, North America. Two years after Magellan's voyage, the Italian Giovanni da Verrazano sailed on behalf of France. He explored the coast from South Carolina to Maine and was the first European to see New York Harbor. To Europeans, however, all that Verrazano had discovered was a huge barrier between Europe and Asia.

On that "huge barrier" of North America lived Indians, some wary and some friendly. Unfamiliar with Indian customs, Europeans often could not distinguish hospitality from malice. When Algonquian Indians attempted to dry out one of Verrazano's sailors, who had almost drowned, by setting him near a campfire, Verrazano feared that they "wanted to roast him for food." In the early years of exploration, survival often depended on local Indians, yet because the Europeans were looking either for treasure or for a Northwest Passage and were not necessarily thoughtful students of human nature, they tended to see cultural differences rather than similarities.

Between 1534 and 1542, King François I of France financed Jacques Cartier to make three expeditions to seek a route through North America and to look out for any riches along the way. All three came to naught. On their second trip, the French sailed up the St. Lawrence River as far as the town of Hochelaga (near present-day Montréal). The Iroquoian speakers there told of a wealthy land to the west. Although the Indians may have been trying to deceive the French, it is possible that the shiny metal they spoke of was the copper that the Hurons to the west mined and traded. The winter was brutal. Even with food and care from the Indians, at the end of the winter almost a quarter of the party was dead. The French found that their survival depended on the native peoples.

Later expeditions fared as badly. The region was cold and remote. The French quarreled with their Indian hosts and fought among themselves. Because their early attempts at finding easy riches failed, the French were in effect demonstrating that European profits in North America would have to rest on exploration, conquest of the natives, and colonization. Needless to say, this principle of European colonialism was gradually established without the consent of the Indians who inhabited the land.

Spanish Outposts

Throughout the sixteenth century, European nations jockeyed for power on their own continent. Because most of these nations were at war with each other, North America was often a low priority. But when the fighting in Europe abated, the Europeans looked across the Atlantic in hopes of gaining an advantage over a rival nation or finding a new source of wealth.

Soon the French and English, who found no gold or jewels along the coast, discovered an easier source of wealth—stealing from the Spanish. Every season, Spanish ships laden with treasure from Mexico and South America moved out of the Caribbean into the Atlantic and north along the coast until they caught the trade winds home. By the middle of the sixteenth century, French ships were lying in wait off Florida or the Carolinas. Because it was cheaper than exploration, preying on Spanish ships became a national policy.

To prevent these costly acts of piracy, King Philip II established a series of forts along both coasts of Florida. At the same time, a group of Huguenots (French Protestants) established a colony, Fort Caroline, near present-day Georgia. For the new commander of the Spanish forts, Pedro Menéndez de Avilés, the task was to destroy the French settlement. On a September morning in 1565, 500 Spanish soldiers surprised the French at Fort Caroline. Although the French surrendered and begged for mercy, they were slaughtered. The religious and nationalist conflicts of Europe had been transplanted to North America (see Map 2–2).

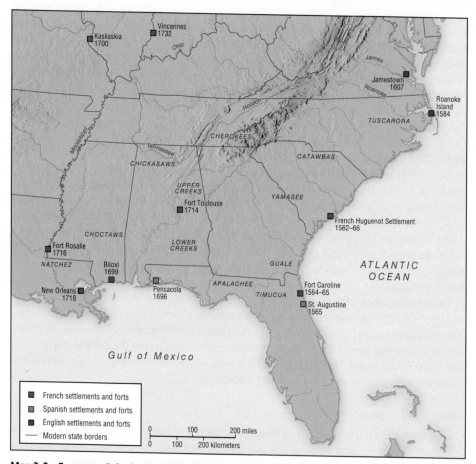

Map 2–2   European Colonization of the Southeast Beginning in the second half of the sixteenth century, the French, Spanish, and English established settlements in the Southeast.
Source: Charles Hudson, *The Southeastern Indians* (Knoxville: University of Tennessee Press, 1976), pp. 430–431.

One of the forts established by the Spaniards, St. Augustine, settled in 1565, is the oldest continuously inhabited city of European origin in the United States. Most of Menéndez's ambitious plans for Spanish settlements, however, were undermined by local Indians whom the Spanish alienated. After attacks by the Orista Indians in 1576 and by England's Francis Drake a decade later, the Spanish abandoned all of their Florida forts except St. Augustine. They faced the reality that this was not a territory either of silver mines or of sedentary Indians who could easily be given out in *encomienda*. Spanish dreams of an empire in this part of North America had been reduced to a small coastal garrison designed to protect the far richer territories to the south. Although the Spanish would later establish other missions in Florida, their presence was peripheral to Spain's American empire.

New France: An Outpost in Global Politics and Economics

The Spanish had given up hopes of an empire along the southeast coast of North America, but they had at least succeeded in scaring off the French from there. After the massacre at Fort Caroline, the French once again turned their focus to the St. Lawrence River. By the beginning of the seventeenth century, the French had discovered the beaver trade. The pelts found a ready market in Europe, where they were turned into felt hats. A trade that began almost as an accident on fishing expeditions soon became the basis for the French empire in modern Canada. The French were drawing the Indians into a global economy, a process that dramatically changed not only the world of the North Americans but that of the Europeans as well.

The Five Nations of Iroquois and the Political Landscape

The French intruded on a region where warfare among Indian tribes had recently been widespread. At least a century previously, five Iroquoian-speaking tribes living in today's New York State (see Map 2–3) had ended a period of feuding among themselves by establishing a league called the Five Nations. The members of this alliance were bound to keep peace among themselves and to coordinate a common defense against outsiders. Their new policy, combined with a relatively dense population due to their practicing agriculture for part of the year, easily rendered them the dominant political entity in the region. They made war against the Algonquian-speaking tribes living primarily to the north of the St. Lawrence, but they also attacked other Iroquoian-speaking groups and may even have annihilated some, such as the Hochelegans. The Hurons, for example, although speakers of an Iroquoian language, were the avowed enemies of the Five Nations when the French arrived. Such schisms would have serious consequences indeed when the Europeans became a factor in the political landscape.

However, despite the endemic warfare, we must not imagine a world of unending violence. Casualties tended to be light, which was not the case in European wars. Most often, the goal was not to kill as many of the enemy as possible, but to take young women and children captive so that they might be adopted to replace deceased clan members. Furthermore, these wars focused violence outward. The cruelty that Indians practiced on their enemies shocked Europeans, but unlike in European society, violence or even crime within a clan or extended family was virtually unknown.

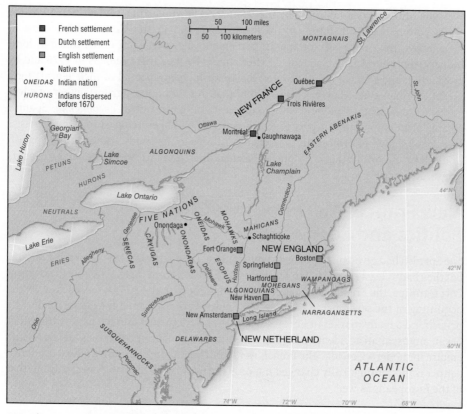

Map 2-3 The Iroquois Region in the Middle of the Seventeenth Century By the middle of the seventeenth century, the French, Dutch, and English had all established trading posts on the fringe of the Iroquois homeland. In the Beaver Wars (ca. 1648–1660), discussed later in the chapter, the Iroquois lashed out at their neighbors, dispersing several Huron tribes.
Source: Matthew Dennis, *Cultivating a Landscape of Peace* (Ithaca, NY: Cornell University Press, 1993), p. 16.

Champlain Encounters the Hurons

After Cartier's last voyage in 1541, the French waited more than half a century before again attempting to plant a settlement in Canada. They were preoccupied with a brutal civil war. In 1594, Henry of Navarre, a Huguenot, emerged the victor, converted to Catholicism, and in 1598 issued the Edict of Nantes, which granted limited religious toleration to the Huguenots. The French could once again look to North America.

The French had continued to fish off Newfoundland, sending ships to the mainland to trade for beaver pelts. The French Crown now realized that extending commerce with the Indians could increase its power and wealth. Several early efforts to establish a permanent trading settlement failed, but in 1608, Samuel de Champlain and a small band retraced Cartier's route up the St. Lawrence River and established a post at Québec (see Map 2–4). Champlain, after several attempts, finally established the first French foothold in Canada, created a trading network along the St. Lawrence River, and learned how to live among people with a culture different from his own.

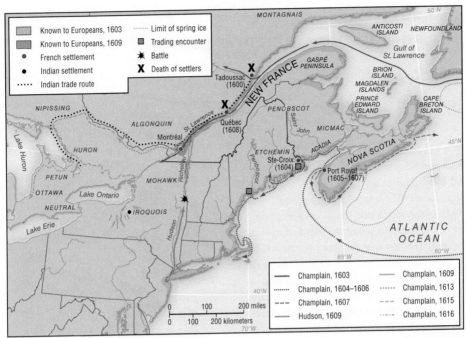

Map 2-4   French Exploration and Settlement, 1603-1616 Between 1603 and 1616, Samuel de Champlain and other French explorers made numerous trips up the St. Lawrence River and along the New England coast as far south as Cape Cod. They established several settlements, and they traded with local Indians and fought with them as well.

As the French government provided them with little support, Champlain's party depended on the aid of their Montagnais Indian hosts (an Algonquian-speaking tribe). To survive in New France, they had to adapt to Indian customs and assist their Indian benefactors in wars against their enemy. Killing the enemy in warfare was relatively easy for an experienced soldier such as Champlain. Indian forms of torture, however, seemed barbaric, not because Europeans did not engage in torture—it was even a part of courtroom protocol to accept evidence elicited under torture—but because Europeans usually did not practice it against other soldiers.

Over the next several years, Champlain established a widespread fur trade in the region, linking the French and the Indians in a transformed transatlantic economy. Peasants were brought to New France in 1614 to raise food for the traders; Jesuits were sent to convert the Native Americans. The missionaries were more successful than the peasants. The persistence and adaptability of the missionaries and their ability to make Catholicism meaningful to Native Americans, as well as their encouragement of trading relationships, eventually gained them many converts.

After Champlain's original trade monopoly expired, his group competed with other Frenchmen in the fur trade. The French government was too busy with conflicts at home and abroad to support any of these outposts. To maintain a competitive edge, each summer Champlain pushed farther up the St. Lawrence River from his base at Québec to intercept the Indian tribes who were bringing pelts to the east. Each winter he also sent some of

STRUGGLES FOR DEMOCRACY

The French and the Indians Learn to Compromise

Should we speak of democracy when people are forced to negotiate because no individual or group has enough power to force all others to acquiesce to their will? That is far from our usual understanding of democracy, in which formalized institutions guarantee that different voices will be heard. Nevertheless, the lack of extreme power on the part of any one group in early America may have helped engender our modern democracy. Europeans maintained outposts of empire; they were far, both literally and figuratively, from being at the center of empire, and as a result they learned to compromise. In the fur-trading regions of Canada, for example, negotiated settlement was the norm for many decades.

Never was this clearer than in the case of murder. Among the Native Americans, if someone was murdered by a fellow tribal member or ally, the killer and his people could atone for the death by offering gifts to the bereaved family or by presenting them with a captive to be adopted. (If someone was killed by an enemy tribe, it was tantamount to a declaration of war.) Among the French, a murder was resolved not by the killer and the kinfolk, but by the

A Colony of Beavers.

The North American Fur Trade Beaver pelts were at the heart of the tensions in New France.

state. And the state demanded as punishment the death of the killer.

In the hunting season of 1682–1683, tensions percolated in the Keewenaw Peninsula of today's Lake Superior. The local Algonkian-speaking Sault Chippewas were embittered because disease had been running rampant, recent Iroquois attacks had gone unavenged by their French allies, and the French were beginning to trade directly with the Siouan

his men to live among the western Hurons and Algonquians to learn their languages and customs. These Indians already traded widely in corn, fish, nets, wampum, and other items. As French traders and Huron and Algonquian hunters created a trade network, each group became dependent on the others.

Creating a Middle Ground in New France

Indians and French traders accommodated each other's cultural practices. Together they created a middle ground neither fully European nor fully Indian, but rather a new world peoples to the west, eliminating the need for the Sault Chippewas to act as middlemen. During this time, the sons of a local chief and a Menominee friend came across two French fur traders whom they robbed and killed. Daniel Dulhut, an officer at the nearest French fort, heard of the event and sent out a party of soldiers to capture the chief, Achiganaga, and all of his sons. Achiganaga's people immediately offered to pay a heavy gift price, including two captive slaves to be adopted by the French.

Dulhut rejected the offer. He wanted the men to stand trial in a French court, but taking the captives through their own people's country to Montreal would be an impossible task; even if his soldiers managed it, they would then have to live with immense Chippewa hostility. Dulhut demanded that the local indigenous groups meet, and once they were assembled, he forced them to serve as a sort of jury at a trial. Achiganaga's son and his friends freely acknowledged what they had done, confident that their proffered gift would be accepted. But the French demanded that the other Indians present execute them. The Indians knew that if they did so, they would in effect be declaring war on the Sault Chippewas and the Menominee, and thus refused. Dulhut offered a compromise: he would not ask that they kill the whole group who had conspired in the murders, but just two of them. If they had been from an enemy group, this would

have been an acceptable punishment—a life for a life.

When it became clear that Dulhut himself was prepared to carry out the executions, the chief of a different Chippewa group tried to avert war by praising him for his mercy in deciding to demand the deaths of only two of the men. He tried to convey to the others that they should accept this plan, lest their relations with the French deteriorate further. Dulhut went ahead and killed Achiganaga's son and his Menominee friend. Because this occurred in Ottawa territory, the Ottawa were deemed responsible by their Indian peers. Their chiefs scrambled to present expensive wampum belts as gifts to Achiganaga and the Menominee chief in an effort to avert war. In a set of remarkable gestures, Dulhut himself gave a great feast for the Ottawa, "to take away the pain I have caused them by pronouncing the death sentence" on their lands, and then presented Achiganaga himself with many gifts. The French traders who lived in the region had persuaded him that it was imperative that he live according to Indian custom as well as French law. Otherwise, the reprisals would be terrible. This was not the lesson the French officer had expected to learn when he came to America, but living with a new reality taught him to let go of some of his expectations. Later, when Europeans once again attempted to assert more control, the settlers would find that they themselves had come to value more open, democratic negotiations.

built from two different traditions. A middle ground came into being in other places in America as well, whenever Europeans and Indians needed each other and, at least for the present, could not achieve what they wanted through the use of force.

As the French drew the Native Americans into a global trade network, the Indians began to hunt more beaver than they needed for themselves, depleting the beaver population. Some historians believe that the introduction of European goods and commerce destroyed Native American cultures from within by making them dependent on those goods and inducing them to abandon their own crafts. Others have pointed out that the trade had different meanings for the French and for the Indians. For the French, trade was important for its cash value; for the Indians, trade goods were important both for the practical uses to which they could be put and for their symbolic value in religious ceremonies.

A métis (or mixed) culture soon emerged. Traders and priests learned to sleep on the cold ground without complaint and to eat Indian foods such as sagamité, a sort of corn-meal mush in which a small animal had been boiled. Many French traders found Indian wives. Most Native Americans accepted the taking of more than one wife, so they were not troubled if the French also had wives at home. Moreover, the Hurons were accustomed to adopting members of different ethnic groups, and the French were not averse to racial mixing. Both the Indians and the French believed mixed marriages strengthened trading and military alliances.

The French were drawn into their Huron and Algonquian allies' political world as well. To keep the furs flowing east, they had to join war parties (usually against the Iroquois), finance their allies' battles, and purchase their loyalty with annual payments the Indians considered "presents" and the French thought of as the price of diplomacy. The French and their Indian allies manipulated each other for their own benefit, and there were costs and benefits on both sides.

The arrival of the French stimulated competition among regional tribes for the positions of brokers between the French and the other Indians with furs to trade. The pace and nature of Indian warfare changed dramatically, for a new motive: control of the lucrative fur trade. Through diplomacy and the liberal dispensing of presents, French officials were usually able to quell the infighting among their allies, but not between their allies and the Five Nations. After the Dutch and English established colonies to the south and made alliances with the Iroquois, maintaining the loyalty of Huron and Algonquian allies became the major French objective in North America in the seventeenth and eighteenth centuries. Because they were receptive to Indian customs, the French were the best diplomats in North America, and their Indian allies the most loyal, but the latter paid dearly in lives lost to warfare and disease.

An Outpost in a Global Political Economy

New France began as a tiny outpost. By the end of the seventeenth century, it had increased in both size and importance. Its French population reached 2,000 in 1650 and 19,000 in 1714. In the same years, the Huron population decreased dramatically, cut in half by epidemics and warfare. The death of many of Huronia's leaders resulted in internal conflict and political instability that left the Hurons vulnerable to their Indian enemies and increasingly dependent on their French allies. At the same time, the French depended on the Hurons and Algonquians to keep bringing them furs. The Hurons operated solely as middlemen, acquiring beaver pelts from other tribes rather than hunting for them.

By the middle of the seventeenth century, the local beaver supply began to diminish. Before the arrival of the French, the Indians had trapped only enough for their own use. The huge European demand, however, led Indians to kill more beaver than could be replaced by natural reproduction. As a result, Europeans (or their Indian middlemen) extended trade routes north and west, drawing larger numbers of Indians into the emerging global economy.

The European demand for beaver coats and hats was insatiable. To increase trade, the French expanded domestic manufacturing of cloth, metal implements, guns, and other goods attractive to the Indians. This pattern, in which the mother country produced goods to be sold or traded in foreign colonies for raw materials, was replicated by England and Holland. None of these nations found either the treasures or the settled Indian populations that Spain did in Mexico and Peru. Instead, they found new products, such as beaver pelts, for which there was a growing demand in Europe.

A new economic theory called mercantilism guided the growth of European nation-states and their colonies: its objective was to strengthen the nation-state by making the economy serve its interests. According to the theory, the world's wealth, measured in gold and silver, could never be increased. As a result, each nation's economic objective must be to secure as much of the world's wealth as possible. One nation's gain was necessarily another's loss. Colonies were to provide raw materials and markets for manufactured goods for the mother country. National competition for colonies and markets was not only about economics but also about politics and diplomacy. The nation's strength would depend on its ability to dominate international trade.

New Netherland: The Empire of a Trading Nation

In many ways, the Dutch venture into North America resembled that of France. It began with an intrepid explorer in quest of a Northwest Passage and a government unwilling to invest heavily in a North American colony. Unlike the French, however, the Dutch government assigned the task of establishing a trading settlement almost entirely to a private company. And because Holland was a Protestant nation, there were no activist Catholic missionaries to spread their religion and oppose the excesses of a commercial economy. Even more than the French and Spanish colonies, New Netherland was shaped by the forces of commerce.

Colonization by a Private Company

The Netherlands had an unusual history in the context of Europe. The seven provinces hugged the coast, and the economy was dominated by merchants whose sailing ventures made them quite cosmopolitan. It had neither a powerful landed aristocracy nor an oppressed peasantry. It was thus no accident that it was home to such Renaissance thinkers as Erasmus and later Descartes. Jews expelled from Spain found a home there, as did zealous Protestants fleeing England. However, being a small, coastal territory also had its disadvantages: the Netherlands was subject to frequent invasion. Most recently, the powerful Spanish had annexed the country, and in the early 1600s the Dutch were in the midst of fighting for their political independence (which they would win in 1648). If anything, their political struggles made them even more ambitious to participate actively in international trade.

It was by chance that the Dutch and not the British claimed the Hudson River valley. Henry Hudson, an English explorer, sailed several times for the English, attempting to find the Northwest Passage by sailing over the North Pole. In 1609, Hudson persuaded a group of Dutch merchants who traded in Asia, the Dutch East India Company, to finance a venture. Sailing on the *Halve Maen* (Half Moon, in English), Hudson headed toward the Chesapeake Bay, which he believed offered a passage to the Pacific. He sailed along the coast, anchoring in New York Harbor and trading with local Algonquian Indians. He pushed up the river as far as Albany, where he discovered that the river narrowed, apparently disproving his theory about a water passage through North America.

The opportunity to profit from the fur trade soon drew investors and traders to New Netherland. Within two years of Hudson's "discovery" of the river that bears his name, Dutch merchants returned to the region, and in 1614 a group called the New Netherland Company secured from their government a temporary monopoly of trade between the Delaware and Connecticut Rivers. The profits drew other Dutch merchants. In 1621, the Dutch West India Company obtained a permit and soon established settlements at Fort Orange (present-day Albany) and New Amsterdam (present-day New York City), purchasing Manhattan from local Algonquian Indians for 60 florins' worth of merchandise. Thirty families arrived in 1624 to serve the fur trade, either by trading with Indians or by providing support for the traders. All profits went to the Company, with the settlers given small salaries.

Until the Company was willing to offer better terms to settlers, the colony grew very slowly. There were 270 inhabitants in 1628 and 500 in 1640. In 1629, the Company began to offer huge plots of land (18 miles along the Hudson River) and extensive governing powers to *patroons*, men who would bring 50 settlers to the new colony. It also offered smaller grants of land to individuals who would farm the land and return to the Company one-tenth of what they produced. Both approaches placed restrictions on land ownership and

self-government, and neither was successful. So in 1640, the Company offered greater rights of self-government and 200 acres to anyone who brought over five adult immigrants. This policy worked better. With its tolerant social attitudes, New Netherland soon became a magnet for peoples from many cultures and nations. As the colony grew, it expanded up the Hudson from the island of Manhattan into New Jersey and Long Island and south to the Delaware River.

The ethnic diversity of the colony increased even further when in 1655 it absorbed the

Peter Stuyvesant A man of strong character, Peter Stuyvesant did his best to govern the Dutch colony of New Amsterdam effectively.

small colony of New Sweden, a privately financed trading outpost on the Delaware that failed when it could not return a quick profit. The varied population of New Netherland was united by no single religion or culture that could have established social order. In most European nations at the time, social order was maintained by a combination of state authority and cohesive religious structures and values. In New Netherland, however, both of these were relatively weak. The governors were caught between the Company, which expected to earn a profit, and the settlers, who wanted to prosper themselves. Peter Stuyvesant, governor from 1647 until the English took over in 1664, was the most successful of the governors, but even he could not fully control New Netherland's people.

In one year alone, when the population numbered less than 1,000, there were 50 civil suits and almost as many criminal prosecutions. The rate of alcohol consumption seems to have been the highest of any North American colony. In 1645, there were only between 150 and 200 houses in New Amsterdam—but 35 taverns! Stuyvesant was unsuccessful in regulating either social life or the economy. He attempted to set prices on such commodities as beer and bread, but he was overruled by the Company, which feared that economic controls would thwart further immigration. In a pattern that would prevail in all of the Dutch and English North American colonies, commerce triumphed.

Slavery and Freedom in New Netherland

The settlers, the Company, and the government of the Netherlands all wanted to make themselves wealthy through commerce. This desire led to the introduction of African slavery into New Netherland. The fur trade did not prove as lucrative as investors had hoped, and the Company found that colonists tended to abandon agriculture for trade. The Company decided that the primary function of New Netherland should be to provide food for its more lucrative plantation colonies in Brazil and the Caribbean. Earlier in the century, the Dutch had seized a portion of northern Brazil from Portugal and developed a sugar-plantation slave economy, which it transplanted to islands in the Caribbean. By that time they had also entered the transatlantic slave trade. In fact, a Dutch warship dropped off the first 20 Africans at the English colony of Jamestown in 1619 in return for food. With its own plantation colonies needing slave labor, the Netherlands became a major player in the slave trade, transporting Africans to the colonies of other nations as well.

In the context of the lucrative Dutch trade in sugar and slaves, New Netherland was only a sideshow. Hoping to make the colony profitable, the Company turned to enslaved Africans. By 1664, there were perhaps 700 slaves in the colony, a considerable portion (about 8 percent) of New Netherland's population.

The Netherlands was perhaps the most tolerant nation of its day, and the Dutch Reformed Church accepted Africans, as well as Indians, as converts, provided they could demonstrate their knowledge of the Dutch religion. The Church did not oppose the institution of slavery, however. Moreover, the strict nature of Dutch Calvinism placed limits on the Church's tolerance. It insisted that its followers be able to read and understand the Bible and the doctrines of the Church.

The primary force for religious tolerance in New Netherland was, in fact, the Dutch West India Company, which saw it as necessary to commercial prosperity. When the head of the Dutch Reformed Church in New Netherland and Governor Stuyvesant attempted to prevent the entry of 23 Dutch Jews expelled from Portuguese Brazil, they were reversed by the Company.

After some early mistakes, the Company also came to advocate a policy of fairness to the local Indian tribes, with the ultimate goal of maintaining peace. They insisted that land must be purchased from its original owners before Europeans could settle on it. Because some settlers were coercing Indians to sell their land cheaply, in 1652 Stuyvesant forbade purchases of land without government approval.

It might appear puzzling that the Dutch, who encouraged toleration of religious minorities and justice toward Native Americans, would also introduce and encourage slavery in North America. The Dutch were not motivated, however, by abstract ideals. Their primary goal was profit through trade: religious and cultural toleration, amicable relations with local Indians, and African slavery all served that end.

The Dutch-Indian Trading Partnership

In the 40 years of New Netherland's existence, its most profitable activity was the fur trade. As the French had done, the Dutch disrupted the balance among regional Indian tribes. The arrival of the Europeans heightened long-standing local animosities. Tribes came to rely on their European allies not only for goods but also for weapons and even soldiers to fight their enemies.

The Dutch began trading near Albany around 1614 and built Fort Orange there a decade later. This small outpost was in a region inhabited by the Mahican tribe, an Algonquian-speaking people who gave the Dutch access to the furs trapped by other Algonquian tribes to the north. The Dutch were assisting the Mahicans in their trade rivalry with the Mohawks (one of the Five Nations of Iroquois) when they were attacked—and defeated—by the Mohawks. The Mohawks, however, asked for peace: their objective was not to eliminate the Dutch but to secure them as trade partners.

By 1628 the Mohawks had defeated the Mahicans and forced them to move into Connecticut, establishing the Mohawks as the most powerful force in the region. The Dutch and the Mohawks abandoned their former hostility for a generally peaceful trading partnership.

By the 1660s, however, New Netherland was in serious economic trouble. The underlying problem was an oversupply of wampum, beads made from the shells of clams. Indians had placed a high value on wampum well before the arrival of Europeans, and the Dutch provided the tools to mass-produce it. They also helped the Indians establish a trade in wampum itself, in which wampum was traded to the Dutch for European goods. The Dutch then exchanged the wampum for furs from the Mohawks and other Indians, shipping the furs to the Netherlands for more European goods. By the middle of the seventeenth century, perhaps as many as 3 million pieces of wampum were in circulation in the area.

By the 1640s English traders in New England had cornered the market in wampum, just when New Englanders were ceasing to use the beads as money. The traders then dumped them into the Dutch market by buying up huge quantities of European goods with them. Almost immediately, the price of manufactured trade goods skyrocketed (due to their relative scarcity) and the value of wampum fell (due to its plentiful supply), leaving the Dutch with too few of the former and too much of the latter. Competition among

Dutch traders increased, pressure on Iroquois trade partners mounted, and profits fell. The economic crisis tipped the delicate balance of violence on the frontier and precipitated a major war.

The Beaver Wars

As the Dutch economic position faltered, the balance of power among many northeastern tribes collapsed. The Iroquois, dependent on the failing Dutch merchants for guns, were now vulnerable. Western Iroquois tribes came under assault from the Susquehannocks, a tribe to the south, while the Mohawks in the east faced renewed pressure from the Mahicans. Simultaneously, the Hurons had cut the Iroquois off from trade with the French to the north. Pressured, the Iroquois lashed out in desperate hostilities, known as the Beaver Wars, which raged between 1648 and the 1660s. They attacked almost all of their Indian neighbors and pushed the last French-allied Hurons to the west.

This warfare was horrendous for all sides. As Indian fought Indian, Europeans ultimately gained the upper hand. The Five Nations won the Beaver Wars, but their victory was hollow. Although the Hurons had been dispersed west, the Iroquois could not secure the French as trade partners. Once the Hurons were gone, the French began trading with other Algonquian tribes to the east. Although the Iroquois remained a powerful force until almost the end of the eighteenth century, the Beaver Wars marked an important turning point. The Indians were never able to replace population lost to warfare, even by raiding other tribes. By the middle of the seventeenth century, the pace of European colonization was increasing, filling the land once hunted by Indians.

Even before the English conquered New Netherland in 1664, the Iroquois were looking for new trade partners. They found them in the English. The transition in New Netherland from Dutch to English rule was relatively quiet. The Dutch had established the colony hoping to make money through trade. Having failed, they had little incentive to fight for its control.

England Attempts an Empire

England came late to empire building. The English did not achieve the necessary political unity until the second half of the sixteenth century. Between 1455 and 1485, England was torn by a dynastic struggle, the Wars of the Roses. King Henry VII and his son, Henry VIII, consolidated the power of the state by crushing resistant nobles. When the pope refused to let Henry VIII terminate his sonless marriage to Catherine of Aragon (a daughter of Ferdinand and Isabel), the king made Protestantism the official religion of the nation, banned Catholicism, and confiscated the land and wealth of the Catholic Church. Henry's daughter Mary, who reigned from 1553 through 1558, reinstated Catholicism, burning Protestants at the stake and throwing the nation into turmoil. Order was finally established under the rule of Henry's other daughter, Elizabeth I (reigning from 1558 to 1603), who reestablished Protestantism and strengthened the state. She, too, did not hesitate to use violence to subdue internal dissent, but in her case, she had the majority of the people behind her rather than against her. She succeeded in stabilizing a political entity worthy of being called a nation, but because the English came late to colonization, they found that the most profitable territories in the Americas were already claimed by others.

Competition with Spain

Queen Elizabeth, although an ardent nationalist, was unwilling to risk her treasury on North American adventures. Others, however, were convinced that a New World empire, even in the inhospitable north, could bring England wealth and glory. By the end of the sixteenth century, nationalists, such as two cousins both named Richard Hakluyt, were making the case for an overseas empire. The Hakluyts united nationalism, mercantilism, and militant Protestantism. They argued that if England had colonies for raw materials and as markets for manufactured goods, it could free itself from economic dependency on Spain and other nations. Moreover, colonies could drain off the growing numbers of the unemployed. The Hakluyts also believed that North American Indians could be relatively easily converted to English trade and religion, assuming they would prefer these to Spanish "pride and tyranie." The English could simultaneously strike a blow against Catholic Spain and advance "the glory of God." Although the Hakluyts' dream was never realized, their plans for an English mercantile empire became a blueprint for colonization.

England's first move was not to establish colonies but to try stealing from the Spanish. The English Crown did not have the money to found a colonial empire that would not immediately deliver profits, and Elizabeth I was unconvinced by colonial propagandists. Most concerned about international power politics in Europe, she was willing to let individual Englishmen try to poach on the Spanish. Her goal was to weaken Spain more than to establish a North American empire.

As early as the 1560s, John Hawkins tried to break into the slave trade, but the Spanish forced him out. The English moved on to privateering, that is, state-sanctioned piracy. In 1570, Sir Francis Drake set off for the Isthmus of Panama on a raiding expedition. Drake was motivated by dreams of glory and a conviction that his Protestant religion was superior to all others. Working in one of Hawkins's slaving expeditions, he had learned to hate the Spanish.

In years to come, Drake led the second expedition to sail around the world, crossed the Atlantic many times, helped defeat the huge Spanish naval fleet, the Armada, and became an architect of England's colonial strategies. He was the English version of the conquistador. His venture into Panama failed to produce any treasure, but it inspired a group of professional seamen, aggressive Protestants, and members of Elizabeth's court to plan for an English colonial empire. This group won the cautious queen's support. The success of Drake's round-the-world expedition (1577–1580) spurred further privateering ventures. He brought back to England enough treasure to pay for the voyage and proof that the Spanish empire was vulnerable. From 1585 to 1604, the English government issued licenses to privateers, sometimes as many as 100 per year. Each venture was financed by a joint-stock company, a relatively new form of business organization that was the forerunner to the modern corporation. These companies brought together merchants who saw privateering as a way to broaden their trade and gentlemen who saw it as a way to increase their incomes.

Rehearsal in Ireland

At the end of the sixteenth century, England embarked on a campaign to bring Ireland, which its people had first invaded in the twelfth century, under its full control. The conquest of Ireland between 1565 and 1576 became the model for England's colonial ventures. Ireland presented the monarchy with the same political problem that all early-modern rulers faced, that is, a set of powerful nobles who put their own interests ahead of those of the nation. Building the nation meant bringing the nobles into line.

England not only subdued the Irish leaders and their people but also forcibly removed some of them to make way for loyal Englishmen, who were given land as a reward for their service to the queen. By paying her followers with someone else's land and financing military expeditions from joint-stock companies, England made the conquest of Ireland relatively cheap. It showed a skeptical queen that establishing colonies was in England's interest, provided that the venture was paid for privately—by privateering, by charters to individuals, or by joint-stock companies.

The English conquest of Ireland provided not only practical experience in how to organize and finance a colonial venture but also a view of cultural difference that was later applied to the Indians. Although the Irish were Catholics and hence fellow Christians, the English thought that people who behaved as the Irish did must be barbarians. According to the English, the Irish "blaspheme, they murder, commit whoredome, hold no wedlocke, ravish, steal, and commit all abomination without scruple of conscience." These attitudes were used to justify an official policy of terrorism. In two grisly massacres, one in the middle of a Christmas feast, hundreds of men, women, and children were slaughtered. The English governor, Sir Humphrey Gilbert, ordered that the heads of all those killed resisting the conquest be chopped off and placed along the path leading to his tent so that anyone coming to see him "must pass through a lane of heads." The English justified such acts by referring to the supposed barbarism of the Irish people. These ideas, similar to early Spanish depictions of the Indians of the Americas, were carried to the New World, England's next stop in its expanding empire.

The Roanoke Venture

Roanoke, England's first colony in what became the United States, was a military venture, intended as a resupply base for privateers raiding in the Caribbean. In 1584, Walter Raleigh received a charter to establish a colony in North America. Only 30 years old at the time, Raleigh was the half-brother of the late Sir Humphrey Gilbert. Elizabeth agreed to let Raleigh establish a combination colony and privateering base north of Spain's settlement at St. Augustine. Raleigh's scouts had found a potential site at Roanoke Island on the Outer Banks of today's North Carolina and had brought back to England two Indians, Manteo and Wanchese. Elizabeth gave the enterprise some support. She knighted Raleigh but refused to let the hotheaded young soldier lead the expedition himself.

The Roanoke expedition left Plymouth in April 1585 under the command of Sir Richard Grenville, an aristocrat who had fought in Ireland. Half of the crew of 600 were probably recruited or impressed (i.e., forcibly seized) from the unemployed poor of Britain. Little value was attached to their lives. When one of the ships separated from the fleet and found its supplies running low, 20 men were dropped off at Jamaica—only 2 of whom were ever heard from again—and another 32 were later left on an island in the Outer Banks.

Roanoke was a poor port, dangerous for small ships and inadequate for larger ones. When the primary ship was almost wrecked and a major portion of the food supply lost, Grenville's fleet departed for England. Colonel Ralph Lane, another veteran of war in

Indians on the Thames

When we think about the cultural encounter between the Old World and the New, we tend to imagine European men coming ashore in a wilderness and meeting Native American people. Often, however, the encounter consisted of Indians docking at European cities for the first time. Over the course of the first century after contact, the colonizers brought hundreds of Native Americans back to Europe with them. Some of these Native Americans went on to take leading roles in the unfolding dramas.

The phenomenon began with Columbus and the Spaniards, but English colonizers also regularly kidnapped Indians. In 1530, an English captain explored the coast of Brazil (not yet firmly under Portuguese control) and reported that "one of the savage kings of the country was contented to take ship with him and to be transported into England." The indigenous man was brought to the court of Henry VIII. "The King and all the Nobilitie did not a little marvaile." The English spent a year teaching him their language, but when they tried to take him home, so that he might

aid them in their efforts to profit in Brazil, "the said Savage king died at sea."

Other English explorers followed suit. Sir Walter Raleigh, for example, in the course of the explorations leading to the founding of Roanoke, ordered that two indigenous boys be taken from the Carolina coast. They were known as Manteo and Wanchese. Now we know that the latter was hiding his true name from those who had kidnapped him: the word he gave them simply meant "boy" in his own language. The two lived in Raleigh's home for two years until the expedition sailed.

Sometimes indigenous people coming to London from the Spanish world did not disclose their Indian origins. Martín Cortés, Malinche's son by the conqueror, was given to Philip II as a page when he was a young man, and in 1554, he accompanied Philip to London for his marriage to Queen Mary. He lived at court, where no one would have guessed that his mother had grown up in an indigenous chieftainship on the coast of Mexico.

At the start of the seventeenth century, when the English became more active in

Ireland, was left in charge as governor. He was supposed to look for a better port, build a fort, and find food for the 100 men left under his command.

Roanoke was established to gain an advantage over the treasure-filled Spanish ships traveling back to Spain. The men left on the island prepared for an attack by Spain and pointed the fort's guns out to sea. Raleigh intended to send another supply ship that summer, but the queen insisted he sail instead to Newfoundland to warn the English there about a probable sea war with Spain. The first settlers of Roanoke were ill equipped to build a self-sustaining colony. Half soldiers and gentlemen and half undisciplined and impoverished young men, no one knew how to build or support a town. Unable to find colonization, interest in Native Americans spiked. In 1603, Bartholomew Gosnold seized some Indians from the Rappahannock River and had them perform daring feats on canoes on the Thames for riveted audiences. (They died of the plague shortly after, and their people were still asking angrily about them when John Smith arrived in their country.) In *The Tempest*, Shakespeare has one character complain of others' selfishness: "When they will not give a doit [a coin] to a lame beggar, they will lay out ten to see a dead Indian." And in *Henry VIII* (1613), a man responds to the sight of a gathering mob by saying, "Have we some Indian with the great tool come to court, the women so besiege us?" When Pocahontas came to London in 1616, she was the talk of the town, and the Virginia Company used her presence to secure investments.

In 1614, an English explorer of the Massachusetts coast seized about 14 Indians to sell in Spain. One of them was later taken to London, working for a shipbuilder. He traveled to Newfoundland with some fishermen, back to London, and then in 1619 sailed with a captain planning to go farther south, to New England. This was Tisquantum, known as "Squanto." No wonder the Pilgrims were greeted by an Indian saying very distinctly, in English, "Welcome."

It is easy for us to imagine the agonizing loneliness of these Indians and to be angry at the ways in which they were used. (If only they had left us diaries and letters!) But we must remember that they also took action and made choices that sometimes had significant consequences. Some of the indigenous in Spain came to know religious men who later advocated for them, and the behavior of don Luis helped convince Spanish authorities that it was worthless to attempt to colonize North America. Wanchese harbored rage against the English and, once home, was instrumental in leading his people away from an alliance, thereby contributing to the destruction of the colony at Roanoke. Pocahontas died in England, but one of her father's advisers accompanied her on the trip. He returned home to warn his countrymen of the danger they faced and to encourage a great rebellion against Jamestown that later followed. Squanto offered his services to the Pilgrims in order to benefit his own clan, but in doing so, he also ensured the colony's survival.

These people were undoubtedly impressed by what they saw in Europe, but they were far from overwhelmed by it. Instead, they used their knowledge to strategize about how best to react to the Europeans.

gold or provide for themselves, the colonists turned to the local Roanoke Indians (an Algonquian-speaking tribe), whom they soon alienated.

The Roanokes were familiar with Europeans through their contacts with the Spanish and through the stories of Wanchese, who had run away from the English and returned home. They were ready to trade with them. However, the English need for more food than the natives could easily supply led to tensions. Thinking that an Indian had stolen a silver cup, the English retaliated by burning an empty village and the surrounding cornfields, which fed both Indians and English. The Indians had to balance the benefits of trade against the costs of English aggression. After a failed ambush attempt, the Roanokes

The Arrival of the English at Roanoke This image derives from a 1585 sketch by the artist John White.

decided to withdraw from Roanoke Island, leaving the English to starve. When Lane learned of this plan, he attacked the Indians, beheading their chieftain Wingina. Indian-English relations deteriorated further, and Wanchese became an avowed enemy.

Not all the colonists, however, treated the Roanokes as an enemy to be conquered. Much of what we know about the Roanoke Colony and its Indian neighbors is due to the work of two sympathetic colonists. John White, a painter, and Thomas Hariot, who later became a great mathematician, were sent to survey the region and describe its inhabitants and natural features. Their illustrations, maps, and descriptions provide the most accurate information that we have about the people of this region before the arrival of large numbers of Europeans.

By June 1585, it was clear that Roanoke had failed in its mission. When Drake and his fleet appeared on their way back from a looting expedition in the Caribbean, the colonists decided to return to England, leaving behind only 15 men.

Yet the English advocates of colonization were not ready to give up. The original plan for a military-style base had failed, but a new vision of colonization would now be tried. Raleigh's commitment was lukewarm, for Roanoke had already cost £30,000 without returning a cent. John White, the painter, remained enthusiastic and assembled a group of settlers. It included 110 people—men, women, and children—who were prepared to raise their own crops, and also one loyal Roanoke Indian, Manteo. In exchange for their investment, Raleigh granted each man 500 acres of land. The new expedition arrived in July 1587. The second attempt to establish a colony at Roanoke was probably doomed by the poisoned relations with the Indians. White soon found that the 15 men who had

John White's Watercolor of Indians Fishing Much of what we know about Algonquian life at the time of the Roanoke expedition comes from the paintings of John White, who was a member of the expedition. Here we see four people fishing from a canoe.

remained had been attacked by Roanokes. As the survival of the colony now depended on support from England, the colonists, who included White's daughter and granddaughter, sent White back to act as their agent in England. No European ever saw any of the colonists again.

The Abandoned Colony

No one had planned to abandon the little colony. Raleigh assembled a supply fleet the next spring, but a sea war looming with the Spanish Armada prevented it from leaving. Finally, in August 1590, after the Armada had been defeated, White arrived in Roanoke

Portrait of an Algonquian Mother and Child by John White This beautiful picture illustrates the indulgence of Algonquian mothers and the sensitivity of the English artist who painted this one.

only to find everyone gone. There were signs of an orderly departure, and the word CROATOAN, Manteo's home island, was carved in a post. White assumed that was where the group had gone. Short of water and with a storm brewing, the fleet decided to put out to sea and return the next year. They never got there.

The colony of Roanoke was not "lost," as legend usually puts it; it was abandoned. Serving no useful economic or military purpose, the people of Roanoke were entirely expendable. John White could not obtain the help of backers and seems to have died shortly thereafter. Raleigh and Queen Elizabeth soon after had a falling out, and he was placed under arrest. After he was released, he did send at least one search party, but no one was ever found.

Time Line

▼**1400–1600**
Five Iroquois nations create the Great League of Peace

▼**1561**
Spanish abduct don Luis de Velasco

▼**1562**
John Hawkins tries to break into the slave trade

▼**1565**
Spanish establish settlement at St. Augustine
Spanish destroy French settlement at Fort Caroline

▼**1565–1576**
The English conquer Ireland

▼**1570**
Paquiquineo returns home to Virginia

▼**1577–1580**
Francis Drake sails around the world for England

▼**1584**
Walter Raleigh receives charter to establish colony at Roanoke

▼**1585**
First settlement at Roanoke established

In 1603, Queen Elizabeth died, and her successor, James I, had Raleigh arrested as a traitor in his efforts to make peace with Spain.

What happened to the abandoned colonists? In 1607, the English returned to the region, establishing a permanent colony at Jamestown, on the Chesapeake. In 1608, Englishmen heard that many Roanoke colonists had made their way up to Virginia and settled among the friendly Chesapeake Indians before being attacked by the Powhatans. In fact, over the next two generations, there were numerous reports of sightings of people with "perfect yellow hair" or "white skin" at various places. One scholar has mapped these purported appearances and finds that a good number fall along a well-known trading path. This makes perfect sense. The seminomadic Algonquian-speaking people who either attacked the colonists or absorbed them peacefully would never have been able to keep such a large group together. The vulnerable newcomers would have been immediately dispersed, just like any other large group of prisoners or starving migrants, and traded along well-worn routes. Theories abound about the fate of the colonists, but this is the only one that has common sense and the realities of Native American life on its side.

The English were beginning to learn that they could not rely on the Indians for food. Unlike the Spanish, they had not found densely settled farming communities who were accustomed to paying tribute. As a result, the English colonies would have to grow their own food. Consequently, the history of the English in North America would by and large be that of the growth of the English population (augmented by Africans and other European immigrants) and the steady decline of the original inhabitants.

Conclusion

European nations established colonies to achieve a political or economic advantage over their rivals. Most of these nations had only recently been unified by force, an experience that gave them the energy to establish colonies and a military model they could

▼**1587**
Second attempt to found colony at Roanoke

▼**1590**
English settlers at Roanoke have disappeared

▼**1607**
English establish permanent colony at Jamestown

▼**1608**
Samuel de Champlain establishes a fort at Quebec

▼**1609**
Henry Hudson arrives at New York, sailing for the Netherlands

▼**1614**
Dutch begin trading in Albany region
French settlers arrive in New France

▼**1621**
Dutch West India Company established

▼**1624**
First Dutch families arrive at Manhattan

▼**1648-1660s**
Beaver Wars fought

▼**1664**
English take over New Amsterdam

use for colonization. The distinctive domestic history of each nation, however, shaped its relations with the Indians it encountered, just as the distinctive societies of the Indian nations shaped their interactions with Europeans. The Spanish came prepared for a new *reconquista*, and the Crown helped sponsor well-armed forces in the New World. There they found large, highly organized groups of native peoples, who had amassed treasure and were accustomed to working for others. The French found no such peoples, but they learned that the Indians there were expert providers of beaver pelts. Rather than uselessly attempting to conquer the nomadic and seminomadic hunters, they worked on establishing alliances to guarantee the trade and became entangled in the Indians' own conflicts. The Dutch, experienced as merchants, also recognized that the goodwill of the Indians was vital for a flourishing trade, and their businessmen worked to make New Amsterdam a crossroads in the international beaver economy. The English, like the Dutch, arrived on the scene late, but rather than joining the northern beaver economy as merchant traders, they still dreamed of competing with Spain in the warmer climes. They did so largely by preying on Spanish ships. The English thought it would be relatively easy to convince the Indians to grow food for them, as the Spanish had done, but they had misunderstood the nature of the societies they were dealing with.

Out of these different interactions between natives and newcomers, a North Atlantic political economy began to emerge, shaped by the forces of trade and the quest for power. Europeans, Indians, and eventually Africans were drawn into a global economy in which the nations of the world competed for advantage. The early years of American colonial history were shaped by impersonal forces that built empires and subjugated peoples. But they were also shaped by individuals. Some set out to find new worlds, whereas others were forced into them. Captives such as Paquiquineo, Wanchese, and Manteo; explorers such as Jacques Cartier and Henry Hudson; soldiers such as Sir Francis Drake and Samuel de Champlain; the poor dragooned into sailing for Roanoke and left there to die; and Huron women who married French traders: all of them left their mark on the New World, even before the English planted their first permanent colonies in North America.

Who, What, Where

Review Questions

1. What were the key European objectives in exploring North America in this period? To what extent did England, France, and the Netherlands achieve their objectives?

2. What do we know about the precontact history of the Five Nations of Iroquois? How did this history affect the world of colonial America? How did the European colonial ventures affect the Iroquois?

3. What was the "middle ground," and how was it created?

Critical-Thinking Questions

1. What were the ramifications of the northern Europeans failing to find cities equivalent to Tenochtitlan anywhere in North America?

2. Did the English, French, and Dutch have profoundly different attitudes toward the Indians at the outset? If the English had been the ones to spearhead the beaver trade, do you think that English traders and trappers might have married Huron women?

3. Early on, the Dutch faced the need to democratize their colony to some extent. Did other colonies of the era face a similar need? Why or why not?

Suggested Readings

Hoffman, Paul. *A New Andalusia and a Way to the Orient: The American Southeast During the Sixteenth Century.* Baton Rouge: Louisiana State University Press, 1990.

Kupperman, Karen. *Roanoke: The Abandoned Colony.* Lanham, MD: Rowman & Littlefield, 2007.

Quinn, David. *North America from Earliest Discovery to First Settlements.* New York: Harper & Row, 1977.

Shorto, Russell. *The Island at the Center of the World.* New York: Doubleday, 2004.

Trigger, Bruce. *Natives and Newcomers: Canada's "Heroic Age" Reconsidered.* Kingston, ON: McGill-Queen's University Press, 1985.

For further review materials and resource information, please visit www.oup.com/us/oakes-mcgerr

CHAPTER 2: COLONIAL OUTPOSTS, 1550–1650
Primary Sources

2.1 LETTER FROM FRAY PEDRO de FERIA TO PHILLIP II, KING OF SPAIN, ABOUT PAQUIQUINEO (1563)

Paquiquineo, a Native American boy, was kidnapped from the Chesapeake by Spanish explorers in 1561. He and a companion were taken to Spain, where they met the king. Paquiquineo refused to convert to Christianity and begged the monarch to send him home. His wish was granted, but he was sent first to Mexico; from there he was to be taken to the northern territories. While in Mexico, he became a Christian and was baptized "don Luis de Velasco," in honor of the viceroy. The following letter offers insight into his frustrating experiences among his captors. It was written by the head of the Dominican order in Mexico City soon after Paquiquineo had been left to his keeping. The friar was alight with zeal: he had in his hands a young man whom he believed would be a perfect intermediary in a major effort to proselytize in the northern territories.

Your Holy Royal Majesty:

In the last fleet there came to New Spain two Indians whom Captain Antonio Velázquez brought before Your Majesty, and whom Your Majesty ordered Captain Pedro Menéndez to return to their homeland as they were not baptized at the time they left the kingdom [of Spain]. As soon as they arrived in this city they got so sick and arrived at such a point that it was not thought they would escape death. For that reason, having learned of their desire to be baptized, as they had asked for it more than once, they were given the sacrament of baptism. Our Lord was moved to give them back their health. The religious [brothers] of this your Convent of Santo Domingo begged your Viceroy to keep them here among us so we might instruct them in the things of our holy Catholic Faith and also so that they would become tied by affection to the friars. It was done, and thus they have been and still are among us, and have been treated like sons and taught the things of our faith. Seeing that they are now Christians and members of the church, and that if they were returned to their land alone without ministers who could keep them from straying from the faith and from Christian law, and if they were to return to their rites and idolatries and thus lose their souls, then their baptism would have caused them to be damned. Permitting all of that to happen would seem to be a great inhumanity, even a grave offense against our Lord, and a disservice to Your Majesty. It is believed that your desire to return them to their land depended on their being pagans, as they were when they left you. Considering as well the fine presence and capacity of this Indian, and what he tells us of his land, that it is well populated with peaceful people, and believing as we do that Our Lord has arranged all of this business and sent this Indian so that he may be the means of saving all of that land, your viceroy, with the zeal of a true Christian and a Catholic and a vassal of Your Majesty . . . communicated with the Provincial and other leading men of our Dominican Order what we might do assuming we received the permission of Your majesty so that the excellent opportunity we had been offered by means of the conversion of this Indian would not be lost. Thus the Order offered to send religious brothers on this project. . . . And to be more effective your Viceroy, desirous of being of service to Our Lord and to Your Majesty, offered to pay expenses himself . . . There then arrived the moment to deal with the captain [of the royal convoy] Pedro Menéndez about the necessary measures for the execution of this business . . . Because he did not have the necessary orders, or because Our Lord ordered it otherwise, wanting the expedition to be better guided by Your Majesty's hands, he denied the departure of the religious . . .

The Archbishop[1] then ordered Pedro Menéndez not to return the Indians to their homelands since no ministers would go with them. If he wanted to bring them back to Spain to go before Your Majesty, of course he could do that. The Indians were at full liberty to go to Spain and even encouraged to do so, but they said that if they were not going to return to their land, they preferred to stay here than to go all the way to Spain. Thus they remained here and are still among us, who take care to teach them the doctrine and all that is appropriate. Your Viceroy takes a special interest in them and oversees their good treatment. . .

Understanding the desire that exists on the part of the Order to serve Our Lord and Your Majesty and the opportunity that exists just now to save those people [of the northern territory] and the misfortune it would be if this opportunity were lost, it seems Your Majesty was well served. Those people are peaceful, and it is believed that they would be even more so if this Indian were to go there and give an account of what he has seen and the benefits he has received. No more than forty or fifty men would have to go with the religious, in one ship, which would be able to pacify the people there. . . . May Our Lord keep the holy person of Your Majesty and augment your territories for his service . . . Mexico City, February 13, 1563.

Fray Pedro de Feria

Source: Archivo General de Indios, Seville, Spain. Record Group Mexico, vol. 280, February 1563. Our own translation.

2.2 RICHARD HAKLUYT, EXCERPT FROM *THE PRINCIPAL NAVIGATIONS, VOYAGES, TRAFFIQUES, AND DISCOVERIES OF THE ENGLISH NATION* (1589–1600)

Toward the end of Queen Elizabeth I's reign, two cousins, both named Richard Hakluyt, became involved in the project of advancing English explorations and conquests overseas. The elder Hakluyt became known to merchants and geographers for his immense collection of letters and documents related to English interactions abroad, and the younger eventually published the collection in three volumes in 1598, 1599, and 1600. The latter Hakluyt conceived of his project as showing the way to young Englishmen who also wished to pursue exploration and conquest. The original spelling has been retained in the case of this document in order to show how differently the English language of earlier centuries reads.

"A brief relation of two sundry voyages made by the worshipful M. William Haukins [Hawkins] of Plimmouth, father to Sir John Haukins knight, late treasurer to her Majesties Navie, in the yeere 1530 and 1532"

Olde M. William Haukins of Plimmouth, a man for his wisedome, valure, experience, and skill in sea causes much esteemed, and beloved of K. Henry the 8, and being one of the principall Sea captaines in the West partes of England in his time, not contented with the short voyages commonly then made onely to the knowne coasts of Europe, armed out a tall and goodly shippe of his owne of the burthen of 250 tunnes, called the Paule of Plimmouth, wherewith he made three long and famous voyages unto the coast of Brasil, a thing in those dayes very rare, especially

---

[1]The Archbishop at the time was a Dominican. He was a friend of the Provincial of the Order and strongly in favor of any plan that would help the Dominicans gain influence in the New World.

to our Nation. In the course of which voyages he touched at the river of Sestos upon the coast of Guinea, where hee trafficqued with the Negros, and tooke of them Elephants teeth, and other commodities which that place yeeldeth: and so arriving on the coast of Brasil, he used there such discretion, and behaved himself so widely with those savage people, that he grew into great familiarity and friendship with them. Insomuch that in his second voyage, one of the savage kinds of the countrey of Brasil, was contented to take ship with him, and to be transported hither into England: whereunto M. Haukins agreed, leaving behind in the Countrey as a pledge of his safetie and returne again, one Martin Cockeram of Plimmouth. This Brasilian king being arrived, was brought up to London and presented to K. Henry the 8, lying as then at White-hall: at the sight of whom the King and all the Nobilitie did not a little marvaile, and not without cause: for in his cheeks were holes made according to their savage maner, and therein small bones were planted, standing an inch out from the said holes, which in his owne Countrey was reputed for a great braverie. He had also another hole in his nether lip, wherein was set a precious stone about the bigness of a pease: All his apparel, behavior, and gesture, were very strange to the beholders.

Having remained here the space almost of a whole yeere, and the king with his sight fully satisfied, M. Hawkins [sic] according to his promise and appointment, purposed to convey him againe into his courntrey: but it fell out in the say, that by the change of aire and alteration of diet, the said Savage king died at sea, which was feared would turn to the losse of the life of Martin Cockeram his pledge. Neverthelesse, the Savages being fully persuaded of the honest dealing of our men with their prince, restored againe the said pledge, without any harme to him, or any man of the company: which pledge of theirs they brought home againe into England, with their ship freighted, and furnished with the commodities of the countrey. Which Martin Cockeram, by the witnesse of Sir John Hawkins, being an officer in the towne of Plimmouth, was living within these fewe yeeres.

Source: Richard Hakluyt, *The Principal Navigations, Voyages, Traffiques, and Discoveries of the English Nation*, edited by Irwin R. Blacker (New York: Viking, 1965), pp. 39–40.

2.3 FATHER PIERRE CHOLONEC, LIFE OF KATERI (1715)

Many Native American people resisted the pressure brought to bear by Christian missionaries to accept Christianity; others chose to convert. In French Canada, the most famous convert was Catherine Tegahkouita, or Kateri as she is usually called today. It has traditionally been assumed that she was simply susceptible to influence by the missionaries, for better or for worse, depending on one's perspective. The story, however, is more complicated: her mother was an Algonkian captive taken by the Iroquois. When her father and his family died of smallpox, she was left without immediate kin and thus was apparently interested in joining a new community that would be more supportive of her. She became a devout Christian, and when she died young, her confessor wrote about her life as he understood it.

From Father Cholonec, missionary of the Society of Jesus, to Father Augustin Le Blanc at Sault de St. Louis, the 27th of August, 1715.
My Reverend Father,
The Peace of our Lord be with you.
The marvels which God is working every day through the intercession of a young Iroquois female who has lived and died among us in the order of sanctity, have induced me to inform you of the particulars of her life, although you have not pressed me in your letters to enter into detail.

You have yourself been a witness of these marvels, when you discharged there with so much zeal the duties of a Missionary, and you know that the high Prelate who governs this church, touched by the prodigies with which God has deigned to honor the memory of this holy maiden, has with reason called her the Genevieve of New France. All the French who are in the colonies, as well as the Indians, hold her in singular veneration. They come from a great distance to pray at her tomb, and many, by her intercession, have been immediately cured of their maladies, and have received from Heaven other extraordinary favors. I will write you nothing, my Reverend Father, which I have not myself seen during the time she was under my care, or which I have not learned from the Missionary who conferred on her the rite of holy Baptism.

Tekakwitha (which is the name of this sainted female about whom I am going to inform you) was born in the year 1656, at Caughnawaga, one of the settlements of the lower Iroquois, who are called Mohawks. Her father was an Iroquois and a heathen; her mother, who was a Christian, was an Algonquin, and had been baptized at the village of Three Rivers, where she was brought up among the French. During the time that we were at war with the Iroquois, she was taken prisoner by them, and remained a captive in their country. We have since learned, that thus in the very bosom of heathenism, she preserved her faith even to her death. By her marriage, she had two children, one son and one daughter, the latter of whom is the subject of this narrative, but she had the pain to die without having been able to procure for them the grace of Baptism. The smallpox, which ravaged the Iroquois country, in a few days removed her husband, her son, and herself. Tekakwitha was also attacked like the others, but she did not sink as they did under the violence of the disease. Thus, at the age of four years, she found herself an orphan, under the care of her aunts, and in the power of an uncle who was the leading man in the settlement.

The smallpox had injured her eyes, and this infirmity having rendered her incapable of enduring the glare of light, she remained during whole days shut up in her cabin. By degrees, she began to love this seclusion, and at length that became her taste, which she had at first endured only from necessity. This inclination for retirement, so contrary to the usual spirit of the young Iroquois, was the principal cause of her preserving her innocence of life while living in such scenes of corruption . . .

Source: Fr. Pierre Cholonec, S.J., *Kateri Tekakwitha, the Iroquois Saint,* trans. by Rev. William Ingraham Kip and Ellen H. Wallworth (Merchantville, NJ: Arx, 2013 [1715]), pp. 3–6.

2.4 JOHN HECKEWELDER, ACCOUNT OF THE ARRIVAL OF THE DUTCH AT MANHATTAN

The Delawares and Mahicans lived on the coast of today's New Jersey and in the Hudson River valley region when the Dutch first arrived at Manhattan in 1609. Gradually, as more Europeans arrived, they were pushed westward, taking their memories and stories with them. By the middle of the eighteenth century, they were living in the Ohio Valley. There, a Moravian missionary named John Heckewelder came to live among them and learn their language. Accounts of his indicate that the Indians told him of the arrival of the Dutch at Manhattan as a humorous tall tale.

A great many years ago, when men with a white skin had never yet been seen in the land, some Indians who were out a fishing, at a place where the sea widens, espied at a great distance something remarkably large floating on the water, and such as they had never seen before. These Indians immediately returning to the shore, apprised their countryman of what they had observed, and pressed them to go out with them and discover what it might be. They hurried out together, and saw with astonishment the phenomenon which now appeared to their sight, but could not agree upon what it was; some believed it to be an uncommonly large fish or animal, while others were of opinion it must be a very big house floating on the sea. At length the spectators concluded that this wonderful object was moving towards the land, and that it must be an animal or something else that had life in it; it would therefore be proper to inform all the Indians on the inhabited island of what they had seen, and put them on their guard. Accordingly they sent off a number of runners and watermen to carry the news to their scattered chiefs, that they might send off in every direction for the warriors, with a message that they should come on immediately. These arriving in numbers, and having themselves viewed the strange appearance, and observing that it was actually moving towards the entrance of the river or bay; concluded it to be a remarkably large house in which the Mannitto (the Great or Supreme Being) himself was present, and that he probably was coming to visit them. By this time the chiefs were assembled at York island, and deliberating in what manner they should receive their Mannitto on his arrival. Every measure was taken to be well provided with plenty of meat for a sacrifice. The women were desired to prepare the best victuals. All the idols or images were examined and put in order, and a grand dance was supposed not only to be an agreeable entertainment for the Great Being, but it was believed that it might, with the addition of a sacrifice, contribute to appease him if he was angry with them. The conjurers were also set to work, to determine what this phenomenon portended, and what the possible result of it might be. To these and to the chiefs and wise men of the nations, men, women and children were looking up for advice and protection. Distracted between hope and fear, they were at a loss what to do; a dance, however, commenced in great confusion. While in this situation, fresh runners arrived declaring it to be a large house of various colors, and crowded with living creatures. It appears now to be certain, that it is the great Mannitto, bringing them some kind of game, such as he had not given them before, but other runners soon after arriving declare that it is positively full of human beings, of quite a different color from that of the Indians, and dressed differently from them; that in particular one of them was dressed entirely in red who must be the Mannitto himself. They are hailed from the vessel in a language they do not understand yet they shout or yell in return by way of answer, according to the custom of their country; many are for running off to the woods, but are pressed by others to stay, in order not to give offence to their visitor, who might find them out and destroy them. The house, some say large canoe, at last stops, and a canoe of a smaller size comes on shore with the red man, and some others in it; some stay with his canoe to guard it. The chiefs and wise men, assembled in council, form themselves into a large circle, towards which the man in red clothes approaches with two others. He salutes after their manner. They are lost in admiration [stunned surprise]; the dress, the manners, the whole appearance of the unknown strangers is to them a subject of wonder; but they are particularly struck with him who wore the red coat all glittering with gold lace,[2] which they could in no manner account for. He, surely, must be the great Mannitto, but why should he have a white skin? Meanwhile, a large *Hackhack* [gourd] is brought by one of his servants, from which an unknown substance is poured out into a small cup or glass, and handed to the supposed Mannitto. He drinks—has the glass filled again, and hands it to the chief standing next to him. The chief receives it, but only smells the contents and passes it on to the next chief, who does the same. The glass or cup thus passes through the circle, without the liquor being tasted by any one, and is upon the point of being returned to the red clothed Mannitto, when one of the Indians, a brave man and a great warrior, suddenly jumps up and harangues the assembly on the impropriety of returning the cup with its contents. It was handed to them, says he, by the Mannitto, that they should drink out of it, as he himself had done. To follow his example would be pleasing to him; but to return what he had given them might provoke his wrath, and bring destruction on them. And since the orator believed it for the good of that nation

---

[2]Note that this is not really how the Dutch officers dressed in 1609. It is, however, how British officers dressed in the eighteenth century, when the story was recorded.

that the contents offered them should be drunk, an as no one else would do it, he would drink it himself, let the consequence be what it might; it was better for one man to die, than that a whole nation should be destroyed. He then took the glass, and bidding the assembly a solemn farewell, at once drank up its whole contents. Every eye was fixed on the resolute chief, to see what the effect the unknown liquor would produce. He soon began to stagger, and at last fell prostrate on the ground. His companions now bemoan his fate, he falls into a sound sleep, and they think he has expired. He wakes again, jumps up and declares, that he has enjoyed the most delicious sensations, and that he never before felt himself so happy as after he had drunk the cup. He asks for more, his wish is granted; the whole assembly then imitate him, and all become intoxicated.

After this general intoxication had ceased, for they say that while it lasted the whites had confined themselves to their vessel, the man with the red clothes returned again, and distributed presents among them, consisting of beads, axes, hoes, and stockings such as the white people wear. They soon became familiar with each other, and began to converse by signs. The Dutch made them understand that they would not stay here, that they would return home again, but would pay them another visit the next year, when they would bring them more presents and stay with them awhile; but as they could not live without eating, they should want a little land of them to sow seeds, in order to raise herbs and vegetables to put into their broth. They went away as they had said, and returned in the following season, when both parties were much rejoiced to see each other; but the whites laughed at the Indians, seeing that they knew not the use of the axes and hoes they had given them the year before; for they had these hanging to their waists as ornaments, and the stockings were made use of as tobacco pouches. The whites now put the handles to the former for them, and cut trees down before their eyes, hoed up the ground, and put the stockings on their legs. Here, they say, a general laughterr ensued among the Indians, that they had remained ignorant of the use of such valuable implement, and had born the weight of such heavy metal hanging to their necks, for such a length of time. They took every white man they saw for an inferior mannitto attendant upon the Supreme Deity who shone superior in the red and laced clothes. As the whites became daily more familiar with the Indians, they at last proposed to stay with them, and asked only for so much ground for a garden lot, as, they said the hide of a bullock would cover or encompass, which hide was spread before them. The Indians readily granted this apparently reasonable request; but the whites then took a knife, and beginning at one end of the hide, cut it up to a long rope, not thicker than a child's finger, so that by the time the whole was cut up, it made an great heap; they then took the rope at one end, and drew it gently along, carefully avoiding its breaking. It was drawn out into a circular form, and being closed at its ends encompassed a large piece of ground. The Indians were surprised at the superior wit of the whites, but did not wish to contend with them about a little land, as they had still enough themselves. The white and red men lived contentedly together for a long time, though the former from time to time asked for more land, which was readily obtained, and thus they gradually proceeded higher up the mahicannittuck [Hudson River], until the Indians began to believe that they would soon want all their country, which in the end proved true.

Source: John Heckewelder, *An Account of the history, manners, and customs of the Indian nations, who once inhabited Pennsylvania and neighboring states* (Philadelphia: Historical Society of Pennsylvania, 1876 [1819]), pp. 71–75 and 321–322.

3

The English Come to Stay

1600–1660

< The Fort at Jamestown

The Predicament of Pocahontas, Alias Rebecca

Because Pocahontas was the subject of a 1995 animated Disney movie, many people do not realize that she was a real girl who lived during difficult times. Born in the 1590s in what is today Virginia, Pocahontas was the daughter of Powhatan, paramount chief of at least 20 tribes, but she herself held no special status. In her world, although men ruled, power passed through the female line. (A chief was thus succeeded by his sister's son, not his own son.) Pocahontas's mother was unimportant (she may even have been a prisoner of war), so Pocahontas was not marked to rule or even to marry a chief. As a child, Pocahontas would have worked alongside other children to protect the village's crops from hungry animals and birds.

When the girl was about 10 years old, events occurred that would eventually lead to immense change for her people. In 1607, the Jamestown colonists arrived and built a permanent fort. Despite the trade opportunities, many of Powhatan's people did not want them there, and some skirmishing occurred. Eventually, an Englishman named John Smith, president of the struggling colony, came upriver to try to trade for corn, and some relatives of Powhatan kidnapped him and brought him to the high chief. Through sign language, he attempted to communicate his desire for trade. For the next several weeks, he was left in the company of young Pocahontas; they tried to teach each other something of their two languages. When Powhatan felt confident that he had made a friend and trade partner of the Englishman, he had him escorted back to the fort. Later he sent advisers to visit, and they took Pocahontas along to translate. In the report that Smith sent back home, he said nothing about Powhatan ever having tried to kill him, or about Pocahontas having rescued him. That was a story he told 17 years later, when all the principals were dead. (In his writings of later years, Smith elaborated on the theme of beautiful young women having rescued him from death everywhere he went.)

Smith returned to England shortly after his sojourn with the Indians ended. Battles escalated between the hungry English colonists—who wanted the Indians to pay them tribute—and the Indians—who had no intention of doing so. Eventually, it was learned that Pocahontas was visiting a village on the Potomac. She was kidnapped and brought to Jamestown, where she was held prisoner for a year.

The English wanted the Indians to agree to pay tribute, or at least to offer a significant ransom. Powhatan, however, could not afford to do that for a politically insignificant child. In the meantime, the colonists taught Pocahontas English and attempted to convert her to Christianity, hoping she could at least be an effective go-between. Pocahontas does seem to have learned English quite easily, but she steadfastly refused to convert to Christianity.

One day in 1613, in frustration, the English took her aboard a war ship and went up the James River, approaching her father's village, training their guns on the shore. They wanted Powhatan to fear for his daughter's life and the lives of his people. At this juncture, a young man named John Rolfe, who had apparently been one of Pocahontas's English teachers, asked the English colonial governor for permission to marry the girl. Messengers were dispatched to

Powhatan, who immediately consented to the marriage. In his world, the daughters of noblemen often had to marry the enemy in an effort to broker peace.

Pocahontas faced a difficult future as a prisoner-wife, though it was a familiar fate for indigenous women. She agreed and found the strength to do what she was expected to do. She took her husband's god as her god and became a Christian. Three days later, she went through the marriage ceremony. When it came time to choose her baptismal name of Rebecca, the English were startled to learn that "Pocahontas" was not her real name, but a childhood nickname. Her real name was Matoaka.

Pocahontas continued to protect her own customs and sense of what was right even after the marriage. She did not always do what Christians thought she should do. John Rolfe appeared to be very happy with her, but he wrote in frustration that the Indians "doe runn headlong, yea with joy, into destruction and perpetuall damnation."

In the spring of 1616, Pocahontas and her husband and young son, Thomas, were asked to travel to England to help rescue the Virginia Company from financial disaster. Several of Powhatan's highest ranking advisers accompanied them, so as to glean needed information about these strangers. Pocahontas worked to establish confidence in the venture. But she also insisted, through her husband, that her people be well compensated for their land. Her experience of England had been enough to convince her that negotiated settlements were the most they could hope for; they could not win wars against Renaissance technology. For the first time, she understood the magnitude of her people's predicament. In 1617, just as they were about to sail for home, Pocahontas succumbed to a European disease and died. She was no more than 21 years old.

The First Chesapeake Colonies

When Queen Elizabeth died in 1603, she was succeeded by her Scottish cousin, King James I, who immediately signed a treaty with Spain ending decades of warfare. With peace established, all those who had lived off privateering and warfare had to look for another source of income. They joined with old advocates of colonization to establish new colonies in North America. In 1606, James granted charters to two groups of English merchants and military men, one in London and the other in Plymouth. The Plymouth group would colonize the northern coast, and the Londoners the Chesapeake region. Each operation was chartered as a private company, which would raise money from shareholders and finance, populate, and regulate its colonies.

Founding Virginia

In 1606, the Plymouth-based company deposited some settlers at the mouth of the Kennebec River in today's Maine, but the climate defeated them within a season. The Virginia Company (named in honor of the recently deceased, never-married queen) had wealthy London backers and met with greater success. Just before Christmas in 1606, it sent out three ships under Captain Christopher Newport, a one-legged veteran Atlantic explorer. When the ships arrived at Virginia on April 26, 1607, the colonists learned that they

The Fort at Jamestown This nine-teenth-century engraving of James-town in 1607 shows the difficulties of unloading goods from a ship in the earliest days of settlement.

were to be governed by a council of seven men. Unfortunately, two of them, Edward Maria Wingfield, an arrogant gentleman and investor in the company, and Captain John Smith, the equally arro-gant but considerably more ca-pable soldier of fortune, despised each other. By the end of the summer, another council member had been executed because he was supposedly a double agent for the Spanish. The early history of Jamestown was marked by internal wrangling. External conflict soon developed as well, as the colonists antagonized their Indian hosts. Almost every-thing that could go wrong did.

The experience of Roanoke notwithstanding, the English still hoped to find a land like Mexico, filled with gold and other less glamorous raw materials. Whatever limited manufac-turing was needed could be performed either by English criminals, sent over to work as their punishment, or by indentured servants, English men and women from the lowest ranks of society who agreed to work for a set period to pay their transportation expenses. The colo-nists expected to trade with the local Indians, who would be the primary suppliers of food.

The Virginia Company planned to get the colony up and running within seven years. During that period, all colonists would work for the Company, which would give them food and shelter. At the end of that time, they would receive grants of land. The Company evidently thought the colony would need a great deal of direction, for about one-third of the original settlers were gentlemen, that is, members of the elite, a proportion of the colony's population that was six times higher than it was in England.

The Company also sent skilled laborers, many with skills of little use in the colony, such as tailors, goldsmiths, and a perfumer. Some were thought necessary to support the gentlemen. Others were to work the gold and precious gems colonists hoped to find. Farmers and ordinary laborers, on the other hand, were in short supply, for it was assumed that the Indians would fill these roles.

Starving Times

Poor planning and bad luck placed the colonists on swampy ground with bad water. The salty water of the James River could be poisonous, and in summer it became a breeding ground for typhoid and dysentery. Some historians have argued that these diseases left the survivors too weak to plant food, whereas others note that many of the healthy seemed to prefer prospecting for gold. The colonists depended on the resentful Powhatan Indians for food, and the resulting malnutrition made the effects of disease worse. These factors, along with skirmishes with the Powhatans, led to appallingly high mortality rates. By September 1607, half of the more than 100 original colonists were dead, and by the following spring

Table 3-1 English Population of Virginia, 1607–1640

Population in Virginia Colony	Immigration to Virginia Colony
104 (April 1607)	104 (April 1607)
38 (Jan. 1608)	
	120 (Jan. 1608, 1st supply)
130 (Sept. 1608)	
	70 (Sept. 1608, 2nd supply)
200 (late Sept. 1608)	
100 (spring 1609)	
	300 (Fall 1609, 3rd supply)
	540 (1610)
450 (April 1611)	
	660 (1611)
682 (Jan. 1612)	
350 (Jan. 1613)	
	45 (1613–1616)
351 (1616)	
600 (Dec. 1618)	
	900 (1618–1620)
887 (Mar. 1620)	
	1,051 (1620–1621)
943 (Mar. 1621)	
	1,580 (1621–1622)
1,240 (Mar. 1622)	
	1,935 (1622–1623)
1,241 (April 1623)	
	1,646 (1623–1624)
1,275 (Feb. 1624)	
1,210 (1625)	
	9,000 (1625–1634)
4,914 (1634)	
	6,000 (1635–1640)
8,100 (1640)	total: 23,951

Source: Data from Carville Earle, *Geographical Inquiry and American Historical Problems* (Stanford, CA: Stanford University Press, 1992), and Virginia Bernhard, "Men, Women, and Children at Jamestown: Population and Gender in Early Virginia, 1607–1610," *Journal of Southern History* 58 (1992).

Note: Although about 24,000 men and women immigrated to Virginia between 1607 and 1640, in 1640 the population stood at only 8,100. Most of the inhabitants fell victim to disease, although the Indian uprising of 1622 took 347 lives.

only 38 were still alive. Although the Company sent over more colonists, they continued to die off at extraordinary rates. As late as 1616, the English population was only 350, although more than five times that number had emigrated from England (see Table 3–1, p. 65).

Troubled Relations with the Powhatans

In Virginia, the English encountered the powerful paramount chieftaincy of the Powhatan Indians. Originally a small tribe of Algonquian-speaking Indians like many others in the region, the Powhatans had attained great power when, through a series of politically motivated marriages, a young chief of theirs had inherited the rulerships of several other tribes, some through his mother and some through his father. This man, called Powhatan in honor of his people, took his larger-than-usual force of warriors and made a series of strategic attacks, then followed up by taking a wife from each of numerous chiefly families in the area. At the time of the arrival of the English, Powhatan's chieftaincy included about 20,000 Indians, divided into about three dozen tribes.

Powhatan hoped to use the English to buttress his power by trading for metal goods and textiles, but he recognized that the strangers might constitute a threat. In his negotiations first with Smith and then with others, he attempted to tie the English into his world as his vassals. But, of course, the English hoped for the inverse. At one point, the English put a fake crown on the kneeling Powhatan's head, imitating the ceremonies in which feudal princes pledged allegiance to a king. The Indians, however, remained unmoved by the ceremony.

With his large force, Lord De La Warr immediately set out to subjugate the Indians. He ordered Powhatan to return all English captives taken in prior skirmishes. When Powhatan refused, De La Warr ordered an attack on an Indian village. The English killed about 75 inhabitants, burned the town and its cornfields, and captured the wife of a chieftain and her children. As the English sailed back to Jamestown, they threw the children overboard and shot them as they swam in the water. So opened the First Anglo-Powhatan War, the first of three conflicts between 1610 and 1646. Eventually, a brief peace was ushered in when Pocahontas married John Rolfe, but it could not last.

Toward a New Economic Order and the Rise of Democracy

The tide finally turned against the Powhatans, not because of a failure in diplomacy or the politics of marriage, but because the English finally found a way to make money in Virginia. Pocahontas's husband, John Rolfe, developed a strain of tobacco that found a ready market in England. It transformed the colony almost overnight. Within three years, Virginia was shipping 50,000 pounds of tobacco to England per year. Suddenly Virginia experienced an economic boom. By 1619, a man working by himself was making £200 in one crop, and a man with six indentured servants could make £1,000, money only the nobility was accustomed to. Once fortunes this large could be made, the race to Virginia was on.

All that was needed to make money in Virginia was land and people to work it. In 1616, the Virginia Company, which had land but no money, offered land as dividends to its stockholders. Those already living in Virginia were given land, and anyone who came over (or brought another person over) was to be granted 50 acres a head (called a headright). The Company was moving toward private enterprise, away from the corporate, company-directed economy of the early years. The leadership of the colony also gave itself grants, laying the basis for its own wealth and power. It was far easier to obtain land in Virginia than in England.

Powhatan and English Dwellings These are reconstructions of typical Powhatan Indian and English homes, ca. 1607. Both are dark and small.

To attract settlers, the Company replaced martial law with common law, guaranteeing colonists all the rights of the English people. The colonists were also granted greater rights to self-government than were enjoyed by those who lived in England. The first elected representative government in the New World, the Virginia House of Burgesses (renamed the General Assembly after the American Revolution), met in Jamestown on July 30, 1619.

These inducements attracted 3,500 settlers to Virginia in three years, three times as many as had come in the preceding 10 years. By accident more than planning, Virginia had found the formula for a successful English colony. It was one that all other colonies generally followed: offering colonists greater opportunities to make money and greater rights of self-government than they had at home. These changes came too late, however, to rescue the Virginia Company, which went bankrupt in 1624. King James I dissolved the Company and turned Virginia into a royal colony under his control.

Toward the Destruction of the Powhatans

As the new colonists spread out, establishing private plantations, English settlers claimed all the Indians' prime farmland on both sides of the James River and began to move up its tributaries (see Map 3–1). At the same time, the Powhatans became increasingly dependent on English goods such as metal tools. Moreover, as the English population began to grow its own food, it had less need of Indian food, the only significant commodity the Indians had to trade. The Indians slowly accumulated a debt to the English and lost their economic independence.

After Powhatan died, his more militant brother, Opechancanough, decided to get rid of the English. He wanted to convince them to go home or at least to limit their spreading. On the morning of March 22, 1622, in an extraordinarily well-planned attack, the Indians struck at most of the plantations along the James River, killing about one-quarter of the colonists. The Second Anglo-Powhatan War, which continued for another 10 years, had begun. This war marked a turning point in English policy. Although some of the English

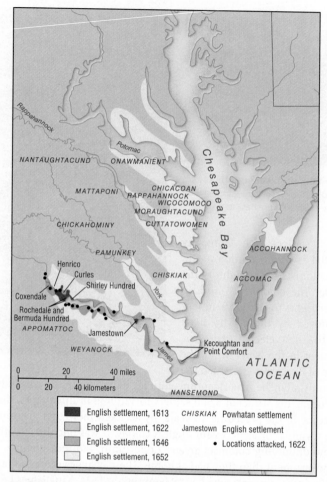

Map 3-1 English Encroachments on Indian Land, 1613–1652 After John Rolfe's development of a marketable strain of tobacco, the English spread out through the Chesapeake region, encroaching steadily on Indian land. Tobacco planters preferred land along the rivers, for casks filled with tobacco bound for England were more easily transported by ship.
Source: Frederic Gleach, *Powhatan's World and Colonial Virginia* (Lincoln: University of Nebraska Press, 1997), and James Horn, *Adapting to a New World: English Society in the Seventeenth-Century Chesapeake* (Chapel Hill: University of North Carolina Press, 1994).

recognized that the Indian attack had been caused by their "own perfidiouse dealing," most decided that the Indians were untrustworthy and incapable of being converted to the English way of life. Therefore, a policy of extermination was justified. Some were almost happy that the Indians had attacked; John Smith concluded that the massacre "will be good for the Plantation, because now we have just cause to destroy them by all meanes possible." Until this point, the English had claimed only land that the Indians were not currently farming. Now they seized territory the Indians had just cleared and planted. In only 15 years' time, the English and Indians in Virginia had become implacable enemies.

Indian resistance only made the English more determined to stay, and with the tobacco economy booming, settlers poured into Virginia. They spread across the Chesapeake to the Eastern Shore and north to the Potomac River. The aged Opechancanough, determined to make one final push, struck again on April 18, 1644, killing about 400 and taking many prisoners.

The Third Anglo-Powhatan War ended, however, in the Indians' total defeat two years later. Opechancanough was killed. The English took complete possession of the land between the James and York Rivers. Henceforth, no Indian was allowed to enter this territory unless he was bringing a message from a chief. Any English person who sheltered an Indian without permission was to be put to death. The land north of the York River was set aside for the Indians, making it the first American Indian reservation. Soon, English settlers moved into that region, too. It was not the last time that the English settlers would break a treaty with the Indians.

A New Colony in Maryland

Virginia's original plan to make money from trading with the local Indians was not entirely forgotten. When tobacco prices dipped in the 1620s, trade became attractive once again. By the late 1620s, an outpost had been established at the northern end of the Chesapeake Bay to obtain beaver furs from the Susquehannocks. Sir George Calvert, the first Lord Baltimore and a Catholic, saw the commercial potential of this region and in 1632 persuaded King Charles I, a Catholic sympathizer, to grant him the land north of the Potomac and south of the Delaware that was "not yet cultivated and planted." This territory became Maryland, the first proprietary colony, that is, a colony owned literally by an individual and his heirs. (Virginia was originally a charter colony, held by a group of private shareholders. Unlike royal colonies, in charter and proprietary colonies the English Crown turned over both financing and management to the shareholders or proprietors.) Maryland, named after the Catholic queen of England, remained the hereditary possession of the Calvert family until the American Revolution, although the majority of the settlers were not Catholics.

As the first proprietary colony, Maryland established a pattern for subsequent proprietorships. The proprietor had extensive powers to grant land and make laws by himself, but perhaps because Calvert knew he would have to compete for settlers with Virginia, which had a representative government, he agreed to a representative assembly. In 1649, that assembly passed the Act of Toleration, which said that no one would be "compelled to the beliefe or exercise of any other Religion against his or her consent." Even though religious toleration was extended only to Christians, Maryland was among the most tolerant places in the world. Moreover, this right was extended to women as well as men. (This experiment in religious toleration faced a crisis, however, in 1689, when Coode's Rebellion overthrew the proprietor, making Maryland temporarily a royal colony and, in 1702, establishing the Anglican Church. In 1715, the Calvert family was restored to power. See Chapter 4 for more on the effects of England's "Glorious Revolution" in America.)

Although Maryland's population increased slowly, the familiar political economy emerged quickly. As in Virginia, attracting colonists required greater opportunities and freedoms—of self-government and of religion—than they enjoyed in England. Even during the conflict with the Powhatan Confederacy, the booming tobacco economy drew settlers to Virginia and, after about 1650, to Maryland as well. Although they had separate governments, Virginia and Maryland had similar political economies, based on tobacco. The defeat of the Indians made more land available for cultivation; the colonies needed only people to work it.

The Political Economy of Slavery Emerges

Chesapeake society in the first half of the seventeenth century was shaped by four forces: weak government, the market for tobacco, the availability of land, and the need for labor. Because government was weak, the forces of plantation agriculture were unchecked, and the profit motive operated without restraint. Those who could take advantage of these opportunities—male and female both—profited wildly, whereas the poor, both white and African, were without defense. In this environment the political economy of slavery took root.

The Problem of a Labor Supply

Once the crises of the early years had passed, the Chesapeake's greatest problem was securing laborers to produce tobacco. As soon as John Rolfe brought in his first successful crop, the Virginia governor began pressing England to send him its poor. The Virginia Company also encouraged the emigration of women, for the young colony was primarily male. No matter how many colonists came, however, the demand for labor always outstripped the supply. By 1660, 50,000 Britons, mostly single men in their 20s, had migrated to the Chesapeake, but the population was still only a little over 35,000. Because of disease and malnutrition, the death rate remained extraordinarily high. It did not help that most of the colonists came from impoverished backgrounds and arrived alone and friendless to face a harsh new situation.

The profits from tobacco were so great and the risk of death so high that landowners squeezed out every penny of profit as quickly as they could. Those with land and servants to work it could become rich overnight. Colonial officials, including members of the legislature, discovered a variety of ways to make themselves wealthy. Great wealth, however, could be achieved only by the labor of others, and the demand for labor was almost insatiable. Perhaps 90 percent of those who migrated to the Chesapeake in the seventeenth century came as servants, and half died before completing their term of service. In England, servants had some basic protections, but in Virginia, working conditions were deadly brutal. In 1623, Richard Frethorne, a young Virginia servant "with weeping tears" wrote to his parents in England, "We must work early and late for a mess of water gruel and a mouthful of bread and beef."

Servants might be beaten so severely that they died, or they might find their indentures (the contract that bound them to service for a period of usually seven years) sold from one master to another. They found little protection from the courts. They were not, in fact, slaves. They would become free if they outlived their period of indenture; they retained all of the rights of English people, and their servitude was not hereditary. But they were far worse off than servants in England.

Some colonists tried to resolve the problem of the labor shortage by purchasing Indian slaves who had been captured by other Indians in wars farther west, but there were not nearly enough of these to meet the demand (see Chapter 4).

The Origins of African Slavery in the Chesapeake

Other New World plantation societies in which labor was in short supply had already turned to African slavery, so it was probably only a matter of time until the Chesapeake did as well. Historians do not know precisely when slavery was first practiced on a widespread basis in the Chesapeake, but Africans first arrived in Virginia in 1619, when a Dutch ship sailing off course sold its cargo of "twenty Negars" to the Virginians. As long as life expectancy was low, it was generally more profitable for a planter to purchase an indentured servant for a period of seven years than a slave for life. Not until life expectancy improved toward the end of the seventeenth century were significant numbers of African slaves imported into the Chesapeake.

All the English plantation colonies followed the same pattern in making the transition from white servitude to African slavery. The transition was quick in some places and slow in others; in Virginia, it took about three-quarters of a century. The primary factors dictating how readily English colonists adopted African slavery were the need for plantation laborers and the availability of African slaves at a good price. If there was any discussion about the justice of slavery, the English claimed that slavery was an appropriate punishment for certain crimes and for prisoners taken in just wars. No white people were ever enslaved in the English colonies, however. It was a practice reserved for "strangers," primarily foreigners of a non-Christian religion. At first, some of the Africans who ended up in the colonies were those who came as the domestic servants of well-to-do colonists, not as chattel slaves. In addition, some buyers in the early years allowed Africans to earn their freedom as did English indentured servants. Still, all the British colonies eventually practiced permanent chattel slavery, and it became critical to plantation economies. African slaves were even brought back to the British Islands, and by the middle of the eighteenth century, 2 percent of London's population was African.

Even before they had substantial contact with African people, the English and other northern Europeans probably harbored prejudice against dark-skinned people. By the second half of the sixteenth century, the English were depicting Africans in derogatory terms, saying that Africans were unattractive, with "dispositions most savage and brutish," a "people of beastly living" who "contract no matrimonie, neither have respect to chastity." Northern Europeans considered African women particularly monstrous, sexually promiscuous, and neglectful of their children. Although these views were not explicitly used to justify slavery, they formed the basis for the racism that would develop along with the slave system.

During the first half of the seventeenth century, African slavery and white and African servitude existed side by side. The Chesapeake was a society with slaves, but it was still not a slave society. The first clear evidence of permanent and generalized enslavement of Africans in the Chesapeake dates to 1639, when the Maryland Assembly passed a law guaranteeing "all the Inhabitants of this Province being Christians (Slaves excepted)" all the rights and liberties of "any natural born subject of England." The first Virginia law recognizing slavery, passed in 1661, said that any English servant who ran away with an African would have to serve additional time not only for himself but for the African as well. Such Africans were clearly already understood to be slaves for life and hence were incapable of serving any additional time.

Such laws reveal the great familiarity that existed between white and black servants. Slaves and white servants worked together, enjoyed leisure together, had sexual relations with each other, and ran away together. As late as 1680, most of the plantation laborers were still white indentured servants. There is no evidence that they were kept separate from Africans by law or inclination.

As long as the black population remained small, the color line was blurry. Not until late in the seventeenth century were laws passed that restricted free African Americans. In fact, in 1660, Anthony Johnson, an African who had arrived in Virginia as a servant in 1621, owned both land and African slaves. In the 40 years that he had been in Virginia, slavery had become institutionalized and recognized by the law, but laws separating the races had yet to be enacted.

The English Enter the Slave Trade

By the sixteenth century, slavery did not exist in England, and its people prided themselves on their "free air." History books in the Anglo-American world have tended to blame the Portuguese and the Spanish for initiating the African slave trade and the Dutch merchants for developing it. Yet by the eighteenth century, British shipping dominated the trade, and English merchants made immense profits from it. Slavery eventually took root everywhere in the Americas, including the English colonies. English traders entered the business as soon as it was feasible to do so, and their actions sped the rise of slavery in the Americas, which in turn encouraged the trade.

In 1562, John Hawkins, from a wealthy seafaring family in Plymouth, decided to break into the Portuguese slave trade. He seized hundreds of Africans, as well as valuable trade goods, from Portuguese ships along the Guinea coast of West Africa and took them to Santo Domingo on Hispaniola to sell. Even after paying the necessary bribes to Spanish officials—as trade with England was illegal—the profits were enormous. Queen Elizabeth I, who had been against the slave trade, began to pay attention, and she later invested Crown resources. On his second voyage, Hawkins experimented with attacking African villages himself, but he found the costs to be high: in one incident, he seized 10 Africans but lost 7 crew members. Hawkins eventually learned that Africans could be his allies in the trade. An emissary from an African king approached him with a proposition: help the king defeat his enemies and share in the slaves taken

Gender and the Social Order in the Chesapeake

The founders of England's colonies hoped to replicate the social order they had known at home. As early as 1619, the Virginia Company began to bring single women to the colony to become brides of the unmarried planters. As in England, it was expected that men would perform all the "outside" labor, including planting, farming, and tending large farm animals. Women would do all the "inside" work, including preserving and preparing food, spinning and weaving, making and repairing clothing, and gardening. In English society, a farmer's wife was not simply a man's sexual partner and companion; she was also the mistress of a successful household economy. Both men and women were vital to the society the English wanted to create in the Chesapeake.

However, the powerful tobacco economy transformed both the economy and society of the New World. With profits from tobacco so high, women went directly into the tobacco fields instead of the kitchen. Children were in the fields as soon as they could work. Only when a man became wealthy did he hire a servant—often a woman—to replace his wife in the fields. As a result, for many years, Virginia society lacked the "comforts of home" that women produced, such as prepared food, homemade clothing, and even soap. Tobacco was everything.

as booty. Hawkins agreed and ended up with hundreds of captives. It was the beginning of a hideous guns-for-slaves cycle that would eventually cripple Africa. For Hawkins, ironically, the voyage ended badly. The Spaniards in the Caribbean, having been punished for their prior illegal dealings with him, refused his merchandise. Then they attacked his fleet off the coast of Veracruz, Mexico, and killed and imprisoned nearly all his men. Hawkins himself barely made it home to England.

It was the lack of a ready legal market in the New World that made the business impossible for the time being. In the first half of the seventeenth century, however, that situation changed as the English established colonies on the mainland of North America and on certain Caribbean islands. In 1630, wealthy Puritans established the colony they hoped would make England rich on Providence Island, off the coast of Nicaragua. The investors had in mind the widespread production of cash crops that grew readily in tropical climates. After only four years, the investors abandoned the importation of indentured English servants and filled the land with Africans—whom enthusiastic captains found they could buy along the Central American coast. After the Pequots lost a war with the New Englanders, Pequot prisoners were also sold on Providence Island. One man wrote with abhorrence of the turn of events; his Puritan brethren were unmoved. Only the constant rebellions frightened them, so they took steps to curb the total number relative to the number of English. Yet by the time the Spanish navy destroyed the colony in 1641, there were more than 380 African slaves and fewer than 350 English settlers.

From 1640 on, the numbers of African slaves grew in Barbados and other English island colonies, and after the 1660s in the Chesapeake as well. As soon as they were available cheaply enough, slaves became widespread wherever cash crops could grow—even in a Puritan colony. The English slave trade had blossomed.

Colonial society also weakened patriarchal controls. Chesapeake governments tried—but failed—to control immigrant women, insisting, for example, that a woman receive government permission before marrying and prosecuting for slander women who spoke out against the government or their neighbors. But colonial government was relatively weak, and women, far from their own fathers, found themselves unexpectedly free from traditional restrictions.

Although women without the protection of fathers were vulnerable in seventeenth-century plantation societies, in a world where men outnumbered women three or four to one, women were often in a position of relative power. Local governments struggled to impose order by prosecuting women for adultery, fornication, and giving birth to illegitimate children. The public, however, was more tolerant of sexual misconduct than government officials were. The first generation of women to immigrate to the Chesapeake region married relatively late—in their mid-20s or later. As a result, they had relatively few children, and it was many decades before Chesapeake society reproduced itself naturally. Perhaps half of all children born in the colony died in infancy, and one marriage partner was also likely to die within seven years of marriage. At least until 1680 or so, to be a widow, widower, or orphan was the normal state of affairs. Widows who inherited their

STRUGGLES FOR DEMOCRACY

The First African Arrivals Exercise Some Rights

One day in 1654, an African American family living on Virginia's Eastern Shore met on their plantation for a family conference. They were all free; in fact, they themselves owned a few slaves. One of these slaves, a man named John Casor, had recently complained that he was really an indentured servant and should have been given his liberty by now. A court investigator reported that "Anthony Johnson's son-in-law, his wife and his own two sons persuaded the old Negro Anthony Johnson to set the said John Casor free."

To modern readers, the Johnson family saga seems a remarkable one. Anthony Johnson arrived as a slave in Virginia in 1621, aboard one of the first ships to bring Africans to the new colony. The following year, the plantation where he worked was attacked by the Powhatan Indians in the uprising of 1622, but Johnson managed to escape death. That same year, he married another newly arrived African named Mary. They went on to spend forty years together and had at least four surviving children. Within a few years, they found a way to gain their freedom—probably by being allowed to raise their own cattle on the side and keep the proceeds. After he was free, Johnson put the money he made into buying slaves and indentured servants, and eventually was able to claim 250 acres of land under the headright system (through which colonists were given 50 acres for each person they brought into the colony). Then in 1653, the Johnson family experienced catastrophe: a fire on their plantation left them nearly destitute. Fortunately, however, they had gained their community's respect and liking over the years, and the court allowed them tax relief for a significant period so they might put themselves back on their feet. And they did indeed collect themselves.

Anthony Johnson found a way to empower himself. Within a few decades, however, it became impossible for any black man in Virginia, no matter how enterprising, to achieve what he achieved. An extraordinary legal constriction of the rights of Africans occurred. From the time of their first arrival, Africans had generally been viewed as slaves for life, unlike indentured servants; nevertheless, the lines of demarcation were at first somewhat fuzzy. Many Africans were freed by their masters after years of service or were encouraged to buy themselves, and once they were free, no laws forbade them from participating in community activities like anyone else. In the 1660s, as the colony became more dependent on plantation agriculture and slave labor, this began to change. The Virginia Assembly gradually passed laws disenfranchising the region's black population on multiple levels. Most of the laws applied to enslaved people only and came to be called "the slave code." But free blacks were not immune. By the 1690s, any slave who became a freedman was required to leave Virginia within six months. And in 1705, people of African descent living in the colony were specifically prohibited from holding office or giving grand jury testimony. For people of African descent, the Virginia Assembly, rather than being an entity that enabled them to voice their concerns, was the instrument that destroyed their hard-won freedoms. By then, the Johnson family had moved away.

husband's possessions were powerful and in demand on the marriage market. Children, however, often lost their inheritances to a stepparent.

A Bible Commonwealth in the New England Wilderness

In 1620, 13 years after the founding of the Virginia Colony, England planted another permanent colony at Plymouth; 9 years after that, it planted one at Massachusetts Bay. In many ways the Virginia and Massachusetts colonies could not have been more different. The primary impetus behind the Massachusetts settlement was religious. Both the Pilgrims at Plymouth and the much more numerous Puritans at Massachusetts Bay sought to escape persecution and to establish new communities based on God's law as they understood it. The Puritans and Pilgrims were middle class, and their ventures were well financed and capably planned for the benefit of the settlers. The environment was much more healthful than that of the Chesapeake, and the population reproduced itself rapidly. Relations with the Indians were better than in the Chesapeake. Nonetheless, despite the colonies' differences, the Puritan movement was in fact originally a product of the same growth of national states in Europe and the expansion of commerce that led to the European exploration of the New World and the foundation of Jamestown. Furthermore, the Puritans themselves often demonstrated the same tendencies as other Englishmen.

The English Origins of the Puritan Movement

In Europe during the sixteenth century, ordinary people and powerful monarchs had vastly different reasons for abandoning the Roman Catholic Church in favor of one of the new Protestant churches. In England, these differing motives led to 130 years of conflict, including a revolution and massive religious persecution. In the 1530s, Henry VIII established his own state religion, the Church of England, for political rather than for pious reasons. After many years of marriage to Catherine of Aragon, Henry still did not have a male heir. With one of Catherine's ladies-in-waiting, Anne Boleyn, already pregnant, Henry pressed the pope for an annulment of his marriage. In 1533, the pope refused the annulment, and Henry removed the Catholic Church as the established religion of England, replacing it with his own Church of England. He confiscated Catholic Church lands, which he redistributed to members of the English nobility in return for their loyalty. In one move, Henry eliminated a powerful political rival, the Roman Catholic Church, and consolidated his rule over his nobility.

Replacing the Catholic Church did not bring stability, however. Henry's successors alternated between Protestantism and Catholicism. Under the reign of Catherine's daughter Mary, hundreds of Protestants left the country to avoid persecution. When Mary's Protestant sister, Elizabeth, ascended the throne, these exiles returned, having picked up the Calvinist doctrine of predestination on the Continent. John Calvin, the Swiss Protestant reformer, insisted that even before people were born, God foreordained "to some eternal life and to some eternal damnation." Although the Church of England adopted Calvin's doctrine of predestination, the Church never held to it thoroughly enough or followed through on other reforms well enough to please those who called themselves Puritans. And because the monarch viewed challenges to the state religion as challenges to the state itself, religious dissenters were frequently persecuted.

What Did the Puritans Believe?

Like all Christians, Puritans believed that humanity was guilty of the original sin committed by Adam and Eve when they disobeyed God in the Garden of Eden. They believed that God's son, Jesus Christ, had given his life to pay (or atone) for the original sin and that, as a consequence, all truly faithful Christians would be forgiven their sins and admitted to heaven after they died. Unlike other Christians, Calvinists insisted there was nothing that people could do to guarantee that God, by an act of "grace," would grant them the faith that would save them from hell.

Protestants rejected the hierarchy of the Catholic Church, maintaining that the relationship between God and humanity should be direct and unmediated. Because every person had direct access to the word of God through the Bible, Protestants promoted literacy and translated the Bible into modern languages.

As Calvinists, Puritans wanted to "purify" the Church of England of all remnants of Catholicism, including rituals and priestly hierarchy. Furthermore, Anglicans (members of the established Church of England) had come to think that Catholics were partly right—that believing Christians *could* earn their way to heaven by good works, a doctrine the Puritans labeled Arminianism. Puritans, in contrast, continued to insist that salvation was the free gift of God and that human beings could not force God's hand. Individuals could only prepare for grace by reading and studying the Bible, so that they understood God's plan, and by attempting to live the best lives they could. Because they could never be certain of salvation, Puritans always lived with anxiety.

Puritanism contained a powerful tension between intellect and emotion. On the one hand, Puritanism was a highly rational religion, requiring all of its followers to study the Bible and listen to long sermons on fine points of theology. As a result, Puritans, male and female, were highly literate. On the other hand, Puritans believed that no amount of book learning could get a person into heaven, and that grace was as much a matter of the heart as of the mind. The Puritan movement always struggled to contain this tension, as some of its believers embraced a more fully rational religion and others abandoned book learning for emotion.

Puritans believed that church membership was only for those who could demonstrate that they were saved. As they were persecuted for their faith, they came to believe that, like the Israelites of old, they were God's chosen people—that they had a covenant or agreement with God, and that if they did his will, he would make them prosper.

The Puritans first attempted to reform the Church of England. Once they saw that the Church would resist more reformation and was moving further from the Calvinist principle of predestination, some Puritans began to make other plans.

The Pilgrim Colony at Plymouth

The first Puritan colony in North America was established in 1620 at Plymouth, by a group of Puritans known as the Pilgrims, "Separatists" who had given up hope of reforming the Church of England. The Pilgrims had already moved to Holland, thinking its Calvinism would offer a better home. It was hard for the Pilgrims to fit themselves into Holland's economy, however, and they found their children seduced by "the manifold temptations of the place."

By 1620 the Pilgrims were ready to accept the Virginia Company of London's offer of land in America for any English people who would pay their own way. With the colony at Jamestown foundering and the Company looking for other opportunities, it filled two ships, the *Mayflower* and the *Speedwell*, with the Pilgrims from Holland, other interested Puritans, and a large number of non-Puritans also willing to pay their own way.

The leaking *Speedwell* had to turn back, but the *Mayflower* arrived at Plymouth, Massachusetts, in November 1620, far north of its destination and outside the jurisdiction of the Virginia Company. Because the Pilgrims had landed in territory that had no legal claim and no lawful government, 41 of the adult men on board signed a document known as the Mayflower Compact. The men bound themselves into a "Civil Body Politic" to make laws and govern the colony and also to recognize the authority of the governor. Although the Compact provided a legal basis for joint government and to a large extent allowed for self-determination on the part of the people, it was by no means a wholly democratic document. By design, it excluded those who were not "Saints," or Puritans, from the body politic. Some of the non-Puritans (called "Strangers") had been talking about mutiny, so the Pilgrims wanted to make their power secure.

Only 1 of the 102 passengers had died en route, but only half of the party survived the harsh first winter. Years later the second governor, William Bradford, remembered the Pilgrims' ordeals. The Indians, he complained, were "savage barbarians . . . readier to fill their sides full of arrows than otherwise." And their new home was "a hideous and desolate wilderness, full of wild beasts and wild men."

In fact, the Plymouth Colony would never have survived had it not been for the assistance of friendly Indians. Like the French in New France and unlike the English at Jamestown, the Pilgrims established diplomatic relations both because they were good diplomats and because the local Indians desperately needed foreign allies. Before the Pilgrims' arrival, Plymouth Bay had been inhabited by as many as 2,000 people. Then European fishermen and traders introduced some fatal disease—possibly viral hepatitis—which was carried along the trading network and killed 90 percent of the local population. Indians "died in heapes as they lay in their houses," their villages filled with the bones of the unburied dead. So recently had Patuxet and Pokanoket Indians inhabited the region that the Pilgrims were able to supplement their meager supplies by rummaging Indian graves, homes, and stores of grain.

The world was vastly changed for Native Americans who survived. Tisquantum, or "Squanto," a Patuxet, had spent the plague years in Europe, having been kidnapped by an exploring Englishman (see Chapter 2). He had only recently made his way back and found that his tribe had almost entirely disappeared. The once-powerful Pokanokets, led by Massasoit, were now paying tribute to the Narragansetts, who had escaped the deadly disease. Squanto persuaded Massasoit that the English might be allies against the Narragansetts. Thus, in the spring of 1621, Squanto offered his assistance to the Pilgrims and showed them how to grow corn.

From the Indian perspective, this assistance was a diplomatic initiative, enabling a treaty between the Pokanokets and the Pilgrims. It worked for the English, too, however. By the time Squanto died in 1622, he had helped secure the future of the Pilgrims' Plymouth Colony. Plymouth remained a separate colony until 1691, when it was absorbed into the larger, more influential Massachusetts Bay Colony. Plymouth demonstrated that New England could be inhabited by Europeans and that effective diplomatic relations with local Indians were critical for a colony's survival.

The Puritan Colony at Massachusetts Bay

In England, increasing numbers of people considered themselves Puritans and yet were not Separatists, like the Pilgrims. Many dreamed of founding colonies, but they wanted to serve as models to other Englishmen, not sever themselves from them. In February 1630, an English Puritan noted in his diary that the faithful had recently sent off ships to New England as well as to a place near Mexico. He was referring to Providence Island, off the coast of Nicaragua. Many Puritans were wealthy landowners and merchants who could not bear to think that the great wealth of the Americas should go mostly to Spain. They wanted an English colony in the tropics and so found an uninhabited island upon which to establish a plantation economy. They first envisioned a labor force of indentured servants, as in the Chesapeake, but rapidly moved to African slavery, with only one Puritan voicing serious opposition. In 1641, the Spanish navy destroyed the fledgling colony.

In the meantime, friends and relatives of the Providence Island Puritans had remained focused on New England and the transport of Puritan settler families. In 1629, the Massachusetts Bay Company, a group of London merchants, had received a charter from King Charles I to establish a colony. The investors in the joint-stock company would have full rights to a swath of land reaching from Massachusetts Bay west across the entire continent. Along with Puritans looking for a new home where they could govern themselves, the company included some who hoped to turn a profit from trade. By the end of the year 1630, Boston and 10 other towns had been founded. By the early 1640s, between 20,000 and 25,000 Britons (not all of them Puritans) had migrated to the Puritan colonies of Plymouth, Massachusetts Bay, Connecticut, Rhode Island, and New Hampshire. Although fewer than half as many migrated to New England as to the Chesapeake region, by 1660 both had populations of a similar size—around 35,000.

New England was able to catch up and keep pace with the Chesapeake for three reasons. First, New England was a much more healthful region. Long, cold winters killed

the mosquitoes that carried fatal diseases, and the water supply was good. Second, Puritans migrated as families. Ninety percent came as part of a family group, a pattern almost exactly the reverse of that in the Chesapeake. In such circumstances, the population soon reproduced itself. Third, most of the settlers were not desperate; they had resources to help them make the transition. Most were prosperous members of the middle range of society. Many of the men were professionals—craftsmen, doctors, lawyers, and ministers—people who profited

Elizabeth Paddy Wensley Far from the grim Massachusetts settler we imagine, Elizabeth Paddy Wensley dressed stylishly by the standards of the 1670s. A mother of five, she was married to the wealthy Boston merchant John Wensley.

from the changing English economy of the late sixteenth and early seventeenth centuries. Again, the contrast with the Chesapeake was dramatic. There, the vast majority of migrants were people with few skills and dim prospects.

The New England Way

The Puritans of Massachusetts Bay Colony were men and women with a mission. Their first governor, John Winthrop, set out the vision of a Bible commonwealth in a sermon he preached aboard the *Arbella* in the spring of 1630, before the ship even docked. God, Winthrop said, had entered into a covenant with the Puritans, just as they had entered into a covenant with one another. Together they had taken enormous risks and begun an extraordinary experiment to see whether they could establish a society based on the word of God: "We shall be as a city upon a hill, the eyes of all people are upon us. So that if we shall deal falsely with our God in this work we have undertaken, and so cause Him to withdraw his present help from us, we shall be made a story and a by-word through the world." This broad vision shaped the development of New England's society.

This communal vision made early New Englanders relatively cohesive. Each town was created by a grant of land by the Massachusetts General Court (the name given to the legislature) to a group of citizens. The settlers in turn entered into a covenant with one another to establish a government and distribute the land they held collectively. This was not a modern democracy, for Puritans believed in hierarchy, and their vision was more communal than individualist. Nonetheless, there was considerably more economic equality and cohesion than in most parts of the world.

At first, the new towns divided up only a portion of the land that they held, reserving the rest for newcomers and the children of the original founders. The land was distributed unequally, according to social status and family size (see Table 3–2). Although New England society was relatively egalitarian, with only a small gap between the richest and poorest, the Puritans set out to create a social hierarchy. The rich and powerful were supposed to take care of the poor, and Puritan towns did assist all those who could not care for themselves. Each town administered itself through a town meeting, a periodic gathering of the adult male property owners to attend to the town's business. In the past, historians pointed to the democratic elements in the town meeting as

Table 3-2 Distribution of Land in Rowley, Massachusetts, 1639–ca. 1642

Acres	No. of Grants
Over 250	0
201–250	1
151–200	1
101–150	0
51–100	7
21–50	22
20 or less	63
No record	1
Total	95

Source: David Grayson Allen, In *English Ways: The Movement of Societies and the Transferal of English Local Law and Custom to Massachusetts Bay in the Seventeenth Century* (Chapel Hill: University of North Carolina Press, 1981), p. 32.

Note: Between 1639 and 1642, the town of Rowley, Massachusetts, distributed a little over 2,000 acres to 95 families—an average of just 23 acres per family—even though the grant to the town was for many thousand acres. Although most grants were for fewer than 20 acres, some families received considerably more. The founders of Rowley wanted to re-create the hierarchical social order they had known in England.

the source of American democracy. More recently, historians have emphasized undemocratic elements. Participation was restricted to adult male property holders, who were only 35 percent of the adult residents, once women are considered. In addition, the habit of deference to the powerful, prosperous, and educated was so strong that a small group of influential men tended to govern each town. Moreover, Puritans abhorred conflict, so great social pressure was used to ensure harmony and limit dissent. If democracy means the right to disagree and majority rule in open elections, then the New England town meeting was not fully democratic. However, even with all these restrictions, the New England town meeting was far more democratic than any form of government in England at the time, where the vast majority of men, not to mention women, were excluded from political participation.

Changing the Landscape to Fit the Political Economy

The Puritans' corporate social vision was generally compatible with a capitalist political economy. Although land was distributed to towns, once those towns transferred parcels of the land to individual farmers, the farmers were free to leave it to their heirs, to sell it to whomever they pleased, and to buy more land from others. Any improvements on the land (from clearing away trees to building homes, fences, dams, or mills) remained the property of the owners. These practices followed English law.

The contrast with Indian patterns of land use was dramatic. Indians held their land communally, not individually. The entire group had to consent to its sale. At first, when Indians "sold" land to the Puritans, they thought that they were giving them the right to use the land only and to share the land with them. They might allow the Puritans to build a village, plant, and hunt, while they retained similar rights over the same parcel of land, including the right to allow it to be used by several groups of Europeans at once.

The Puritans' notion of exclusive land rights was a cornerstone of their political economy. Because a man could profit from the improvements made on his land and pass those improvements on to his heirs, he had incentives to make them. Moreover, not only the land but its products became commodities to be sold. Thus, like other European colonists, the Puritans turned their Indian neighbors into commercial hunters. For centuries, the Indians had taken only as many beaver as they needed, but now that they found themselves fenced out of their former lands, they could no longer live part of the year by farming and became more committed to hunting. Overhunting led to the disappearance of beaver in the region.

The Puritans themselves cleared the forests of trees. They found a ready market for timber in England, as New England's trees were much taller and straighter than any known in Europe. The English navy came to depend on New England for its masts. Although the bounty of the land had seemed limitless, by 1800 much of southern New England had been stripped of its forests and native wildlife.

Prosperity did not come to Massachusetts immediately. For the first decade, the colony maintained a favorable balance of trade with England only by sending back the money that new immigrants brought with them in return for goods from the mother country. New England's cold climate made it impossible to develop a cash crop such as tobacco. In the 1640s and 1650s, the government encouraged local manufacturing (to cut down on imports) and export of raw materials. Through government policy and individual initiative, New Englanders eventually made great profits from selling timber, wood products, and fish and by acting as merchants. In the meantime, successful family farms were the mainstay of the local economy.

The Puritan Family

Like most early-modern western Europeans, Puritans thought of the family as the society in microcosm, or "a little Church, and a little commonwealth." There was no sharp distinction between home and the wider world. Although Harvard College was founded in 1636 (to train ministers) and the Massachusetts General Court established a system of public education in 1647, most early instruction and virtually all vocational teaching took place at home. Parents were required to teach their children to read the Bible.

The family was also the center of the Puritans' economy. Farmers, of course, worked at home, as did almost all craftsmen. Women also performed tasks critical to the survival of the family. Although tasks were assigned by gender, in the absence of her husband a woman could assume his responsibilities, selling the products he had made or even fighting off Indians. The family, like society, was a hierarchy, with the husband at the top and his wife as his "deputy."

Puritans lived in fear of lawlessness, and they used the family as an instrument of order. Puritans considered excessive affection and particularly excessive maternal love a danger. Children were subjected to strict discipline not out of cruelty but from deep religious convictions. Considering that Puritan women bore on average eight or nine children and that families were confined in small houses over long New England winters, this harmony was probably necessary for survival.

Despite the importance of control, Puritan households were hardly prisons. If Puritans believed that men were the natural heads of the household and that women bore particular responsibility for Eve's original sin, they also believed that both were equally capable of God's grace. Puritans distrusted the passion of love, which could lead to impulsiveness and disorder. They had great respect, however, for the natural affection that grew over the course of marriage and encouraged playfulness when it helped rather than impeded social harmony.

So successful were the early Puritans in establishing tight-knit communities that only two years after their great migration to America had begun, Reverend Thomas Welde could write proudly back to England, "[H]ere I find three great blessings, peace, plenty, and health. . . . I profess if I might have my wish in what part of the world to dwell I know no other place on the whole globe of the earth where I would be rather than here."

Dissension in the Puritan Ranks

Yet not everyone lived in such bliss. The Puritan movement embodied tensions that created individual and social turmoil. Puritans had difficulty balancing emotion and intellect, the individual and the community, spiritual equality and social hierarchy, and anxiety over salvation and the satisfaction of thinking oneself a member of a chosen people. The Puritans also had no mechanisms for handling dissent, which they interpreted as a replay of original sin. The migration to a strange land, populated by people they thought of as savages, as well as the pressure of thinking that the whole world was watching them, only increased the Puritans' desire to maintain a strict order.

Roger Williams and Toleration

The Massachusetts Bay Colony was only a year old when trouble appeared in the person of Roger Williams, a brilliant and obstinate young minister. No sooner had he landed than he announced that he was really a Separatist and would not accept appointment at a church unless it repudiated its ties to the Church of England. Massachusetts Bay was already walking a fine line between outward obedience to the laws of England and inner rejection of the English way of life, and an explicit repudiation of the established church was thought to be an act of political suicide.

Without a church of his own, Williams began preaching to those who would listen. Saying that the king had no right to grant land owned by the Indians, he questioned the validity of the Massachusetts charter and argued for strict separation of church and state, as well as strict separation of the converted and the unconverted. Williams went so far as to advocate religious toleration, with each congregation or sect governing itself completely free from state interference.

These doctrines were heresy to both Puritan church and state. In 1635, when Williams violated an order to stop preaching his unorthodox views, the magistrates decided to ship him immediately to England, where he might be imprisoned or even executed. John Winthrop warned Williams of his fate, giving him time to sneak away to Narragansett Bay, outside the jurisdiction of Massachusetts Bay. Williams and some followers established the new colony of Rhode Island, which was chartered in 1644. The colony, which became a refuge for dissenters of all sorts, was referred to by Massachusetts Puritans as "the sewer of New England."

Anne Hutchinson and the Equality of Believers

One of Puritanism's many tensions concerned the position of women. By insisting on the equality of all true believers before God and the importance of marriage, Protestantism and especially its Puritan branch undermined the starkly negative image of women that prevailed in sixteenth-century Europe. When Puritan ministers preached that women and men were both "joynt Heirs of salvation" and that women, rather than being a "necessary evil," were in fact "a necessary good," they were directly criticizing both the Catholic legacy and common folk belief.

Puritanism extended women respect, but it also insisted they be subordinate to men. In their hierarchical society, woman's position was clearly beneath that of man. Puritanism struggled to find the balance between women's spiritual equality and their earthly subordination: although most Puritan women deferred to male authority, others seized the opportunity that Puritanism seemed to offer. Without exception, the Puritan authorities put them back in their place.

Anne Hutchinson was just over 40 when she, her husband, and their 12 children followed the Reverend John Cotton to Massachusetts Bay. Cotton was a popular preacher who placed particular emphasis on the doctrine of predestination. Hutchinson pushed that doctrine to its logical, if unsettling, conclusion. She claimed that she had experienced several direct revelations, one telling her to follow Cotton to Boston. At informal Bible discussion meetings at her Boston home, which even the new governor attended, Hutchinson challenged the Puritan doctrine of "preparation": if God had truly chosen those whom he would save, it was unnecessary for Puritans to prepare themselves for saving grace by leading sin-free lives. Nor was good behavior a reliable sign of salvation. Hutchinson did not favor sin; she simply believed her neighbors were wrong in thinking that good works would save them. She accused them of the heresy of Arminianism. By claiming that the Holy Spirit spoke directly to her, Hutchinson opened herself to charges of another heresy, antinomianism.

Hutchinson's views were so popular that many residents—possibly a majority—became her followers. Once she accused certain ministers of being unconverted, the colony leaders mounted a campaign against her and her allies. In 1637, they moved the site of the election for governor outside Boston, where her strength was greatest, so that John Winthrop could win. Then, after her most prominent ally among the ministers had been banished, Hutchinson was put on trial for slandering the ministry, convicted, and ordered to leave the colony. Followed by 80 other families, she and her family found temporary refuge in Roger Williams's Rhode Island. (She later moved to New Netherland, where she was killed in an Indian war.) The fact that Hutchinson's ideas came from a woman made them even more dangerous to the Massachusetts leadership. John Winthrop suggested that she might be a witch. Without any evidence at all of sexual misconduct, ministers asserted that Hutchinson and her female followers were driven by lust and that unless they were punished, it would lead to communal living, open sex, and the repudiation of marriage.

It is sometimes asserted that Puritans came to New England in search of religious freedom, but they never would have made that claim. They wanted the liberty to follow their own religion but actively denied that opportunity to others. Puritans insisted on their right to keep out nonbelievers. "No man hath right to come into us," John Winthrop wrote, "without our consent."

Puritan Indian Policy and the Pequot War

The Puritan dissidents were all critical of the Puritans' Indian policy. Roger Williams insisted on purchasing land from the Indians instead of simply seizing it, and the men in the Hutchinson family refused to fight in the Pequot War of 1637. The Puritans had been fortunate in settling in a region in which the Indian population had recently been decimated and in having the English-speaking Squanto's diplomatic services. The Puritan communities expanded so rapidly, however, that they soon intruded on land populated by Indians who had no intention of giving them exclusive rights to it.

Within a few years of the founding of the Massachusetts Bay Colony, small groups of Puritans were spreading out in all directions (see Map 3–2). The Reverend John Wheelwright, Anne Hutchinson's brother-in-law and most ardent supporter, took a party into what is now New Hampshire. Others settled in Maine. In 1638, New Haven, Connecticut, was founded by the Reverend John Davenport and a London merchant, Theophilus Eaton, who purchased land from local Indians. Four years earlier, the first Puritan settlers had reached the Connecticut River in western Massachusetts. In 1636, the Reverend Thomas Hooker led his followers to the site of Hartford, Connecticut.

The Pequot War grew out of conflicts among Europeans about who would govern the fertile Connecticut River valley and among Native Americans about who would trade with the Europeans. Until the arrival of the English, the Dutch had controlled trade along the Connecticut River. They had granted trading privileges to the Pequots, which frustrated other tribes, who could trade only through these middlemen. When the English arrived, the Pequots' enemies attempted to attract them to the valley as trading rivals to the Dutch. The Pequots, afraid of losing their monopoly, made the mistake of inviting Massachusetts

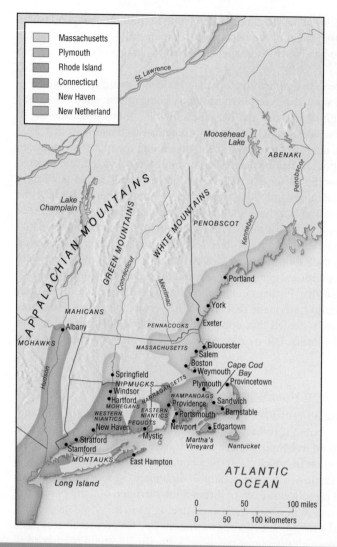

Map 3-2 New England in the 1640s This map shows the land settled by each of the New England colonies, the regions inhabited by Indian tribes, and the region of Dutch settlement. *Source:* John Murrin et al., *Liberty, Equality, Power* (Orlando, FL: Harcourt College Publishers, 1995), p. 73.

Time Line

▼**1533**
Henry VIII breaks with Roman Catholic Church, establishes Church of England

▼**1603**
Queen Elizabeth I dies, succeeded by King James I

▼**1606**
James I grants two charters for North American settlement to Virginia Company

▼**1607**
English found Jamestown

▼**1608**
John Smith named president of Virginia's council

▼**1609**
John Smith returns to England

▼**1610–1614**
First Anglo-Powhatan War

▼**1612–1617**
John Rolfe develops a marketable strain of tobacco

▼**1614**
John Rolfe and Pocahontas marry

▼**1616**
Virginia Company offers a 50-acre headright to each immigrant

Bay to establish a trading post in the region. They were counting on their ability to control not only their Indian enemies but also the Dutch and English. As hundreds of settlers poured in, the Pequots became alarmed. They appealed to their one-time enemies, the Narragansetts, to join with them to get rid of the English. The Narragansetts, however, had already been approached by the Puritans to join them in fighting the Pequots. That is where the Narragansetts calculated that their long-term advantage lay. They themselves were in desperate need of land, having been squeezed beyond endurance by the English settlements. Their leaders recognized the greater power of the English as allies than the Pequots.

The Pequots were caught in a rivalry for their lands between the parent colony in Massachusetts and the new offshoot in Connecticut. The Connecticut group struck first, avenging an attack by the Pequots, which in itself was in revenge for an attack on their allies. At dawn on May 26, 1637, 90 Connecticut men accompanied by 500 Narragansett allies attacked a Pequot village at Mystic filled with women, children, and old men. The raiders knew most of the warriors were away from home. As his men encircled the village, the commander, Captain John Mason, set a torch to the wigwams, shouting, "We must burn them." Those Pequots who escaped the fire ran into the ring of Mason's party, who killed between 300 and 700 Indians, while losing only two of their own men. The Narragansetts' Indian allies were horrified by the brutal attack.

Deeply demoralized, the remainder of the Pequot tribe was easily defeated. Prisoners were sold into slavery in the colony of Providence Island. By 1638, the Puritans declared the Pequot tribe dissolved, and in 1639 Connecticut established its dominance over the Pequots' land. In that year Connecticut established its own government, modeled after that of Massachusetts. In 1662, it became a royal colony. The Puritans had demonstrated that where ecological changes were insufficient to destroy the Indians, they were more than willing to use violence.

Conclusion

By the middle of the seventeenth century, the New England and Chesapeake colonies had already become quite different. Although the forces of capitalism shaped each region, other factors—disease, demographic patterns, relations with the Indians, and the objectives of the founders—left their distinctive imprints. The early history and relatively quick settlement

▼**1619**

First meeting of Virginia General Assembly

First Africans arrive in Virginia

Virginia Company pays for transportation of women to Virginia

▼**1620**

Pilgrims found colony at Plymouth; Mayflower Compact signed

▼**1622–1632**

Second Anglo-Powhatan War

▼**1624**

Virginia Company dissolved; Virginia becomes a royal colony

▼**1625**

James I dies, succeeded by King Charles I

▼**1629**

Massachusetts Bay Company receives charter to establish colony in North America

▼**1630**

Massachusetts Bay Colony founded

▼**1632**

George Calvert receives charter for Maryland

continued

of New England was shaped by the extraordinary cohesiveness and relatively high social standing and degree of wealth of the Puritan settlers, which made them uniquely successful. By contrast, New France and New Netherland were rough frontier societies for many decades, and the Chesapeake colonies were still raw outposts, populated largely by suffering indentured servants and African slaves long after New England had achieved a secure order. All of the North American colonies, except those of New England, were outposts in the transatlantic political and economic order, created to enrich their mother countries and enhance those countries' power. New England was the exception, but so successful was New England in achieving a stable society that we sometimes forget that it was the exception and not the rule.

Who, What, Where

Anglo-Powhatan Wars 66

Antinomianism 83

Arminianism 76

Calvinism 76

Charter colony 69

Headright 66

Hutchinson, Anne 82

Indentured servants 78

Jamestown 75

Maryland 69

Massachusetts Bay 77

Pequot War 83

Plymouth 63

Pocahontas 62

Powhatan 62

Proprietary colony 69

Royal colony 67

Smith, Captain John 64

Squanto 77

Virginia 62

Williams, Roger 82

Winthrop, John 82

Time Line *continued*

▼**1636**
Harvard College founded
Roger Williams exiled from
  Massachusetts

▼**1637**
Anne Hutchinson and her
  followers exiled
Pequot War

▼**1638**
New Haven founded

▼**1639**
First law mentioning slavery, in
  Maryland
Connecticut establishes its
  government

▼**1644**
Rhode Island receives charter

▼**1644–1646**
Third Anglo-Powhatan War

▼**1647**
Massachusetts establishes
  system of public education

▼**1649**
Act of Toleration passed in
  Maryland

▼**1661**
First Virginia law mentioning
  slavery

▼**1691**
Plymouth Colony absorbed into
  Massachusetts

Review Questions

1. What were the objectives of the founders of Virginia? Why did the colony survive, in spite of poor planning?

2. What were the objectives of the founders of the Puritan colonies at Plymouth and Massachusetts Bay? Compare the early years of these colonies to those of the Virginia Colony.

3. What role did gender play in the social order of the Chesapeake and New England colonies?

Critical-Thinking Questions

1. Were the more amicable native-white relations in early New England, as compared to those in Virginia, the result of greater tolerance on the part of the New Englanders or greater willingness to compromise on the part of the Indians?

2. What factors other than religious commitment help explain the success of the Puritan colonies in Massachusetts?

3. Which society was more democratic in its original formulation, the New England colony or the Chesapeake colony? Explain your answer.

4. Are you more impressed by the ease or the slowness that the Chesapeake demonstrated in adopting African slavery? Explain your answer.

Suggested Readings

Eltis, David. *The Rise of African Slavery in the Americas.* New York: Cambridge University Press, 2000.

Miller, Perry. *The New England Mind: The Seventeenth Century.* Cambridge, MA: Harvard University Press, 1967.

Morgan, Edmund. *American Slavery, American Freedom: The Ordeal of Colonial Virginia.* New York: Norton, 1975.

Rountree, Helen. *Pocahontas, Powhatan, Opechancanough: Three Indian Lives Changed by Jamestown.* Charlottesville: University of Virginia Press, 2005.

Silverman, David. *Thundersticks: Firearms and Violent Transformation in Native America.* Cambridge, MA: Harvard University Press, 2016.

For further review materials and resource information, please visit www.oup.com/us/oakes-mcgerr

CHAPTER 3: THE ENGLISH COME TO STAY, 1600–1660

Primary Sources

3.1 EDWARD WATERHOUSE'S REPORT ON THE UPRISING OF 1622

In March of 1622, the Powhatans launched a major attack, striking without warning at many sites up and down the James River. About a quarter of the colony's population was killed in one day. We do not know if the Powhatans hoped the surviving colonists would leave forever or would simply be content to stay in Jamestown and operate a trading post, leaving the Indians with their lands. Almost immediately, Edward Waterhouse sent this report back to London, in which he hatched the idea of exterminating the Indians.

These small and scattered Companies [of Indians] had warning given from one another in all their habitations to meete at the day and houre appointed for our destruction, at all our severall Townses and places seated upon the River; some were directed to goe to one place, some to another, all to be done at the same day and time, which they did accordingly: some entering their Houses under colour of trucking [trading], and so taking advantage, others drawing our men abroad upon faire pretencs, and the rest suddenly falling upon those that were at their labours.

. . . Thus have you seen the particulars of this massacre, out of Letters from thence written, wherein treachery and cruelty have done their worst to us, or rather to themselves; for whose understanding is so shallow, as not to perceive that this must needs bee for the good of the Plantation after, and the losse of this blood to make the body more healthfull, as by these reasons may be manifest.

First, Because betraying of innocency never rests unpunished: And therefore *Agesilaus*,[1] when his enemies (upon whose oath of being faithfull hee rested) had deceived him, he sent them thankes, for that by their perjury, they had made God his friend, and their enemy.

Secondly, Because our hands which before were tied with gentlenesse and faire usage, are now set at liberty by the treacherous violence of the Savages, not untying the Knot, but cutting it: So that we, who hitherto have had possession of no more ground then their waste, and our purchasse at a valuable consideration to their owne contentment, gained; may now by right of Warre, and law of Nations, invade the Country and destroy them who sought to destroy us: whereby wee shall enjoy their cultivated places, turning the laborious Mattocke into the Victorious Sword (wherein there is more both ease, benefit, and glory) and possessing the fruits of others labours. Now their cleared grounds in all their villages (which are situate in the fruitfullest places of the land) shall be inhabited by us, whereas heretofore the grubbing of woods was the greatest labour.

Thirdly, Because those commodities which the Indians enjoyed as much or rather more than we, shall now also be entirely possessed by us. The Deere and other beasts will be in safety, and finitely increase, which heretofore not onely in the generall huntings of the King (whereat foure or five hundred Deere were usually slaine) but by each particular Indian were destroied at all times of the yeare, without any difference of Male, Damme, or Young. . . .

Fourthly, Because the way of conquering them is much more easie then of civilizing them by faire meanes, for they are a rude, barbarous, and naked people, scattered in small companies,

---

[1] Agesilaus was a king of Sparta who lived from 444 BCE to 360 BCE. In making reference to him, Waterhouse is showing off his classical education, and thus proving his credentials as a "gentleman" to anyone who might read his work.

which are helps to Victories, but hinderances to Civilitie: Besides that, a conquest may be of many, and at once, but civility is in particular, and slow, the effect of long time, and great industry. Moreover, victorie of them may bee gained many waies; by force, by surprise, by famine in burning their Corne, by destroying and burning their Boats, Canoes and Houses, by breaking their fishing Weares, by assailing them in their huntings, whereby they get the greatest part of their sustenance in Winter, by pursuing and chasing them with our horses, and blood-Hounds to draw after them, and Mastives to teare them, which take this naked, tanned, deformed Savages, for no other then wilde beasts, and are so fierce and fell upon them, that they feare them worse than their old Devill which they worship, supposing them to be a new and worse kind of Devils then their owne. By these and sundry other wayes, as by driving them (when they flye) upon theire enemies, who are round about them, and by animating and abetting their enemies against them, may their ruine or subjection be soone effected . . .

Fiftly [sic], Because the Indians, who before were used as friends, may now most justly be compelled to servitude and drudgery, and supply the roome of men that labour, whereby even the meanest [poorest] of the Plantation may imploy themselves more entirely in their Arts and Occupations, which are more generous, whilest Savages performe their inferiour workes of digging in mynes, and the like, of whom also some may be sent for the service of the Sommer Ilands [in the Caribbean].

Sixtly, This will forever hereafter make us more cautelous and circumspect, as never to bee deceived more by any other treacheries, but will serve for a great instruction to all posterities there, to teach them that *Trust is the mother of Deceipt*, and to learne them that of the *Italian, Chi no fida, non s'ingamuu*, Hee that trusts not is not deceived; and make them know that kindnesses are misspent upon rude natures, so long as they continue rude; as also, that Savages and Pagans are above all other for matter of Justice ever to be suspected. Thus upon this Anvile shall wee now beate out to our selves an armour of proofe, which shall for ever after defend us from barbarous Incursions, and from greater dangers that otherwise might happen. And so we may truly say according to the French Proverb, *Aquelq chose Malheur est bon*, Ill lucke is good for something.

Source: Edward Waterhouse, "A Declaration of the State of the Colony and Affaires in Virginia, with a Relation of the Barbarous Massacre in the Time of Peace and League, Treacherously Executed by the Native Infidels upon the English." Imprinted at London for Robert Mylbourne, 1622. Appearing in Susan Myra Kingsbury, ed., *The Records of the Virginia Company of London*, vol. III (Washington, DC: United States Government Printing Office, 1933), pp. 541–564.

3.2 LETTER FROM RICHARD FRETHORNE TO HIS PARENTS ABOUT LIFE IN VIRGINIA (1623)

Almost nothing is known about Richard Frethorne, other than what a letter he sent home to his parents tells us. Frethorne was a young indentured servant who arrived in Jamestown in December of 1622, a few months after the uprising described in the previous source. Life in Virginia was not what he had expected, and he wrote to beg his parents to try to buy him out of his indenture. Someone apparently turned the missive over to the Company, as it was found in their records. The spelling here has been modernized, as the original is too idiosyncratic to read with ease.

Loving and kind father and mother,

My most humble duty remembered to you, hoping in God of your good health, as I myself am at the making hereof. This is to let you understand that I your child am in a most heavy case by reason of the nature of the country is such that it causeth much sickness, as the scurvy and the bloody flux and divers other diseases, which maketh the body very poor and weak. And when we are sick, there is nothing to comfort us, for since I came out of the ship, I never ate anything but peas and loblolly (that is, water gruel). As for deer or venison, I never saw any since I came into this land. There is indeed some fowl, but we are not allowed to go and get it, but must work hard both early and late for a mess of water gruel and a mouthful of bread and beef. . . . People cry out day and night—Oh that they were in England without their limbs—and would not care to lose any limb to be in England again, yea, though they beg from door to door. For we live in fear of the enemy every hour, yet we have had a combat with them on the Sunday before Shrovetide, and we took two alive and make slaves of them. But it was by policy, for we are in great danger, for our plantation is very weak by reason of the dearth and sickness of our company. . . . [W]e are but 32 to fight against 3000 if they should come. And the nighest help that we have is ten miles of us, and when the rogues overcame this place last they slew 80 persons. How then shall we do, for we live even in their teeth [that is, close by]? They may easily take us, but that God is merciful and can save with few as well as with many . . .

And I have nothing to comfort me, nor there is nothing to be gotten here but sickness and death, except that one had money to lay out in some things for profit. But I have nothing at all—no, not a shirt to my back but two rags, nor no clothes but one poor suit, nor but one pair of shoes, but one pair of stockings, but one cap, but two bands. My cloak is stolen by one of my own fellows. . . . I have not a penny, nor a penny worth, to help me to either spice or sugar or strong waters, without which one cannot live here. For as strong beer in England doth fatten and strengthen them, so water here doth wash and weaken these here, only keeps life and soul together. But I am not half a quarter so strong as I was in England, and all is for want of victuals: for I do protest unto you that I have eaten more in a day at home than I have allowed me here for a week. You have given more than my day's allowance to a beggar at the door . . .

If you love me, you will redeem me suddenly, for which I do entreat and beg. And if you cannot get the merchants to redeem me for some little money, then for God's sake get a gathering [that is, take up a collection] or entreat some good folks to lay out some little sum of money in meat and cheese and butter and beef. . . .

Good father, do not forget me, but have mercy and pity my miserable case. I know, if you did but see me, you would weep to see me. . . . Wherefore, for God's sake, pity me. I pray you to remember my love to all my friends and kindred. I hope all my brothers and sisters are in good health, and as for my part I have set down my resolution that certainly will be; that is, that the answer of this letter will be life or death to me. Therefore, good father, send as soon as you can . . . I thought no head had been able to hold so much water as hath and doth daily flow from mine eyes. But this is certain: I never felt the want of father and mother till now; but now, dear friends, full well I know and rue it, although it were too late before I knew it. Your loving son,
Richard Frethorne
Virginia, 3rd April, 1623.

Source: Susan Kingsbury, ed., *The Records of the Virginia Company*, vol. 4 (Washington, DC: US Government Printing Office, 1935), pp. 58–62.

3.3 EXCERPTS FROM ANNE HUTCHINSON'S TRIAL TRANSCRIPT (1637)

When the Massachusetts Bay Colony was still very young, Anne Hutchinson, a merchant's wife, held meetings in her house for those who wished to discuss religion. She was accused of promoting a schism, or division within the spiritual community, and on November 7, 1637, was brought to trial in Boston. She stonewalled the prosecution by avoiding their questions, arguing that she had not actually been accused of any specific wrongdoing. Nevertheless, she was found guilty and banished from the colony.

Gov. John Winthrop:

Mrs. Hutchinson, you are called here as one of those that have troubled the peace of the commonwealth and the churches here: you are known to be a woman that hath had a great share in the promoting . . . those opinions that are the cause of this trouble, and to be nearly joined not only in affinity and affection with some of those the court had taken notice of and passed censure upon, but you have spoken divers thing . . . very prejudicial to the honour of the churches and ministers thereof, and you have maintained a meeting and an assembly in your house that hath been condemned by the general assembly as a thing not tolerable nor comely in the sight of God nor fitting for your sex, and notwithstanding that was cried down you have continued the same. Therefore we have thought good to send for you to understand how things are, that if you be in an erroneous way we may reduce you that so you may become a profitable member here among us. Otherwise if you be obstinate in your course that then the court may take such course that you may trouble us no further. Therefore I would entreat you to express whether you do assent and hold in practice to those opinions and factions that have been handled in court already, that is to say, whether you do not justify Mr. Wheelwright's sermon and the petition.

Mrs. Anne Hutchinson:

I am called here to answer before you but I hear no things laid to my charge.

Source: David Hall, ed., *The Antinomian Controversy, 1636–1638: A Documentary History* (Durham, NC: Duke University Press, 1990).

3.4 LETTER FROM ANNE BRADSTREET TO HER CHILDREN (UNDATED)

Anne Dudley Bradstreet, born to a prosperous London family, came to the Massachusetts Bay Colony in 1630 where first her father and then her husband later served as governor. She was well educated and, in 1650, a volume of her poems was published in London under the title *The Tenth Muse Lately Sprung Up in America*. It was met with a positive reception. This letter to her children is undated but was probably written later in her life.

To My Dear Children

This book by any yet unread,
I leave for you when I am dead,
That being gone, here you may find
What was your living mother's mind.
Make use of what I leave in love
And God shall bless you from above.

A.B.

My dear children,—

I, knowing by experience that the exhortations of parents take most effect when the speakers leave to speak, and being ignorant whether on my death bed I shall have opportunity to speak to any of you much less to all, thought it the best whilst I was able to compose some short matters (for what else to call them I know not) and bequeath to you, that when I am no more with you, yet I may be daily in your remembrance (although that is the least in my aim in what I now do) but that you may gain some spiritual advantage by my experience. I have not studied [that is, aimed] in this you read to show my skill, but to declare the Truth, not to set forth myself, but the Glory of God. If I had minded the former it had been perhaps better pleasing to you, but seeing the last is the best, let I be best pleasing to you.

The method I will observe shall be this—I will begin with God's dealing with me from my childhood to this day.

In my young years, about 6 or 7 as I take it, I began to make conscience of my way, and what I knew was sinful as lying, disobedience to parents, etcetera, I avoided it. If at any time I was overtaken with the like evils, it was a great trouble. I could not be at rest 'till by prayer I had confessed it unto God. I was also troubled at the neglect of private duties, though too often tardy that way. I also found much comfort in reading the Scriptures, especially those places I thought most concerned my condition, and as I grew to have more understanding, so the more solace I took in them.

In a long fit of sickness which I had on my bed, I often communed with my heart, and made my supplication to the most high who set me free from that affliction.

But as I grew up to be about 14 or 15, I found my heart more carnal, and sitting loose from God, vanity and the follies of youth took hold of me.

About 16, the Lord laid his hand sore upon me and smote me with the small pox. When I was in my affliction, I besought the Lord, and confessed my pride and vanity and he was entreated of me, and again restored me. But I rendered not to him according to the benefit received.

After a short time I changed my condition and was married and came into this country, where I found a new world and new manners, at which my heart rose. But after I was convinced it was the way of God, I admitted to it and joined to the church at Boston.

After some time I fell into a lingering sickness like a consumption, together with a lameness, which correction I saw the Lord sent to humble and try me and to do me good: and it was not altogether ineffectual.

It pleased God to keep me a long time without a child which was a great grief to me, and cost me many prayers and tears before I obtained one, and after him gave me many more, of whom I now take the care, that as I have brought you into the world, and with great pains, weakness, cares and fears brought you to this, I now travail in birth again of you till Christ be formed in you.

Among all my experiences of God's gracious dealings with me I have constantly observed this, that he hath never suffered me long to sit loose from him, but by one affliction or another hath made me look home, and search what was amiss—so usually thus it hath been with me that I have no sooner felt my heart out of order, but I have expected correction for it, which most commonly hath been upon my own person, in sickness, weakness, pains, sometimes on my soul, in doubts and fears of God's displeasure, and my sincerity towards him. Sometimes he hath smote a child with sickness, sometimes chastened by losses in estate, and these times (through his great mercy) have been the times of my greatest getting and advantage, yet I have found them the times when the Lord hath manifested the most love to me. Then have I gone to searching, and have said with David, Lord search me and try me, see what ways of wickedness are in me, and lead me in the way everlasting: and seldom or never but I have found either some sin I lay under which God would have reformed, or some duty neglected which he would have performed. And by his help I have laid vows and bonds upon my soul to perform his righteous commands.

If at any time you are chastened of God, take it as thankfully and joyfully as in greatest mercies. For if ye be his, ye shall reap the greatest benefit by it. It has been no small support to me in times of darkness, which the Almighty hath hid his face from me, that yet I have had abundance of sweetness and refreshment after affliction and more circumspection in my wailing after I have been afflicted. I have been with God like an untoward child, that no longer than the rod has been on my back (or at least in sight) but have been apt to forget him and myself too. Before I was afflicted I went astray, but now I keep thy statutes.

I have had great experience of God's hearing my prayers, and returning comfortable answers to me, either in granting the thing I prayed for, or else in satisfying my mind without it; and I have ben confident it hath bene from him, because I have found my heart through his goodness enlarged in thankfulness to him.

I have often been perplexed that I have not found that constant joy in my pilgrimage and refreshing which I supposed the most of the servants of God have, although he hath not left me altogether without the witness of his Holy Spirit, who hath oft given me his word and set to his seal that it shall be well with me. I have sometimes tasted of that hidden manna that the world knows not, and have set up my Ebenezer, and have resolved with myself that against such a promise, such tastes of sweetness, the fates of Hell shall never prevail. Yet have I many sinkings and droopings, and not enjoyed that felicity that sometimes I have done. But when I have been in darkness and seen no light, yet have I desired to stay myself upon the Lord. And, when I have been in sickness and pain, I have thought if the Lord would but lift up the light of his countenance upon me, although he ground me to powder, it would be but light to me. Yea, often have I thought were it Hell itself and could there find the love of God toward me, it would be a Heaven. And, could I have been in Heaven without the love of God, it would have been a Hell to me. For, in Truth, it is the absence of presence of God that makes Heaven or Hell.

Many times hath Satan troubled me concerning the verity of the Scriptures, many times by atheism. How could I know whether there was a God if I never saw any miracles to confirm me, and those which I read of, how did I know, but they were feigned. That there is a God my reason would soon tell me by the wondrous works that I see, the vast frame of the Heaven and the earth, the order of all things, night and day, summer and winter, spring and autumn, the daily providing for this great household upon the earth, the preserving and directing of all to its proper end. The consideration of these things would with amazement certainly resolve me that there is an Eternal Being.

But how should I know he is such a God as I worship in Trinity, and such a Saviour as I rely upon? Though this hath thousands of times been suggested to me, yet God hath helped me over. I have argued thus with myself. That there is a God I see. If ever this God hath revealed himself, it must be in his word, and this must be it or none. Have I not found that operation by it that no humane invention can work upon the soul? Hath not judgments befallen diverse who have scorned and contend it? Hath it not been preserved through all ages maugre [that is, despite] all the heathen tyrants and all of the enemies who have opposed it? Is there any story but that which shows the beginning of times, and how the world came to be as we see? Do we not know the prophecies in it fulfilled which could not have been so long foretold by any but God himself?

When I have got over this block, then have I another put in my way. That admit this be the true God whom we worship, and that be his word, yet why may not the popish religion be the right? They have the same God, the same Christ, the same word. They only interpret it one way, we another.

This hath sometimes stuck with me, and more it would, but the vain fooleries that are in their religion, together with their lying miracles, and cruel persecutions of the saints, which admit were they as they term them, yet not so to be dealt withal.

The consideration of these things and many the like would soon turn me to my own religion again.

But some new troubles I have had since the world has been filled with blasphemy, and sectaries, and some who have been accounted sincere Christians have been carried away with them, that sometimes I have said, "Is there faith upon the earth?" And I have not known what to think; but then I have remembered the words of Christ that so it must be, and that, if it were possible, the very elect should be deceived. "Behold," saith our Saviour, "I have told you before," that hath stayed my heart, and I can now say, "Return, o my soul, to thy rest, upon this rock Christ Jesus will I build my faith, and if I perish, I perish." But I Know all the powers of Hell shall never prevail against it. I know whom I have trusted, and whom I have believed, and that he is able to keep that I have committed to his charge.

Now to the King, immortal, eternal, and invisible, the only wise God, be honor and glory forever and ever. Amen.

This was written in much sickness and weakness, and is very weakly and imperfectly done; but if you can pick any benefit out of it, it is the mark which I aimed at.

Source: Adelaide Amore, ed., *A Woman's Inner World: Selected Poetry and Prose of Anne Bradstreet* (Lanham, MD: University Press of America, 1982).

4

De Yndio 1º y Mestiza

Continental Empires

1660–1720

< **Eighteenth-Century Spanish Illustration of New World Racial Mixture**

AMERICAN PORTRAIT

Mercy Lewis Learns to Fear the Devil

In 1692, 19-year-old Mercy Lewis lived in Salem, Massachusetts, as a respected servant in the Putnam household. Her duties were not onerous—she was charged with caring for the family's youngest child, Ann—and it was expected that she, like most servant girls, would eventually make a good marriage and start a family of her own. But Mercy's future did not turn out that way. Living at the fringe of great continental empires could often be costly, even for relatively prosperous white colonists.

Mercy's earliest memories almost certainly were of a horrible day in August of 1676, when almost all her family members died. Her grandparents, George Lewis and his wife Ann, had come from England in the 1640s and settled Casco Bay in Maine. They lived near the border with French Canada. Their nearest neighbors were the Wabanaki Indians, who had gradually been forced to live within a smaller and smaller territory. The Indians had managed to survive at all only because they could play the English Protestants and French Catholics off against each other, buying arms from one side or the other at different times. That August, with French support, the Wabanaki declared war against the English colonists and moved up and down the frontier, killing and taking captives. Among the dead were Mercy's two grandparents, two of her uncles, one aunt, and at least two cousins. Among the captured were one young aunt and several more cousins. Mercy survived only because her parents heard what was happening, grabbed their child, and fled to a small island, where they hid along with a number of others.

Mercy bore the psychological scars years later. In 1691, warfare with the Wabanaki had exploded anew, and although Mercy no longer lived on the Maine border, everyone in Salem—which was not very far away from the frontier—trembled at the news. When soon after the news of war, two girls in the home of the minister, Samuel Parris, began to claim that they were the victims of witchcraft, Mercy paid close attention. Parris's daughter and niece named women who held little power in their world—an enslaved woman named Tituba and two older white women. Suddenly Mercy herself began to experience the effects of witchcraft. "She was Choked and blinded her neck twisted her teeth and mouth shut," her master's brother reported. Later she was "drawn toward the fier by unseen hands as she sat in a Chare." He had to use all his strength to prevent Mercy from being drawn into the fire. Soon enough, Mercy's young charge, Ann, also "fell afflicted." They named others, and a great crisis unfolded: the Salem witch hunt of 1692.

The girls temporarily gained great power. They could rage or cower, letting all emotion get the better of them, and not be punished; they were seemingly only rewarded. More and more the adults in their lives explicitly associated the devil, who they thought was stalking them, with the Indians making war upon them. Several other people who had once lived in Casco Bay also became involved; they probably suffered from what we would today call post-traumatic stress disorder. Twenty people were hanged and several others died in prison before enough people came to their senses and put a stop to the train of events.

Years later, Ann Putnam asked the congregation in Salem for their forgiveness "and to be humbled before God for that sad and humbling providence" that had rendered her "an instrument for the accusing of several persons of a grievous crime." She said that it was "a great delusion of Satan that deceived me in that sad time." Mercy had gone off to New Hampshire and bore a child out of wedlock—which, at that time, was unusual, and probably a sign of some discomposure of mind.

Early settlers managed to live with the knowledge that they were displacing other people, but in handling the effects of the violence that they themselves, or their parents and grandparents, unleashed, they often did not go unscathed.

The Plan of Empire

Trying to make sense of the haphazard development of Britain's American colonies, the English political theorist Edmund Burke explained in 1757, "The settlement of our colonies was never pursued upon any regular plan; but they were formed, grew, and flourished, as accidents, the nature of the climate, or the dispositions of private men happened to operate." In comparison, the Spanish and French governments more actively directed their colonies, though the portions of their empires that would one day become the United States were so marginal that they, too, received relatively little attention. The British colonies were all private ventures, chartered by the government but little supervised or supported. So long as mainland colonies contributed little to the national wealth and cost the government less, they received the loosest of controls and were permitted to develop each in its own way.

The result was a period of significant instability at the end of the seventeenth century, as local colonial governments struggled to control their inhabitants, police their borders, and establish successful economies. In many of the colonies, elites vied for control, whereas in others poor people rose up against insecure leadership. As expanding populations and aggressive traders pushed against native populations, violence exploded. At the edges of empire, the British, French, and Dutch—and their Indian allies—collided. In the midst of these struggles, colonists such as Mercy Lewis found themselves caught in—and taking advantage of—the crosscurrents.

Turmoil in England

In the middle of the seventeenth century, the British government was thrown into turmoil as Parliament and the king struggled over the future direction of the nation. Two issues were at stake: religion and royal power. The uneasy balance that Elizabeth I had established between Puritans and the Church of England collapsed under her successors James I (r. 1603–1625) and Charles I (r. 1625–1649). Archbishop of Canterbury William Laud moved the Church of England away from the Calvinist belief in predestination, brought back worship that smacked of Catholicism, and persecuted Puritans, prompting Presbyterian Scotland to revolt.

Parliament refused to appropriate the funds that King Charles requested to quash the revolt. Instead, in 1628, Parliament passed the Petition of Right, which reasserted such basic freedoms as no taxation except by act of Parliament, no arbitrary arrest or imprisonment, and no quartering of soldiers in private homes. After years of stalemate, in 1642 Charles raised an army and moved against the Parliament, beginning the English Civil War. It concluded in 1647 with Parliament's victory. Two years later, Charles was beheaded. Oliver Cromwell, a Puritan, ruled as Lord Protector until his death in 1658. When Cromwell's son and successor proved an inept leader, Charles II was invited to reclaim the Crown in 1660.

Although the monarchy had been restored, its authority had been diminished. Britain had been transformed into a constitutional monarchy in which the power of the Crown was balanced by that of Parliament. Britain also found a middle way between Calvinist Protestantism and Catholicism. When the Catholic King James II (r. 1685–1688) tried to fill the government with Catholics and to rule without the consent of Parliament, he was removed in a bloodless revolution, known as the Glorious Revolution (1688). It brought Mary, James's Protestant daughter, and her Protestant husband, William of Orange (Holland), to the throne.

The Political Economy of Mercantilism

After the reassertion of Parliament's authority in 1688, the British state became increasingly strong and centralized. Britain then embarked on a course that would make it the world's most powerful nation by the early nineteenth century.

Throughout the political turmoil of the seventeenth century, Britain's economic policies were guided by a theory called mercantilism, which held that the chief object of a nation's economic policies was to serve the state. Mercantilism was developed to facilitate the consolidation of the new European nation-states, which required vast amounts of money to support their growing military and bureaucracies. Mercantilists considered the economy and politics as zero-sum games; one side's gain was another's loss. Wealth was defined exclusively as hard money, that is, gold and silver. With only a finite amount of gold and silver in the world, a nation could best improve its position by capturing a share of other nations' money. Mercantilism thus led to rivalry between nations. Between 1651 and 1696, the mercantilist British government passed a series of trade regulations, the Navigation Acts, requiring that all goods shipped to England and its colonies be carried in ships owned and manned by the English (including colonists). All foreign goods going to the colonies had to be shipped via Britain, where they could be taxed, and some colonial products (tobacco, sugar, indigo, and cotton, to start) had to be sent first to England before being shipped elsewhere. In mercantilist doctrine, the mother country was to produce finished products, and the colonies, raw materials. Hence, when the colonies began to manufacture items such as woolen cloth and hats, Parliament restricted those industries.

New Colonies, New Patterns

Lacking tight English control, each colony developed differently. In the second half of the seventeenth century, two important new English colonies, Pennsylvania and South Carolina, were established, and New Netherland was seized from the Dutch. As a rule, the most successful colonies offered the most opportunity to free white people and the greatest amount of religious toleration.

New Netherland Becomes New York

By the middle of the seventeenth century, the British were ready to challenge their chief trade rival, the Dutch, whom they defeated in three wars between 1652 and 1674. The Navigation Acts cut the Dutch out of international trade, and Britain began to challenge Dutch dominance of the slave trade. In 1663, King Charles II chartered the Royal Africa Company to carry slaves out of Africa to the British West Indies. Britain also made a move for New Netherland.

James, the Duke of York and King Charles II's younger brother, persuaded Charles to grant him the territory between the Connecticut and Delaware Rivers (present-day Pennsylvania, New Jersey, New York, and part of Connecticut), which was occupied by the Netherlands. In 1664, James sent a governor, 400 troops, and several warships that easily conquered the small colony of New Amsterdam. In 1665, James gave away what is now New Jersey to two of his royal cronies, Lords John Berkeley and George Carteret; and in 1667, New York's governor gave the territory on the western side of the Connecticut River to Connecticut. New Netherland had become New York.

The new colony was part Dutch (in New York City and along the Hudson) and part English (on Long Island, where New England Puritans had migrated). The first governors attempted to satisfy both groups. The governors confirmed Dutch landholdings, including huge estates along the Hudson, and guaranteed the Dutch religious freedom. The governors also distributed 2 million more acres of land, most of it in enormous chunks called manors. The owners of these manors, like feudal lords, rented land to tenants and set up courts on their estates.

If religious toleration attracted diverse peoples to the region, feudal land policies and England's failure to restore self-government kept others away. Without an elective legislature to raise taxes, the governors, following English mercantilist policy, used customs duties to raise the revenue necessary to run the colony and send a profit to James. These attempts to regulate trade and direct the economy angered local merchants and harmed the economy. Eventually, James gave in to popular discontent and, in 1683, allowed New York to have an elective assembly.

At its first meeting, this group of English and Dutch men passed a "Charter of Libertyes and Priviledges," which, had the king approved it, would have guaranteed New Yorkers a number of civil liberties and the continuing right to self-government by their elected assembly. The charter expressed the principles of liberalism starting to spread through both Britain and the Netherlands. Liberalism places an emphasis on individual liberty and holds that all human beings are equally entitled to enjoy the freedom and fulfillment to be found in their social lives—their work, families, and churches. The charter would have guaranteed all free men the right to vote and to be taxed only by their elective representatives. It also provided for trial by jury, due process, freedom of conscience for Christians, and certain property rights for women, the latter two items reflecting Dutch practices. However, the king refused to approve the charter on two grounds: it would give New Yorkers more rights than any other colonists, and the New York Assembly might undermine the power of Parliament. Without secure self-government, New Yorkers fell to fighting among themselves, and political instability in combination with feudal land holdings slowed New York's population growth.

New Amsterdam/New York

Today it is called Wall Street, and it represents the center of world finance, but in 1660, it was literally a wall that marked the northernmost edge of settlement on the island of Manhattan. Although some of the street grid remains—and today's Broad Street was once a huge canal—most of the other traces of the Dutch settlement of New Amsterdam have disappeared.

Lower Manhattan did not become a business and commercial center until the nineteenth century, however. Until then, it was a little urban village, first Dutch and then English. Even after the English takeover in

New Amsterdam New Amsterdam was an urban village in a global economy.

Diversity and Prosperity in Pennsylvania

Pennsylvania demonstrated the potential of a colony that offered both religious toleration and economic opportunity. Its founder, William Penn, was a Quaker and the son of one of King Charles II's leading supporters. After his restoration to the throne, Charles had a number of political debts to repay, and giving away vast chunks of North America was a cheap way of doing it. As a Quaker, Penn was eager to get out of England. In

1664, the town retained its Dutch character and distinctive Dutch architectural styles. The original New Amsterdam was home to a variety of crafts- and tradespeople: not only the merchants, brokers, lawyers, and shipmasters one would expect in a commercial port but also druggists, painters, printers, tailors, and boardinghouse keepers. The homes and workshops were built in the Dutch style, out of red and yellow brick, with leaded-glass casement windows and terracotta tiles on the roofs. The comfortable feel of such homes was not unlike a middle-class home in Amsterdam.

Because buildings often functioned as both homes and workshops, they might contain not only the nuclear family but also the employees of the family business and slaves, both Indian and African. (In 1703, 40 percent of New York's households contained African slaves.) If New Amsterdam and its successor, New York, looked and felt like a European town, the presence of large numbers of Africans and Indians gave the little settlement a distinctive New World character.

From its earliest years, New Amsterdam was an urban village in a global economy, home to immigrants and natives, all buying and selling in a global market. The Kierstede family built its house at the corner of what today are Pearl and Whitehall Streets, looking out on the East River. Hans Kierstede, a German religious refugee, came to New Amsterdam and served as its first surgeon. His wife, Sara Roelofs, had been born in Amsterdam and lived as a child near present-day Albany, where she played with the local Indians and learned their languages. In New Amsterdam, she built a backyard shed where Indian women crafted goods to sell in the market across the street from the Kierstedes' home. In 1664, Sara Roelofs Kierstede served as a translator when Peter Stuyvesant negotiated a treaty with the local Indians. The Lenape Indian Sachem Oratam was so pleased with her translating abilities that he gave her some 2,000 acres of land on the Hackensack River, in present-day Bergen County, New Jersey.

When archeologists excavated the family home late in the twentieth century, they found bits and pieces of the cultures that mixed on the island of Manhattan: pipes made in Holland and imported even after the English takeover; a German wineglass; a piece of a sword; hair curlers for curling wigs; whistles carved from clay pipes and traded to the Indians for furs; and ceramic gambling tokens, similar to ones found at plantations in the South and the West Indies.

New Amsterdam was a crossroads of empire. There people—and goods—from both sides of the Atlantic, Europeans, Indians, and Africans, met and traded with each other, creating a new world made out of bits and pieces from each of their cultures.

1661 alone, 4,000 English Quakers were jailed, and Penn was imprisoned four times. The Quakers were a radical sect of Protestants who believed that God offered salvation to all and placed an "inner light" inside everyone. Hardworking, serious, and moral, Quakers rejected violence and refused to serve in the military or pay taxes for its support.

Penn received his charter in 1681. To raise money, he sold land to a group of wealthy Quaker merchants, who received government positions and economic concessions in return. To attract ordinary settlers, Penn promised self-government (although stacked in favor of the merchant elite), freedom of religion, and reasonably priced land.

In 1682, when Penn arrived at Philadelphia (Greek for "city of brotherly love"), the colony already had 4,000 inhabitants. Penn had clear ideas about how he wanted his colony to develop. He expected the orderly growth of farming villages, neatly laid out along rivers and creeks, and mapped the settlement of the city along a grid, with each house set far enough from its neighbors to prevent the spread of fires. He wanted harmonious relations with local Indians.

Penn's policies attracted a wide variety of Europeans. Soon Pennsylvania was populated by self-contained communities, each speaking a different language or practicing a different religion. Pennsylvania's early history was characterized by rapid growth and prosperity. However, this progress undermined Penn's plans for a cohesive, hierarchical society. People lived where and how they wanted, pursuing the economic activities they found most profitable.

While moving away from the inequalities of the Old World, Pennsylvania replicated those of the New World. Many of its European immigrants were indentured servants or redemptioners, people who worked for a brief period to pay back the ship's captain for the cost of transportation to the colony. And by 1700, the Pennsylvania Assembly had passed laws recognizing slavery, although not unanimously. That slavery could take root in a colony where some questioned its morality suggests both the force of its power in shaping early America and the weakness of the opposition.

Indians and Africans in the Political Economy of Carolina

Like Pennsylvania and Maryland, South Carolina was a proprietary colony. One of the proprietors, Anthony Ashley Cooper, the Earl of Shaftesbury, and his secretary, John Locke, drafted the Fundamental Constitutions for the new colony. Locke later became a leading political philosopher, and the Constitutions reflect the liberal, rights-guaranteeing principles that he later developed more fully.

The Constitutions provided for a representative government and widespread religious toleration. At the same time, they embodied the traditional assumption that liberty could be guaranteed only in a hierarchical society. Shaftesbury and Locke tried to set up a complex hierarchy of nobles at the top and hereditary serfs at the bottom. The Constitutions also recognized African slavery, and Carolina was the first colony that introduced slavery at the outset. The Constitutions never went into full effect, for the first Carolina representative assembly rejected many of its provisions. Predictably, the attempt to transplant a British-style nobility failed. The only aristocracy that the Carolinas developed was one of wealth, supported by the labor of slaves.

The first settlers arrived at Charles Town (later moved and renamed Charleston) in 1670. The area had a semitropical climate, wonderfully fertile soil, and a growing season of up to 295 days a year. The region had once been explored by the Spanish, who still claimed it. It was inhabited by mission Indians, that is, Indians who had converted to Catholicism.

As happened so often when Europeans arrived, Indian tribes competed to trade with them, and rival groups of Europeans struggled to dominate the trade. In the colonial period, Indian wars usually pitted one group of Europeans and their Indian allies against another group of Europeans and their native allies, with the Indians doing most of the fighting. Such wars were an extension of Europe's market economy: Indians fought for

Chickasaw Map This eighteenth-century French copy of a Chickasaw map represents an indigenous conception of the local political landscape.

European goods, and Europeans fought for a monopoly over Indian products. The English were particularly successful in achieving dominance because of their sophisticated market economy. London's banks had perfected the mechanisms of credit, which financed a fur trade in the forests half a world away.

The Westos elbowed their way ahead of other tribes by offering the Carolina traders a commodity more valuable even than deerskins: Indian slaves. In fact, until about 1690, slaves were the most valuable commodity sold by the Carolina colony.

Carolina merchants quickly established control over the entire Southeast (see Map 4–1), pushing out the Spanish, the French, and even the Virginians. At the same time, Indian tribes fought to become the chief slave supplier. In 1680, in the Westo War, the Carolina traders sent their allies, the Savannah Indians, out to destroy the Westos, who were the

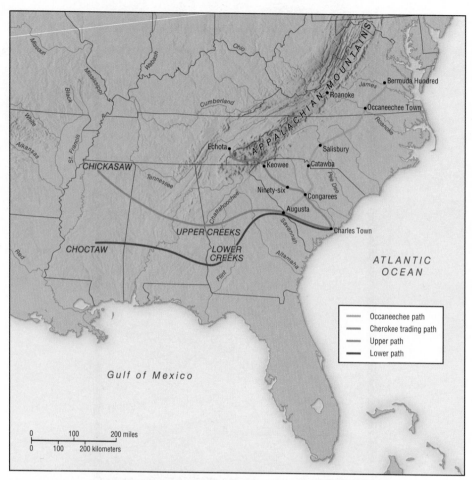

Map 4-1   Trade Routes in the Southeast Beginning in the seventeenth century, English traders from Virginia and later Carolina followed several paths to trade with Southeastern Indians as far west as the Mississippi.
Source: Adapted from W. Stitt Robinson, *The Southern Colonial Frontier* (Albuquerque: University of New Mexico Press, 1979), p. 103.

Virginians' link to the Native American trade of the Southeast. The Carolinians vanquished the Spanish by sending in other Indian allies to destroy the mission towns. In this way, the Carolina traders eliminated their European rivals. At the same time, the Chickasaws emerged to replace the Westos and, like them, obliterated less powerful tribes in order to obtain a steady supply of slaves. All together, between 1670 and 1715, somewhere between 25,000 and 50,000 Indians were enslaved, with many more killed in the slaving raids. The slave trade increased dramatically the level of violence among Native Americans.

This violence was turned against the Carolinians in the Yamasee War (1715–1716). Although the Yamasees had been reliable trading partners for 40 years and had fought with the British in Queen Anne's War (see later in the chapter), South Carolina traders cheated them out of their land and enslaved their women and children. In retaliation, the Yamasees and their allies attacked, pushing the settlers almost back to Charleston before they were stopped. The war killed 400 white South Carolinians (7 percent of the population, more than in King Philip's War in New England), crippled the Indian slave trade, forced the colony to abandon frontier settlements, and revealed the fragility of the entire South Carolina venture. When international war began again in 1739, the frontier regions were, as they had been a quarter of a century earlier, dangerous and unstable for settlers, traders, and Indians alike.

The Barbados Connection

Carolina was part of a far-flung Atlantic political economy based on trade, plantation agriculture, and slavery. Many of the early Carolina settlers had substantial experience with African slavery in Barbados, a small Caribbean island settled in 1627 that within a decade became a major source of the world's sugar. By then, it had an African majority and was Britain's first slave society. By the end of the seventeenth century, Barbados was the most productive of all Britain's colonies, its per-person income much higher than in England.

This income was not shared equally, however. Owners of the largest plantations became fabulously wealthy, and even lesser planters enjoyed a high standard of living. Conditions for African slaves, however, were brutal. The British magnified differences between Europeans and Africans to enhance the distinction between landowners and slaves. Barbadians were the first to portray Africans as beasts, and the racism of Caribbean planters was intense. Slave codes were the harshest of any in the Atlantic world, prescribing that male slaves convicted of crimes could be burned at the stake, beheaded, starved, or castrated. When Caribbean slavery was imported into Carolina, these attitudes came with it. The Carolina slave code was the harshest in North America. Laws and attitudes separated whites from blacks, but differences among Europeans were minimized, as some restrictions against Irish Catholics and Jews were lifted after Barbados became a slave society. In 1650, Barbados allowed the immigration of Jews and other religious minorities six years before England did. As in the Chesapeake, increasing freedom for Europeans developed alongside the enslavement of Africans.

The sugar plantations of Barbados and Britain's other Caribbean islands made their extraordinary profits from the labor of African slaves. British planters worked Africans harder than European indentured servants. Profits came from keeping labor costs down, as well as from the growing demand for sugar. It is important to remember that the New World slave system would not have grown as it did without European demand for plantation crops. African slaves were imported into Carolina from the outset, but only after 1690 did the colony develop a staple crop—rice—that increased the demand for slave labor. After rice became the region's major cash crop, African slaves became more valuable. By 1720, Africans composed more than 70 percent of Carolina's population. With a black majority, a lethal environment, and wealth concentrated in an elite, Carolina resembled the Caribbean islands more than it did the other English colonies on the mainland. In only a few decades, Carolina had become a slave society, not simply a society with slaves: slavery stood at the center of everything.

The Transformation of Virginia

At the same time that a newly vigorous England was planting new colonies, those established earlier were reshaped. In the final quarter of the seventeenth century, the older colonies experienced political and sometimes social instability, followed by the establishment of a lasting order. In Virginia, the transition was marked by a violent insurrection known as Bacon's Rebellion. Significantly, the rebels sought not to overthrow the social and political order but to secure a legitimate government that could protect economic opportunity. In its aftermath, Virginia became a slave society.

Social Change in Virginia

As Virginia entered its second half-century, the health of its population finally began to improve. Apple orchards had matured, so Virginians could drink cider instead of impure water. Ships bringing new servants arrived in the fall, a healthy time of year. Increasingly, they lived to serve out their periods of indenture and set out on their own to plant tobacco. However, most of the best land in eastern Virginia had already been claimed, and the land to the west was occupied by Indian tribes with peace treaties with the English. In addition, the government was controlled by a small clique of men using it as a means of getting rich. Taxes, assessed in tobacco, were extraordinarily high, and as taxes rose, the price of tobacco began to fall. Caught in a squeeze, many ordinary planters went to work for others as tenants or overseers.

Still, servants kept coming to the colony, most from the lower ranks of society. Restless and unhappy, they joined in a series of disturbances beginning in the middle of the century. The elite responded by lengthening the time of service and stiffening the penalties for running away.

Bacon's Rebellion and the Abandonment of the Middle Ground

When the revolt came, it was led not by one of the poor or landless but by a member of the elite. Nathaniel Bacon was young, well educated, wealthy, and a member of a prominent family. Bacon made an immediate impression on Virginia's ruling clique, and Governor Berkeley invited him to join the colony's Council of State. For unknown reasons, Bacon cast his lot with Berkeley's enemies among the elite. The instability of elites created political factions in a number of colonies. When ruling elites, such as Berkeley's in Virginia, levied exorbitant taxes and ignored their constituents, they left themselves open to challenge.

The contest between Bacon and Berkeley might have remained minor had not Bacon capitalized on the discontent of the colony's freedmen (men who had served out their indentures). In 1676, Bacon's Rebellion was triggered by a routine episode of violence on the middle ground inhabited by Indians and Europeans. Seeking payment for goods they had delivered to a planter, a band of Doeg Indians killed the planter's overseer and tried to steal his hogs. Over the years, Europeans and Indians who shared the middle ground had adapted the Indian custom of providing restitution for crimes committed by one side or the other. Although this practice resulted in sporadic violence, it also helped maintain order. But this time, the conflict escalated, as Virginians sought revenge, prompting further Indian retaliation.

Soon an isolated incident escalated into a militia expedition of 1,000 men, an extraordinarily large force at the time. For six weeks the war party laid siege to the reservation of the Susquehannocks, a tribe drawn unwillingly into the conflict, who in turn avenged themselves on settlers on the frontier.

When Berkeley refused to fight the Susquehannocks, the frontier planters were infuriated. They complained that their taxes went to Berkeley's clique instead of being used to police the frontier. Planter women used their gossip networks to spread the idea that Berkeley was "a greater friend to the Indians than to the English."

With his wife's encouragement, Nathaniel Bacon agreed to lead a wholesale war on "all Indians whatsoever." After his rebels massacred some formerly friendly Occoneechees, Bacon marched on the government at Jamestown with 400 armed men, demanding to fight "all Indians in general, for that they were all Enemies." Berkeley agreed, and then changed his mind, but it was too late. By then Bacon was in control, and Berkeley fled to the Eastern Shore.

By the time a royal commission and 1,000 soldiers arrived in January 1677 to put down the disorder, Bacon had died, and Berkeley had regained control. Twenty-three rebel leaders were executed, then the king removed Berkeley from office. After Bacon's death, support for the rebellion quickly dissipated.

After Bacon's Rebellion, the government remained in the hands of the planter elite, but the rebels had achieved their primary objective. The frontier Indians had been dispersed, and their land was now free for settlement. Those in power became more responsive to white freedmen. Other factors also improved economic conditions: tobacco prices began to climb, and planters replaced servants with slaves.

Virginia Becomes a Slave Society

With new colonies such as New York and Pennsylvania offering greater opportunity to poor whites, the supply of European indentured servants to the Chesapeake dried up just when more Africans were becoming available. Britain entered the slave trade on a large scale at the end of the seventeenth century, authorizing private merchants to carry slaves from Africa to North America in 1698. It seemed planters could not get enough slaves to meet their needs. In 1680, only 7 percent of Virginia's population was African in origin, but by 1700 the proportion had increased to 28 percent, and half the labor force was enslaved (see Table 4–1). Within two decades, Virginia had become a society in which slavery was central to the political economy and the social structure. With the bottom tier of the social order enslaved and hence unable to compete for land or wealth, opportunity for all whites necessarily improved.

As the composition of Virginia's labor force changed, so did the laws to control it. Although all slave societies had certain features in common, each colony enacted its own slave code to maintain and define the institution. By 1705, Virginia had a thorough slave code in place.

All forms of slavery have certain elements in common: perpetuity, kinlessness, violence, and the master's access to the slave's sexuality. First, slavery is a lifelong condition. Second, a slave has no legally recognized family relationships. Third, slavery rests on violence or its threat, including the master's sexual access to the slave.

American slavery added other elements. First, slavery in all the Americas was hereditary, passed on from a mother to her children and to their children, for all time. Second, compared with other slave systems, including that of Latin America, manumissions—the

Table 4-1 Population of British Colonies in America, 1660 and 1710

Colony	1660			1710		
	White	Black	Total	White	Black	Total
Virginia	26,070	950	27,020	55,163	23,118	78,281
Maryland	7,668	758	8,426	34,796	7,945	42,741
Chesapeake	33,738	1,708	35,446	89,959	31,063	121,022
Massachusetts	22,062	422	22,484	61,080	1,310	62,390
Connecticut	7,955	25	7,980	38,700	750	39,450
Rhode Island	1,474	65	1,539	7,198	375	7,573
New Hampshire	1,515	50	1,565	5,531	150	5,681
New England	33,006	562	33,568	112,509	2,585	115,094
Bermuda	3,500	200	3,700	4,268	2,845	7,113
Barbados	26,200	27,100	53,300	13,000	52,300	65,300
Antigua	1,539	1,448	2,987	2,892	12,960	15,852
Montserrat	1,788	661	2,449	1,545	3,570	5,115
Nevis	2,347	2,566	4,913	1,104	3,676	4,780
St. Kitts	1,265	957	2,222	1,670	3,294	4,964
Jamaica				7,250	58,000	65,250
Caribbean	36,639	32,932	69,571	31,729	136,645	168,374
New York	4,336	600	4,936	18,814	2,811	21,625
New Jersey				18,540	1,332	19,872
Pennsylvania				22,875	1,575	24,450
Delaware	510	30	540	3,145	500	3,645
Middle Colonies	4,846	630	5,476	63,374	6,218	69,592
North Carolina	980	20	1,000	14,220	900	15,120
South Carolina				6,783	4,100	10,883
Lower South	980	20	1,000	21,003	5,000	26,003
Totals	109,209	35,852	145,061	318,574	181,511	500,085

Source: Jack P. Greene, *Pursuits of Happiness* (Chapel Hill: University of North Carolina, 1988), pp. 178–179.

freeing of slaves—in the American South were quite rare. Finally, slavery in the South was racial. Slavery was reserved for Africans and some Indians. The line between slavery and freedom was defined as one of color.

Slave codes also defined gender roles. Two early pieces of legislation denied African women the privileges of European women. A 1643 statute made all adult men and African women taxable, assuming that they (and not white women) were performing productive labor in the fields. In 1662, another law said that children were to inherit the status of their mother, not their father.

The same laws that created and sustained racial slavery also increased the freedom of whites. New World plantation slavery was developed in a world in which the freedom of most Europeans also was limited in various ways. In fact, two-thirds of the Europeans who migrated to British America before the American Revolution were unfree—servants or redemptioners. (When Africans are added, virtually all of whom were enslaved, the total increases to 90 percent.) The increase in freedom for whites was the product of

Table 4-2 Codifying Race and Slavery

1640—Masters are required to arm everyone in their households except Africans (Virginia)

1643—All adult men and African women are taxable, on the assumption that they were working in the fields (Virginia)

1662—Children follow the condition of their mother (Virginia)

1662—Double fine charged for any Christian who commits fornication with an African (Virginia)

1664—All slaves serve for life; that is, slavery is defined as a lifelong condition (Maryland)

1664—Interracial marriage banned; any free woman who marries a slave will serve that slave's master until her husband dies, and their children will be enslaved (Maryland)

1667—Baptism as a Christian does not make a slave free (Virginia)

1669—No punishment is given if punished slave dies (Virginia)

1670—Free blacks and Indians are not allowed to purchase Christian indentured servants (Virginia)

1670—Indians captured elsewhere and sold as slaves to Virginia are to serve for life; those captured in Virginia, until the age of 30, if children, or for 12 years, if grown (Virginia)

1680—In order to prevent "Negroes Insurrections": no slave may carry arms or weapons; no slave may leave his or her master without written permission; any slave who "lifts up his hand" against a Christian will receive 30 lashes; any slave who runs away and resists arrest may be killed lawfully (Virginia)

1682—Slaves may not gather for more than four hours at other than owner's plantation (Virginia)

1682—All servants who were "Negroes, Moors, Mollattoes or Indians" were to be considered slaves at the time of their purchase if neither their parents nor country were Christian (Virginia)

1691—Owners are to be compensated if "negroes, mulattoes or other slaves" are killed while resisting arrest (Virginia)

1691—Forbidden is all miscegenation as "that abominable mixture"; any English or "other white man or woman" who marries a "negroe, mulatto, or Indian" is to be banished; any free English woman who bears a "bastard child by any negro or mulatto" will be fined, and if she can't pay the fine, she will be indentured for five years and the child will be indentured until the age of 30 (Virginia)

1691—All slaves who are freed by their masters must be transported out of the state (Virginia)

1692—Special courts of "over and terminer" are established for trying slaves accused of crimes, creating a separate system of justice (Virginia)

1705—Mulatto is defined as "the child of an Indian, the child, grandchild, or great grandchild of a negro" (Virginia)

1705—Africans, mulattoes, and Indians are prohibited from holding office or giving grand jury testimony (Virginia)

1705—Slaves are forbidden to own livestock (Virginia)

1705—"Christian white" servants cannot be whipped naked (Virginia)

1723—Free blacks explicitly excluded from militia (Virginia)

1723—Free blacks explicitly denied the right to vote (Virginia)

Note: Slavery is a creation of law, which defines what it means to be a slave and protects the master's rights in his slave property. Slave codes developed piecemeal in the Chesapeake, over the course of the seventeenth century. Legislators in the Chesapeake colonies defined slavery as a racial institution, appropriate only for Africans, and protected it with a series of laws, which, in the process, also created a privileged position for whites.

several sorts of policies. First, it depended on the widespread availability of cheap land, which whites could obtain only by dispossessing the Indians who inhabited it. Second, it depended on British government policies, such as permitting self-government in the colonies, which were designed to attract immigrants. Third, it depended on specific laws that improved the conditions of whites, often at the same time limiting the freedom of blacks. For example, in 1705, Virginia made it illegal for white servants to be whipped without an order from a justice of the peace (see Table 4–2).

New England Under Assault

New England's prosperity led to problems, both internal and external. How would a religion born in adversity cope with good fortune? A combination of internal colonial conflicts and a growing population encroaching on Indian lands led to the region's deadliest Indian war in 1675.

Social Prosperity and the Fear of Religious Decline

In many ways, the Puritan founders of the New England colonies saw their dreams come true. Although immigration virtually halted as the English Revolution broke out, natural increase kept the population growing, from about 23,000 in 1650 to more than 93,000 in 1700. Life expectancy was higher than in England, and families were larger.

Most New Englanders enjoyed a comfortable, if modest, standard of living. By the end of the century, the simple shacks of the first settlers had been replaced by two-story frame homes. By our standards, these homes would still have been almost unbearably cold in the winter, when indoor temperatures routinely dropped into the 40s. Still, New Englanders were beginning to enjoy the prosperous village life their ancestors had once known in England.

For Puritans, such good fortune presented a problem. Prosperity became a cause for worry, as people turned their minds away from God to more worldly things. In the 1660s and 1670s, New England's ministers preached a series of jeremiads, lamentations about spiritual decline. They criticized problems ranging from public drunkenness and sexual license to land speculation and excessively high prices and wages. If New Englanders did not change their ways, the ministers predicted, "Ruine upon Ruine, Destruction upon Destruction would come, until one stone were not left upon another."

Most of the churches were embroiled in controversy in the 1660s concerning who could be members. The founders had assumed that most people, sooner or later, would have the conversion experience that entitled them to full church membership. By the third generation, however, many children and grandchildren of full members had not had the experience of spiritual rebirth. In 1662, a group of ministers adopted the Half-Way Covenant, which set out terms for church membership and participation. Full church membership was reserved for those who could demonstrate a conversion experience. Their offspring could still be "half-way" members of the church, receiving its discipline and having their children baptized. Those who wished to maintain the purity and exclusivity of the church resisted. Rather than settle this question, the Half-Way Covenant aggravated tensions always present in the Puritan religion.

Turmoil broke out as well in the persecution of Quakers, despite Charles II's having issued a protection order. In 1660, Massachusetts had executed the Quaker Mary Dyer, who had returned to Boston after her banishment. The Quakers had been brazen in their defiance of authority, not only returning to the colony when they knew it meant certain death but also even running naked through the streets or in church.

King Philip's War

Although New England's colonies developed along a common path, conflicts among them were intense and led to the region's deadliest Indian war. As in Bacon's

King Philip's (Metacom's) Map, 1668 A map of the lands that Metacom (known by New Englanders as King Philip) sold in 1668. Note that Metacom's understanding of what it meant to "sell" land differed from English conceptions of property ownership. He insisted that the Indians who were living on the land could continue to do so.

Rebellion, the underlying cause of the war was the steady encroachment of English settlers on Native American lands. In the 1660s, Rhode Island, Massachusetts, and Plymouth all claimed the land occupied by the Wampanoags, Massasoit's tribe, now ruled by his son Metacom, known by the colonists as King Philip. By 1671, the colonies had resolved their dispute and ordered King Philip and his people to submit to the rule of Plymouth. No longer able to play one colony against another, King Philip prepared for war, as did the colonists of all the colonies except Rhode Island, which attempted to mediate. In June 1675, King Philip's men attacked the Plymouth village of Swansea.

During the next year, New Englanders attacked entire villages of noncombatants, and the Indians retaliated in kind. At the beginning of the war, New Englanders looked down on the Indians' traditional methods as evidence of depravity, saying they fought "more like wolves than men." By the end of the war, however, both sides committed brutalities, including scalping and putting their victims' heads on stakes. That was the fate of King Philip. His wife and nine-year-old son were sold into slavery, along with hundreds of captives.

The New Englanders won King Philip's War, but the cost was enormous. The casualty rate was one of the highest for any American war ever. About 4,000 Indians died, many of starvation after the New Englanders destroyed their cornfields. The war eliminated any significant Native American presence in southeastern New England and killed 2,000 English settlers (1 out of every 25). The Indians pushed to within 20 miles of Boston, attacked more than half of New England's towns, and burned 1,200 homes. It took the region decades to rebuild.

Indians and the Empire

New England's relations with Indian tribes were not simply a local concern. They were of deep interest to the British Empire, as Andros's participation demonstrated. The British government had to balance the desires of its colonists against the empire's larger objectives. As the French expanded their presence in North America, using friendly Indians to check their advance became one of those objectives. In 1673 the French explorers Jacques Marquette and Louis Joliet had traveled down the Mississippi River as far south as the Arkansas River, and nine years later René-Robert Cavelier, Sieur de La Salle, reached the mouth of the river and named the surrounding territory Louisiana, in honor of King Louis XIV. Biloxi was founded in 1699, New Orleans in 1718, and the forts at Cahokia and Kaskaskia several years later. The French and their Indian allies controlled the Great Lakes region and the eastern shore of the Mississippi all the way to its mouth, while the British were confined to the East Coast.

This geopolitical reality dictated Britain's Indian policy. Andros saw a role for Native Americans as trade partners and allies in Britain's conflict with the French. He welcomed the Indian survivors of King Philip's War into New York and refused to send them back to New England for execution and enslavement, thus becoming the "father" who offered protection to his Indian "children." The British and the Iroquois, who dominated all the other tribes in the region, joined in a strong alliance known as the Covenant Chain, which enhanced the positions of both New York and the Iroquois. The Iroquois became the middlemen between other tribes and the merchants at Albany and were allowed to push as far north and west against French-allied tribes as they could.

With New York dominating the British-Indian alliance, the New England colonies were effectively hemmed in. New York used the Mohawks to make a claim to Maine and blocked New England's movement to the west. Albany became the undisputed center of the Indian trade. In every way, King Philip's War proved exceedingly costly for the New England colonies.

The Empire Strikes

As Britain regained political stability at the end of the seventeenth century, it tried to bring more order to its "accidental empire" by making the colonies play a larger role in its governance. As the Glorious Revolution that removed King James II from the British throne secured constitutional government for Britain's subjects on both sides of the Atlantic, it also made Britain strong and stable enough to challenge France for world supremacy. Between 1689 and 1763, the Anglo-French rivalry drew the colonies into four international wars that shaped them in important ways.

The Dominion of New England

When James II ascended the throne, he decided to punish New England for its disloyalty to the Crown during the Puritan Revolution. There were also reports that New Englanders were defying the Navigation Acts by smuggling. In France, Louis XIV had centralized his administration and brought both his nation and his empire under firm control, and James decided to try similar tactics. In North America, he began unilaterally to revoke the charters of the colonies. By 1688, Massachusetts, Plymouth, Connecticut, New York, New Jersey, New Hampshire, and Rhode Island had been joined together into the Dominion of New England, and Edmund Andros was named its governor.

Before James II and Andros were deposed by the Glorious Revolution of 1688, they wreaked considerable havoc in New England. Massachusetts, New York, and Maryland all suffered revolts. James's attempt to strengthen rule over the colonies failed, but it marked a turning point: the colonies' last period of significant political instability before the eve of the American Revolution.

James's attempt to tighten control affected Massachusetts most seriously. He ordered it to tolerate religious dissenters; some feared he would impose Catholicism on the colony. He took away liberties that residents had enjoyed for over half a century: juries were now to be appointed by sheriffs, town meetings were limited to once a year, and town selectmen could serve no more than two two-year terms. All titles to land had to be reconfirmed, with the holder paying Andros a small fee. Andros claimed the right to levy taxes on his own and began seizing all common lands. Some Boston merchants allied themselves with Andros, hoping to win his favor. This alliance revealed a growing rift in the region between those who welcomed commerce and a more secular way of life and those who wished to preserve the old ways. Most people in Massachusetts, however, despised Andros and feared the road he was leading them down.

The Glorious Revolution in Britain and America

The Glorious Revolution made it clear that Parliament, not an autocratic monarch, would henceforth play the leading role in government. It also determined, after almost a century and a half of conflict, that the Anglican religion would prevail. The Glorious Revolution ushered in a period of remarkable political stability that enabled Britain to become the world's most powerful nation.

In the next century Britain's North American colonies looked to this moment in British history as a model of constitutional government. Their understanding of events in Britain was shaped by political philosopher John Locke's *Two Treatises of Government* (1690). Since the time that he and Shaftesbury had written Carolina's Fundamental Constitutions more than 20 years earlier, Locke had become increasingly radical. The *Treatises* boldly asserted fundamental human equality and universal rights and provided the political theories that would justify a revolution.

The *Treatises* have become the founding documents of political liberalism and its theory of human rights. Locke argued that governments were created by people, not by God. Man was born "with a Title to perfect Freedom," or "natural rights." When people created governments, they gave up some of that freedom in exchange for the rights that they enjoyed in society. The purpose of government was to protect the "Lives, Liberties," and "Fortunes" of the people who created it, not to achieve glory or power for the nation or to serve God. Moreover, should a government take away the civil rights of its citizens, they had a "right to resume their original Liberty." This right of revolution was Locke's boldest and most radical assertion. Once news of the Glorious Revolution reached Massachusetts, its inhabitants poured into the streets, seized the government, and threw the despised Andros in jail. They proclaimed loyalty to the new king and lobbied for the return of their charter. Rhode Island and Connecticut soon got their charters back, but Massachusetts, which was perceived as too independent, was made a royal colony in 1691, with a royal governor. Although Massachusetts lost some of its autonomy and was forced to tolerate dissenters, the town meeting was restored. At the same time, New Hampshire became a royal colony.

Maryland's Colonists Demand a New Government

In 1688, King James II of Britain fell in what came to be known as the Glorious Revolution. As a result, in 1689, rebellions against the authorities occurred in three British colonies—New York, Massachusetts, and Maryland. Though the rebellions collapsed in Boston and New York, in Maryland, the rebels set up their own governing assembly and were eventually recognized as the legitimate colonial government. This was a significant marker in early American history, though whether it signaled a step forward in the forging of democracy is still debated.

In England, the Glorious Revolution occurred when the king's second wife bore a son, which caused the largely Protestant population to fear that their Catholic king would establish a Catholic dynasty. Rebel leaders invited his Protestant daughter, Mary (from his first marriage), and her Dutch husband, William of Orange, to invade their island nation, and they did

so successfully, with little bloodshed. In Maryland, some comparable issues were at stake. Maryland had been established as a proprietary colony in the hands of the Catholic Calvert family; for decades it had served as a haven not only for Catholics but other relatively disempowered sects as well. Key governing positions remained in the hands of the Calvert family or their close connections, and this led to periodic outbursts of resentment and even rebellion among the largely Protestant settlers.

After James II was overthrown, the Catholic colonial government of Maryland did not immediately recognize the Protestant William and Mary as their sovereigns. Crises at the apex of a powerful state often make room for rebellion among the populace, which happened in the colonies. The fact that the reigning authorities of Maryland were also Catholic strengthened the rebellion. Rumors spread that the colonial government

The citizens of Maryland and New York also took the opportunity presented by the Glorious Revolution to evict their royal governors. In Maryland, tensions between the tobacco planters and the increasingly dictatorial proprietor, Charles Calvert, Lord Baltimore, had been building for several decades. Four-fifths of the population was Protestant, but the colony's government was dominated by Catholics, who allocated to themselves the best land. When Protestant planters protested, Baltimore imposed a property qualification for voting and appointed increasingly dictatorial governors. When news of the Glorious Revolution reached Maryland in 1689, a group led by John Coode, a militia officer, took over the government in a bloodless coup (known as Coode's Rebellion), proclaimed loyalty to William and Mary, and got the new government in Britain to take away Baltimore's proprietorship. In 1691, Maryland became a royal colony, and in 1702, the Anglican Church was made the state church, ending Maryland's experiment with religious toleration.

had not only failed to move quickly to support William and Mary but also had in fact entered into negotiations with the Catholic French king and had requested that they send Indians from their inland territories to massacre the discontented Protestant settlers of Maryland. Of course, there was not a shred of truth to these rumors, but many people believed them. Fear of Indian attack was a central part of colonial life.

In July of 1689, within two months of receiving the news from London, a man named John Coode stepped forward to lead the people in marching on the state house in St. Mary's City. Coode was born in Cornwall in 1648 and came to Maryland as a young Anglican minister but found himself unfit for such a profession. He married a wealthy widow and set himself up as a planter. He had protested the Calvert family government before, and now he found a far larger and more enthusiastic audience for his complaints. Surrounded by hundreds of armed men, the proprietary government stepped down without firing a shot. In August, Coode took the remarkable and politically dangerous step of calling for the election of a new assembly. The people were not only protesting; they were choosing to constitute their own governing body, without waiting for word from the king.

Fortunately for Coode and his cohort, in February of 1690 they received official word from William and Mary that the new assembly could continue to govern. They had been doing an excellent job of maintaining the peace, and the new Protestant monarchs had little desire to side publicly with the Calvert family. Results were different in New York and Massachusetts, where the rebel governments were dissolved. In Maryland, the people had demonstrated that in certain circumstances, they had the power to reject an imposed government and replace it with one of their own choosing. Despite this, the change did not open up new economic opportunities for the common man or woman, and already successful Protestant settlers gained more political power than they had had before. Catholics and Quakers suddenly found themselves legally excluded from holding office. Increasing the power of the majority to govern the country ended up putting certain minorities more at risk, since they no longer had a royal power supporting them. Was this democracy or the tyranny of the majority?

New York's rebels were less successful. A group of prosperous Dutch traders led by Jacob Leisler took over the government. Unlike Coode in Maryland, Leisler was not willing to cede power to the new king's appointees. As a result, the new governor put the rebel leaders on trial, and Leisler and his son-in-law were executed, their bodies decapitated and quartered.

The Rights of Englishmen

Although the Glorious Revolution restored self-government to the North American colonies, the colonists and their British governors interpreted that event somewhat differently. Colonists felt it gave them all the rights of Englishmen. These rights were of two sorts: civil rights, from trial by jury to freedom from unreasonable searches, and the rights of self-government, including taxation only by their own elected representatives, self-rule, and civilian, not military, rule. The colonists believed that their legislatures were the local equivalent of Parliament and that, just as the citizens of Britain were governed by Parliament, so they should be governed by their own elective legislatures.

The British government held differently. First, it believed that the colonies were dependents of the mother country that needed a parent's protection and that owed that parent obedience. Second, the good of the empire as a whole was more important than that of any one of its parts. A colony was valued, as one British official put it, by what it contributed to "the gain or loss of *this* Kingdom." Third, colonial governments were subordinate to the British government. Finally, the British government had complete jurisdiction over every aspect of colonial life. The views of Britain and its colonists of how the empire should function radically diverged.

Conflict in the Empire

Between 1689 and 1713, Britain fought two wars against France and her allies, King William's War (1689–1697) and Queen Anne's War (1702–1713). Competition for the Indian alliances and the colonies' struggle over trade and territory made the European-Indian borderline uncertain and dangerous.

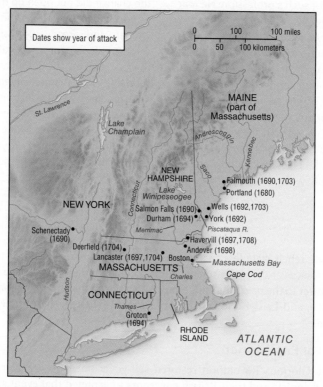

Map 4–2 Frontier Warfare During King William's and Queen Anne's Wars During these international conflicts, the New England frontier was exposed to attack by French Canadians and their Indian allies. *Source:* Adapted from Alan Gallay, ed., *Colonial Wars of North America, 1512–1763* (New York: Garland, 1996), p. 247.

King William's War and Queen Anne's War followed a similar pattern. Each was produced by a struggle for power between France and England, and each resulted in a stalemate. The North American phase of each war began with a Canadian-Indian assault on isolated British settlements on the northern frontier (see Map 4–2). King William's War started with the capture of the British fort at Pemaquid, Maine, and the burning of Schenectady, New York, and Falmouth, Maine. Queen Anne's War began in 1704 with a horrific raid on Deerfield, Massachusetts, in which half the town was torched and half the population was killed or captured.

In the first war, the British colonies responded with massive retaliation, sending raiding parties into ambitious but ultimately unsuccessful attacks on Québec. In 1690, Massachusetts governor Sir William Phips set out to seize Québec in an attack by land and sea. The failed expedition cost 1,000 lives and £40,000 and drove American colonists away from the northern frontier.

Queen Anne's War followed much the same course. Canadian-Indian attacks on frontier villages were met with raids on Indian villages. Again, New England attempted a two-pronged attack on Québec. When 900 troops (and 35 female camp followers) were killed as their ships sank in the St. Lawrence River, the commander canceled the expedition. Like King William's War, Queen Anne's War ended badly for New Englanders who had been eager to remove the twin threats of Catholicism and French-backed Indians to the north.

The imperial wars merged with and were survived by long-standing conflicts with Indian tribes. In North America, European rivals almost never confronted each other directly but instead mobilized their Indian allies and made war on those of their adversaries. These tactics, in addition to an expanding colonial population and the Native American attempt to monopolize trade, made conflict on the frontiers endemic.

Massachusetts in Crisis

If the imperial wars provide a window into international tensions, the Salem witchcraft trials reveal a society in crisis internally, one coping with economic development, the conflict between old and new ways of understanding the world, and the threats presented by political instability, imperial war, and conflict with the Indians. In 1692, Massachusetts executed 20 people who had been convicted of witchcraft in Salem. Even in a society that believed in witchcraft, the execution of so many people at once was an aberration that revealed deep tensions.

The Social and Cultural Contexts of Witchcraft

Although the majority of New England's colonists were Puritan, many seem to have believed in magic. They subscribed to such tenets of Puritanism as predestination, but they also believed that they could use supernatural powers to predict the future, protect themselves from harm, and hurt their enemies. Although the ministry identified the use of magic with the devil, many New Englanders were influenced by folk religion. Before the development of scientific modes of explanation for such catastrophes as epidemics, droughts, and sudden death, people looked for supernatural causes.

In 1692, the inhabitants of Massachusetts were unusually anxious. They were without an effective government because they had not yet received their new charter. King William's War had just begun, with the French Catholics of Canada and their Algonquian

Indian allies raiding the northern and eastern frontiers. Slaves reported that the French were planning to recruit New England's Africans as soldiers. These sources of stress increased underlying tensions, many of which concerned gender. Although men and women both attempted to use magic, the vast majority of those accused of witchcraft were women. Almost 80 percent of the 355 persons officially accused of practicing witchcraft were women, as were an even higher proportion of the 103 persons actually put on trial. Because most of these women had neither sons nor other male heirs, they could control property, which made them an anomaly in Puritan society. By the end of the seventeenth century, local land was an increasingly scarce commodity, and any woman who controlled it could be seen as threatening to the men who wanted it.

In addition, declining opportunity also disrupted the tight Puritan social order. Because land was scarce, it became difficult for young couples to start out. Consequently, the age of marriage increased, and the number of women who were pregnant on their wedding days began to climb, as did the number of women who gave birth without marrying at all. Courts increasingly shifted the burden of child support from fathers to mothers. By the end of the seventeenth century, New Englanders were more inclined than ever to hold women responsible for sin.

Witchcraft at Salem

In this context of strain and anxiety, on February 29, 1692, magistrates John Hathorne and Jonathan Corwin went to Salem to investigate recent accusations of witchcraft. By the time the investigation and trials ended, 156 people had been jailed and 20 executed. As in previous more minor witchcraft scares, most of the accused were women past the age of 40, and most of the accusers were women in their late teens and 20s.

Most of the accused fell into categories that revealed the stresses in Puritan society. Many, like Sarah Good, were the sort of "disagreeable" women who had always attracted accusations of witchcraft. Others had ties to Quakers or Baptists. Several were suspiciously friendly with the Indians. Enslaved women, like Tituba, who was probably an Arawak Indian, were also vulnerable. Notably, some of the accusers, like Mercy Lewis, had been orphaned or displaced by the recent Indian wars, and they described the devil they feared as "a Tawney, or an Indian color." In addition, most of the accusers lived in Salem Village, an economic backwater, whereas most of the accused lived in or had ties to the more prosperous merchant community of Salem Town. The pattern of accusations suggested resentment on a variety of levels.

By late September, accusations were falling on wealthy and well-connected men and women, such as the wife of the governor. Accusers were paraded from town to town to root out local witchcraft, and other people were drawn to Salem like medieval pilgrims. Finally, the leading ministers of Boston, most of whom believed in witchcraft but had been skeptical of the trials, stepped in, and the governor adjourned the court. No one was ever convicted of witchcraft in New England again.

The End of Witchcraft

The epidemic of panic and resentment was eventually brought under control. Although many colonists continued to believe in witchcraft, magic, and the occult, by the end of the seventeenth century they more often believed that the universe was orderly and that events were caused by natural, and knowable, forces. By the eighteenth century, educated people took pride in their rational understanding of nature and disdained a belief in the occult as mere superstition. This change in thinking reflected a new faith not only in human reason but also in the capacity of ordinary people to shape their lives. Increasing numbers of people, especially those who were well educated, prosperous, and lived in cities, believed that they could control their destinies and were not at the mercy of invisible evil forces. The seed of individualism had been planted in New England's rocky soil.

The witchcraft trials ended New England's belief in itself as a covenanted society with a collective future. Because Puritans had believed that God had chosen them for a mission, they read special meaning into every event, from a sudden snowstorm to an Indian attack. By the eighteenth century, however, they began to evaluate events separately, rather than always as part of God's master plan.

Empires in Collision

As late as the middle of the eighteenth century, Native Americans still outnumbered Europeans on the North American continent. At the end of the seventeenth century in the territory that became the United States, Britain was the only European power with a substantial presence (see Map 4–3). The French and Spanish both had mainland outposts north of the Rio Grande, but these nations concentrated their resources on more valuable colonies: for the Spanish, Mexico and Latin America, and for the French, the West Indies. Nonetheless, imperial ambitions brought European powers into conflict in North America, where they jostled against each other and the Native Americans.

France Attempts an Empire

After its civil wars of religion ended early in the seventeenth century, France was free to establish foreign colonies. After 1664, France's minister Jean-Baptiste Colbert tried to formulate a coherent imperial policy, directed from Paris. He envisioned a series of settlements, each contributing to the wealth of the nation through the fur trade and fishing in North America and plantation agriculture in the West Indies. France tried to direct the development of its New World empire, but it could not control small settlements so far away.

Colbert attempted to control every aspect of life in Québec. He subsidized emigration and had female migrants investigated to make sure that they were healthy and morally sound. To encourage reproduction, dowries were offered to all men who married by the age of 20. Agriculture developed and the population grew, more from natural increase than immigration. Colbert's attempt to make Québec a hierarchical society on the Old World model failed, however. First, very few French men and women were willing to settle in Canada. Between 1670 and 1730, perhaps fewer than 3,000 moved to mainland North America (and only a few thousand more to the West Indies). Second, those who did move resisted being controlled from Paris.

Eventually, Native Americans were more successful than Colbert in shaping the fur trade, the mainstay of the Québec economy. The French depended on their Indian trading partners to supply them with furs and serve as military allies. When Indians tried to trade their furs to the British, the French built forts—at considerable cost—to intercept them. French traders smuggled furs to the British in return for British fabrics that the Indians preferred. Moreover, to maintain the allegiance of their Algonquian allies, the French gave

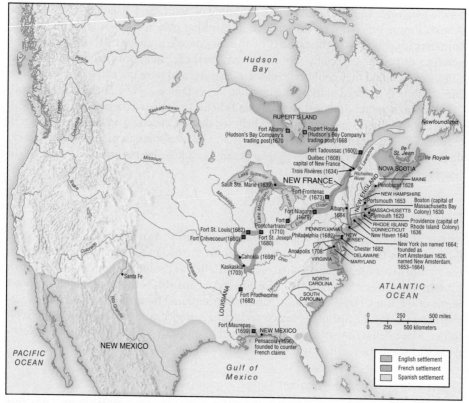

Map 4-3   Colonial North America, East of the Mississippi, 1720 This map shows the expansion of European settlement. English settlement was concentrated in a strip down the East Coast from Maine to North Carolina, with pockets of settlement in Canada and Carolina. French settlements formed a ring along the St. Lawrence River, from the Great Lakes south along the Mississippi, and along the Gulf Coast. The Spanish had outposts along the Gulf and in Florida.
Source: Adapted from Geoffrey Barraclough, ed., *The Times Concise Atlas of World History* (Maplewood, NJ: Hammond, 1994), p. 67.

them ammunition, knives, cloth, tobacco, and brandy. When the declining revenues from the fur trade are balanced against all these costs, it is questionable whether Canada was of any economic benefit to France, which maintained the fur trade more for political than for economic reasons.

It was for political reasons that France established outposts in present-day Louisiana and Mississippi, including Fort Biloxi (1699), Fort Toulouse (1717), and New Orleans (1718), all in the territory named Louisiana. (At the same time France built a number of forts in the north—such as Fort Niagara [1720] and Fort St. Frédéric [1731]—to guard against English encroachments.) When the French explorer La Salle reached the mouth of the Mississippi River in 1682 and claimed it for France, the Spanish mainland empire was cut in two, and the British faced a western rival. British traders had pushed into the lower Mississippi region looking for deerskins and Indian slaves. When the French arrived, tribes such as the Choctaws and Mobilians looked to the French for protection from

The French Settlement at Biloxi The French outpost at Biloxi was moved to higher ground in 1720. Here we see both temporary dwellings, thrown up in haste, and a more permanent storehouse to the left, with the entire settlement a hive of activity.

the British and their allies. Within several decades, the French had established trading posts as far north as the Illinois Territory. Farther west, French settlement of the lower Mississippi Valley led to conflict with the Natchez Indians, whom they conquered and sold into slavery.

The early history of the Louisiana Colony resembled that of the British settlement at Jamestown. As in Virginia, the first settlers were ill suited to the venture, top-heavy with military personnel and pirates. Louisiana itself was so unattractive that it could not attract colonists, so France began deporting criminals to the colony. Debilitated by the unhealthful environment, colonists could not even grow their own food. Caught up in wars on the continent, the French did not adequately support the colony, so its survival depended on the generosity of local Indians. In 1719, after African slaves began to be smuggled into the colony from the Caribbean, France permitted the importation of African slaves, but the colony still foundered.

Unlike the Chesapeake, colonial Louisiana never developed a significant cash crop. Because the colony was not important to French economic interests, French mercantilist policies protected Caribbean plantations at the expense of those in Louisiana. Although Louisiana had a slave majority by 1727, it was not a slave society. Louisiana's economy was one of frontier exchange among Europeans, Indians, and Africans, rather than one of commercial agriculture. Marginal to France's empire, Louisiana was largely ignored, and Europeans, Indians, and Africans depended on each other for survival. They intermarried and worked together. As late as 1730, Native Americans still made up more than 90 percent of the population, and social and economic relations remained fluid.

The situation could not have been more different in France's Caribbean empire. There, by the end of the eighteenth century, most of the native population had been killed by disease or war. It was soon replaced by African slaves. By 1670, the islands of Martinique and Guadeloupe were producing significant amounts of sugar with African slave labor. Between 1680 and 1730, 380,000 Africans were imported into those islands and the French colony of Saint-Domingue on the island of Santo Domingo, where they outnumbered Europeans by an astonishing ratio of 7.6 to 1. By the middle of the eighteenth century, Saint-Domingue was producing more sugar than any colony in America and would become the world's greatest producer of coffee. In a few decades, the French West Indies had been transformed into slave societies, in which slavery shaped every aspect of life. They were by far the most valuable part of France's New World empire.

The Spanish Outpost in Florida

Like France's colony at Louisiana, Spain's settlement at St. Augustine, Florida, was intended to be a self-supporting military outpost. Unable to attract settlers and costly to maintain, Florida grew so slowly and unsteadily that the Spanish considered abandoning it and moving the population to the West Indies.

When the British established their colony at Carolina, however, Florida again became important to Spain—and it gained a new source of settlers in runaway slaves. The British and Spanish began fighting, usually using Indian and African surrogates. Spanish raiders seized slaves from Carolina plantations, paid them wages, and introduced them to Catholicism. Soon, as Carolina's governor complained, slaves were "running dayly" to Florida. In 1693, Spain's king offered liberty to all British slaves who escaped to Florida.

The border between the two colonies was violent—and, for Africans, a place of opportunity. Africans gained valuable military experience and, in 1738, about 100 former slaves established the free black town of Gracia Real de Santa Teresa de Mose near St. Augustine. Mose's leader was the Mandinga captain of the free black militia, Francisco Menéndez. A former slave who had been reenslaved, he persisted in petitioning for his freedom. Spain freed Menéndez and other Africans like him and reiterated the policy that British slaves who escaped to Florida should be free. The persistence of Menéndez and the other escaped slaves established the first free black community on the North American continent.

Conquest, Revolt, and Reconquest in New Mexico

In the West, New Mexico developed into a colonial outpost on the far edge of a world empire, irrelevant to Spain's economy or political power. Early in the seventeenth century, the Spanish considered abandoning the settlement, but Franciscan missionaries persuaded Spain to stay so the priests could minister to the Native Americans. In the eastern half of the continent, Indians could play the European powers against each other, but in the West, only Spain was a presence, reducing the Pueblo Indians' leverage. When the Pueblo Indians rose up against the Spanish at the end of the seventeenth century, the survival of New Mexico was in doubt.

Spain had established its colony in New Mexico by conquest. Although Coronado's party had explored the region from Arizona to Kansas (1541–1542), it had not planted a permanent settlement. In 1598, Juan de Oñate was appointed governor and authorized to establish a colony. Like his great-grandfather Cortés, Oñate persuaded some local Pueblos to accept him as their ruler, and others he overcame by force. His harsh means proved effective, and the Spanish soon dominated the entire Southwest. In 1610, they established their capital at Santa Fe, and the colony, called New Mexico, began to grow slowly. The New Mexico Colony was to serve as an outpost against the French, just as St. Augustine was to defend against the English. The most important "business" in the colony was to convert the Pueblo Indians to Catholicism.

Franciscan priests established a series of missions in New Mexico. Although there were never more than 50 or so Franciscans at any time, they claimed to have converted about 80,000 Indians in less than a century. Most of these conversions, however, were in name only. The Indians deeply resented the priests' attempts to change their customs and beliefs. By forcing the Indians to adopt European sex roles and sexual mores, the Franciscans undermined not only Pueblo religion but also their society.

Spanish rule fell harshly on the Pueblos. Although Spanish law forbade enslavement of conquered Indians, some Spanish settlers openly defied it. More common was the *encomienda* system. Oñate rewarded his lieutenants by naming them *encomenderos*, which entitled them to tribute from the Indians living on the land they had been awarded. Some *encomenderos* also demanded labor or personal service. Women working in Spanish households were vulnerable to sexual abuse by their masters. Facing such burdens, the Indian population declined from about 40,000 in 1638 to only 17,000 in 1670.

A combination of Spanish demands for labor and tribute and a long period of drought left the Pueblos without the food surpluses that they had been selling to the nomadic Apaches and Navajos. Those tribes began to raid the Pueblos, taking by force what they could no longer get by trade. Under siege, Pueblos turned once again to their tribal gods and religious leaders.

The Pueblo at Acoma The Acoma Pueblo sits atop a mesa that rises 400 feet aboveground. In January 1699, Spanish soldiers destroyed the pueblo and killed 800 of its inhabitants, in retaliation for the killing of a dozen soldiers. All the male survivors over the age of 12 and all female survivors were sentenced to 20 years of servitude to the Spanish, and the men over the age of 25 each had a foot cut off as well. The pueblo was rebuilt after its destruction.

When the Spanish punished the Indians who returned to their traditional religion, they pushed the Pueblos into revolt. A medicine man named Popé united the leaders of most of the Pueblos, promising that if the Indians threw out the Spanish and prayed again to their ancient gods, food would be plentiful. Indians would never have to work for the Spanish again, he said, and Indian customs would be restored.

Popé's revolt began on August 10, 1680, when the Spanish were low on supplies. First, the Indians seized all horses and mules, immobilizing the Spanish. Next, they blocked the roads to Santa Fe. Then they destroyed all the Spanish settlements, one at a time. At day's end, more than 400 Spanish had been killed. The Pueblos laid siege to Santa Fe, forcing Spanish survivors to retreat to El Paso. In the most successful Indian revolt ever in North America, the Spanish had been driven from New Mexico.

The Pueblos held off the Spanish for 13 years, until the mid-1690s, but the struggles took a heavy toll. Contrary to Popé's promise, the drought continued. Warfare took more lives, and the population continued to drop.

The revolt taught the Spanish lessons. The new Franciscan missionaries were far less zealous than their predecessors. The *encomienda* was not reestablished, and brutal exploitation was less common. Slowly the Spanish colony began rebuilding (see Map 4–4).

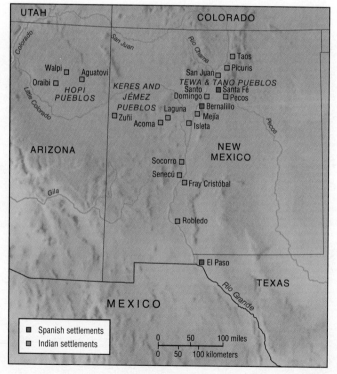

Map 4–4 Region of Spanish Reconquest of New Mexico, 1692–1696 This map includes the pueblos reconquered by the Spanish, as well as Spanish settlements.
Source: Adapted from Oakah L. Jones Jr., *Pueblo Warriors and Spanish Conquest* (Norman: University of Oklahoma Press, 1966), p. 37.

Eighteenth-Century Spanish Illustration of New World Racial Mixture In this case, the union of an Indian ("Yndio") and a "Mestiza" produces a "Coyote" child. The Spanish developed a large vocabulary so that they could make racial distinctions with great precision.

De Yndio y Mestiza
Coyote.

The population was divided into four groupings, from a small elite at the top to enslaved Indians at the bottom. The elite, a hereditary aristocracy of 20 or so families, included government officials. They developed codes of honor to distinguish themselves from lower orders. This local nobility prided itself on its racial purity, considering white skin a clear sign of superiority. It scorned those of mixed blood, many of whom, of course, were the illegitimate children of elite Spanish men and the Indian women they coerced. Aristocratic men placed a high value on the personal qualities of courage, honesty, loyalty, and sexual virility. Female honor consisted of extreme modesty and sexual purity.

The second group was landed peasants, most of them *mestizos*, half-Spanish and half-Indian. In this highly color-conscious colonial society, the *mestizos* often prized the Spanish part of their heritage and scorned the Indian. Next came the Pueblo Indians, living in their own communities. The *genízaros*, Indians who had left their own communities by choice or whose ancestors had been enslaved, lived in Spanish settlements. Sometimes these urban immigrants were outcasts, such as women who had been raped by Spanish men. A century after their first conquest, the Pueblo Indians had in some regards begun to adopt the values of their conquerors.

Native Americans and the Country Between

Spain paid little attention to its impoverished outposts in New Mexico, leaving them vulnerable to the Indians to the east. When the French in Louisiana started arming their Comanche, Wichita, and Pawnee trading partners, New Mexicans—Spanish and Pueblos alike—were challenged.

The Indians of the Great Plains, however, profited from the conflict, obtaining guns from the French and horses from the Spanish. After the Pueblo revolt, the Spanish left behind hundreds of horses that Pueblo and Apache Indians passed on to the Plains Indians. By the middle of the eighteenth century, all the Plains Indians were on horseback, which transformed their lives dramatically. They became more effective buffalo hunters, thus making them better fed, clothed, and housed. Their new mobility gave them an increasing sense of freedom, too. But the horses—and the better living conditions they helped make possible—attracted other Indians to the Great Plains. In fact, most of the

Indians we now associate with the Great Plains—Sioux, Arapaho, Cheyenne, Blackfoot, Cree—did not arrive there until the eighteenth century.

The result was increased warfare among the Plains Indians, and those with the best access to horses fared the best. For example, the Comanches came to dominate the southern plains, from western Kansas to New Mexico, where they intruded on both the Apaches and the Spanish. The Comanches raided the Apaches, taking not only their horses but also their women and children as captives, some of whom they sold as slaves—*genízaros*—to the Spanish. The Comanches cut the Apaches off from French traders to the east. The Apaches in turn moved west and south, bringing them into conflict with the Pueblos and the Spanish. In defense, the Spanish built a string of armed settlements in current-day Texas, but they could not withstand the Comanches, and even the New Mexican settlements were endangered.

Eventually, the new horse-centered way of life took its toll. Although some tribes grew stronger at the expense of others, all suffered from the increasing violence. European diseases proved deadly as well. Under such pressures, gender roles changed. Men sought distinction as warriors, demonstrating success by the number of scalps or captives they seized. Yet so many fell in battle that they were soon outnumbered by women, which led to an increased frequency of polygamy, as surviving warriors took multiple wives. As men's status as warriors and hunters rose, that of women—the agriculturalists—fell.

Time Line

▼**1598**
Juan de Oñate colonizes New
   Mexico for Spain

▼**1610**
Santa Fe established

▼**1627**
Barbados settled

▼**1628**
Parliament passes Petition
   of Right

▼**1642–1647**
English Revolution

▼**1649**
King Charles I beheaded

▼**1651–1696**
Navigation Acts passed to
   regulate trade

▼**1652–1674**
Three Anglo-Dutch Wars

▼**1660**
British monarchy restored,
   Charles II crowned king

▼**1662**
Half-Way Covenant

▼**1664**
British seize New Netherland,
   renaming it New York

▼**1665**
New Jersey established

▼**1669**
Fundamental Constitutions
   written for South Carolina

▼**1670**
Carolina settled

▼**1673**
Marquette and Joliet explore
   Mississippi for France

▼**1675–1676**
King Philip's War

▼**1676–1677**
Bacon's Rebellion

▼**1680**
Pueblo Revolt in New Mexico
   reestablishes Indian rule
Westo War, Carolina defeats the
   Westos

Conclusion

After a period of considerable instability, by the beginning of the eighteenth century, almost all of the British North American colonies had developed the societies that they would maintain until the American Revolution. For the most part, the colonies were prosperous, with a large white middle class. The efforts to replicate a European hierarchical order had largely failed. Each region had found a secure economic base: farming and shipping in New England, mixed farming in the middle colonies, and single-crop planting in the southern ones. The southern colonies had become slave societies, although slavery was practiced in every colony. For the most part, the colonies had figured out how to control their own populations, whether by affording them increased opportunity and political rights, in the case of Europeans, or by exercising tighter control, in the case of enslaved Africans. These strong economic foundations, when combined with political stability, were the preconditions for the rapid population growth of the eighteenth century, when the British population on the mainland would far surpass that of the French and Spanish colonies. The French and Spanish colonies on the mainland were still little more than frontier outposts, although both nations maintained imperial visions for North America. Native Americans remained a strong presence, but the competition among the European powers—and even the individual colonies—for the loyalty of the Indian tribes, their trade, and their land remained a source of conflict.

▼**1681**
William Penn granted charter for Pennsylvania

▼**1683**
New York's assembly meets for first time

▼**1685**
King Charles II dies and James, Duke of York, becomes King James II

▼**1686**
Massachusetts, Plymouth, Connecticut, Rhode Island, and New Hampshire combined in Dominion of New England; New York and New Jersey added two years later

▼**1688**
Glorious Revolution

▼**1689**
Leisler's Rebellion in New York, Coode's Rebellion in Maryland
William and Mary become King and Queen of Britain; Dominion of New England overthrown

▼**1689–1697**
King William's War

▼**1690**
Publication of John Locke's *Two Treatises of Government*

▼**1691**
Massachusetts made a royal colony
Maryland made a royal colony
New Hampshire made a royal colony

▼**1692**
Salem witchcraft trials

▼**1696**
Reconquest of New Mexico

▼**1702–1713**
Queen Anne's War

▼**1715–1716**
Yamasee War

▼**1718**
French establish settlement at New Orleans

Who, What, Where

Review Questions

1. What was Britain's plan of empire? What role were the American colonies supposed to play in it?

2. What effect did political turmoil and the change of leadership in Britain have on the American colonies in the second half of the seventeenth century?

3. Describe Indian-white relations in the American colonies in the second half of the seventeenth century. Why was competition between the colonies an important element?

Critical-Thinking Questions

1. Many of the American colonies experienced a period of political instability in the last quarter of the seventeenth century. In many cases, ranging from the Salem witch trials to Popé's Rebellion of 1680, the sources of the instability appear specific and local, yet they may also reveal a pattern. To what extent were these instances of instability local, and to what extent may they reveal larger processes at work in the colonies of European imperial powers?

2. In this period, a number of colonies became slave societies. What forces propelled these changes? Were different outcomes possible?

3. What patterns, if any, do you see in Native Americans' accommodation and resistance to European expansion in North America in this period?

Suggested Readings

Bailyn, Bernard. *The New England Merchants in the Seventeenth Century.* Cambridge, MA: Harvard University Press, 1955.

Green, Jack P. *Pursuits of Happiness: The Social Development of Early Modern British Colonies and the Formation of American Culture.* Chapel Hill: University of North Carolina Press, 1988.

Isaac, Rhys. *The Transformation of Virginia.* Chapel Hill: University of North Carolina Press, 1982.

Norton, Mary Beth. *In the Devil's Snare: The Salem Witchcraft Crisis of 1692.* New York: Knopf, 2002.

Weber, David. *The Spanish Frontier in North America.* New Haven, CT: Yale University Press, 1992.

For further review materials and resource information, please visit www.oup.com/us/oakes-mcgerr

CHAPTER 4: CONTINENTAL EMPIRES, 1660–1720
Primary Sources

4.1 THE NAVIGATION ACT OF 1651

The Navigation Act of 1651 was the first in a series of acts that would number nearly 200 and end with the American revolutionary crisis. The act laid out a system later called *mercantilism*, which ensured a favorable balance of trade for Britain by forcing the colonies to ship certain raw materials to the mother country and pay for manufactured goods of greater value in exchange. This maximized the inflow of specie—gold and silver—for the mother country.

For the increase of the shipping and the encouragement of the navigation of this nation, which under the good providence and protection of God is so great a means of the welfare and safety of this Commonwealth: be it enacted by this present Parliament, and the authority thereof, that from and after the first day of December, one thousand six hundred fifty and one, and from thence forwards, no goods or commodities whatsoever of the growth, production or manufacture of Asia, Africa or America, or of any part thereof; or of any islands belonging to them, or which are described or laid down in the usual maps or cards of those places, as well of the English plantations as others, shall be imported or brought into this Commonwealth of England, or into Ireland, or any other lands, islands, plantations, or territories to this Commonwealth belonging, or in their possession, in any other ship or ships, vessel or vessels whatsoever, but only in such as do truly and without fraud belong only to the people of this Commonwealth, or the plantations thereof, as the proprietors or right owners thereof; and whereof the master and mariners are also for the most part of them of the people of this Commonwealth, under the penalty of the forfeiture and loss of all the goods that shall be imported contrary to this act; as also of the ship (with all her tackle, guns and apparel) in which the said goods or commodities shall be so brought in and imported; the one moiety to the use of the Commonwealth, and the other moiety to the use and behoof of any person or persons who shall seize the goods or commodities, and shall prosecute the same in any court of record within this Commonwealth.

And it is further enacted by the authority aforesaid, that no goods or commodities of the growth, production, or manufacture of Europe, or of any part thereof, shall after the first day of December, one thousand six hundred fifty and one, be imported or brought into this Commonwealth of England, or into Ireland, or any other lands, islands, plantations or territories to this Commonwealth belonging, or in their possession, in any ship or ships, vessel or vessels whatsoever, but in such as do truly and without fraud belong only to the people of this Commonwealth, as the true owners and proprietors thereof, and in no other, except only such foreign ships and vessels as do truly and properly belong to the people of that country or place, of which the said goods are the growth, production or manufacture; or to such ports where the said goods can only be, or most usually are first shipped for transportation; and that under the same penalty of forfeiture and loss expressed in the former branch of this Act, the said forfeitures to be recovered and employed as is therein expressed.

And it is further enacted by the authority aforesaid, that no goods or commodities that are of foreign growth, production or manufacture, and which are to be brought into this Commonwealth in shipping belonging to the people thereof, shall be by them shipped or brought from any other place or places, country or countries, but only from those of their said growth, production, or manufacture, or from those ports where the said goods and commodities can only, or are, or usually have been first shipped for transportation; and from none other places or countries, under the same penalty of forfeiture and loss expressed in the first branch of this Act, the said forfeitures to be recovered and employed as is therein expressed.

Source: "The Navigation Act, Ordinance of 1651, October 9th, 1651," in *American History Leaflets: Colonial and Constitutional. Number 19, Extracts from the Navigation Acts 1645–1696,* edited by Albert Bushnell Hart and Edward Channing (New York: A. Lovell and Company, 1895), pp. 6–7.

4.2 LETTER FROM WILLIAM PENN TO HIS BACKERS (1683)

William Penn was the son of a wealthy English admiral. As a young man, he converted to the Quaker faith and suffered imprisonments. In 1682, the King paid a debt to Penn's father by giving him lands in the New World, and the younger Penn immediately set off to govern them, founding "Pennsylvania" that same year. In 1683, after touring the lands and meeting with the Lenni Lenape, or Delaware Indians, he wrote a letter describing his experiences with them to his backers in London. That same year, a printed version was published. In 1684, Penn returned to England but went back to Pennsylvania for an extended stay from 1699 to 1701.

August 6, 1683

. . . Every King hath his Council, and that consists of all the Old and Wise men of his Nation, which perhaps is two hundred People: nothing of Moment Is undertaken, be it War, Peace, Selling of Land or Traffick, without advising with them; and which is more, with the Young Men too. 'Tis admirable to consider, how Powerful the Kings are, and yet how they move by the Breath of their People.

I have had occasion to be in Council with them upon Treaties for Land, and to adjust the terms of Trade; their Order is thus: The King sits in the middle of an half Moon, and hath his Council, the Old and Wise on each hand; behind them, or at a little distance, sit the younger Fry, in the same figure. Having consulted and resolved their business, the King ordered one of them to speak to me; he stood up, came to me, and In the Name of his King saluted me, then took me by the hand, and told me, That he was ordered by his King to speak to me, and that now it was not he, but the King that spoke, because what he should say, was the King's mind. He first pray'd me, To excuse them that they had not yet complied with me the last time; he feared, there might be some fault in the Interpreter, being neither Indian nor English; besides, it was the Indian Custom to deliberate, and take up much time in Council, before they resolve; and that If the Young People and Owners of the Land had been ready as he, I had not met with so much delay. Having thus introduced his matter, he fell to the Bounds of the Land they had agreed to dispose of, and the Price (which now is little and dear, that which would have bought twenty Miles, not buying now two). During their time that this Person spoke, not a man of them was observed to whisper or smile; the Old, Grave, the Young, Reverend In the Deportment; they do speak little, but fervently, and with Elegancy: I have never seen more natural Sagacity, considering them without the help (I was agoing to say, the spoil) of Tradition; and he will deserve the Name of Wise, that Outwits them in any Treaty about a thing they understand.

When the Purchase was agreed, great Promises past between us of Kindness and good Neighbourhood, and that the Indians and English must live In Love, as long as the Sun gave light. Which done, another made a Speech to the Indians, in the Name of all the Sachamakers or Kings, first to tell them what was done; next, to charge and command them, To Love the Christians, and particularly live In Peace with me, and the People under my Governement: That many

Governors had been in the River, but that no Gouvernour [sic] had come himself to live and stay here before; and having now such a one that had treated them well, they should never do him or his any wrong. At every sentence of which they shouted, and said, Amen, In their way.[1]

The Justice they have Is Pecuniary: In case of any Wrong or evil Fact, be it Murther itself, they Attone by Feasts and Presents of their Wampum, which Is propositioned to the quality of the Offence or Person Injured, or of the Sex they are of: for in case they kill a Woman, they pay double, and the Reason they render is, That she breedeth Children, which men cannot do. 'Tis rare that they fall out, if Sober; and if Drunk, they forgive It, saying, It was the Drink, and not the Man, that abused them.

We have agreed, that in all Differences between us, Six of each side shall end the matter: Don't abuse them, but let them have Justice, and you win them: The worst Is, that they are the worse for the Christians, who have propagated their Vices, and yielded them Tradition for ill, and not for good things, but as low an Ebb as they're at, and as glorious as the Condition looks, the Christians have not out-liv'd their sight with all their Pretensions to an higher Manifestation: What good then might not a good People graft, where there is so distinct a Knowledge left between Good and Evil? I beseech God to incline the Hearts of all that come into these parts, to out-live the Knowledge of the Natives, but a fixt Obedience to their greater Knowledge of the Will of God; for it were miserable indeed for us to fall under the just censure of the poor Indian Conscience, while we make profession of things so far transcending.

Source: Albert Book Myers, ed., *William Penn's Own Account of the Lenni Lenape or Delaware Indians* (Somerset, NJ: Middle Atlantic Press, 1970 [1683]), pp. 36–41.

4.3 MARY ROWLANDSON, EXCERPTS FROM *THE SOVEREIGNTY AND GOODNESS OF GOD* (1682)

In 1675 and 1676, a brutal war was waged between the Massachusetts colonists and the New England Indians. Initially, the Indians scored some major victories, but they did not have permanent access to food, ammunition, and new recruits as the colonists did. During the war, Mary Rowlandson, a clergyman's wife and mother of four, was kidnapped along with several of her children from Lancaster, Massachusetts, and experienced, together with her captors, the hunger that plagued the Indians as they retreated.

My Child being even ready to depart this sorrowful world, they bade me carry it out to another Wigwam (I suppose because they would not be troubled with such spectacles) Whither I went with a very heavy heart, and down I sat with the picture of death in my lap. About two houres in the night, my sweet Babe, like a lamb departed this life, on *Feb. 18. 1675*, it being about six years and five months old. . . . I cannot but take notice, how at another time I could not bear to be in the room where any dead person was, but now the case [was] changed; I must and could ly down by my dead Babe, side by side all the night after. I have thought since of the wonderfull goodness of God to me, in preserving me in the use of my reason and senses, in that distressed time, that I did not use wicked and violent means to end my own miserable life. In the morning . . . I went to take up my dead child in my arms to carry it with me, but they bid me let it alone: there was no resisting, but goe I must and leave it. . . . I took the first opportunity I could get, to go look after my dead child: when I came I askt them what they had done with it? Then they told me it was

---

[1]This paragraph was not in the original letter. Penn did not actually stay for many years, but he had hoped to.

upon the hill: then they went and shewed me where it was, where I saw the ground was newly digged, and there they told me they had buried it. *There I left that Child in the Wilderness, and must commit it, and my self also in this Wilderness-condition, to him who is above all.* God having taken away this dear Child, I went to see my daughter *Mary*, who was [for a while] at this same *Indian Town*, at a *Wigwam* not very far off, though we had little liberty or opportunity to see one another; she was about ten years old. . . . When I came in sight, she would fall a weeping; at which they were provoked, and would not let me come near her, but bade me be gone; which was a heart-cutting word to me. I had one Child dead, another in the Wilderness, I knew not where, the third they would not let me come near to. . . .

[two weeks later]

On the Saturday, they boyled an old Horses leg which they had got, and so we drank of the broth, as soon as they thought it was ready . . . The first week of my being among them, I hardly ate anything; the second week, I found my stomach grow very faint for want of something; and yet it was very hard to get down their filthy trash: but the third week, though I could think how formerly my stomach would turn against this or that, and I could starve or die before I could eat such things, yet they were sweet and savory to my taste. . . . And here I cannot but take notice of the strange providence of God in preserving the heathen: They were many hundreds, old and young, some sick, and some lame, many had *Papooses* at their backs, the greatest number at this time with us, were *Squaws*, and they traveled with all they had, bag and baggage, and yet they got over the River; and on *Munday*, they set their *Wigwams* on fire, and away they went: On that very same day came the English Army after them to this River, and saw the smoak of their Wigwams, and yet this River put a stop to them . . .

On *Munday* (as I said), they set their *Wigwams* on fire, and went away. It was a cold morning, and before us there was a great Brook with ice on it; some waded through it, up to the knees & higher, but others went till they came to a Beaver dam, and I amongst them, where through the good providence of God, I did not wet my foot.[2] I went along that day mourning and lamenting, leaving farther my own Country, and traveling into the vast and howling Wilderness, and I understood something of Lot's Wife's[3] Temptations, when she looked back: We came that day to a great Swamp, by the side of which we took up our lodging that night. When I came to the brow of the hill, that looked toward the Swamp, I thought we had been come to a great Indian Town (though there were none but our own Company). The Indians were as thick as the trees; it seemed as if there had been a thousand Hatchets going at once: if one looked before one, there was nothing but Indians, and behind one, nothing but Indians, and so on either hand, I myself in the midst, and no Christian soul near me. . . .

On the morrow morning we must go over the River, i.e. Connecticot, to meet with King *Philip*, two *Cannoos* full, they had carried over, the next Turn I myself was to go; but as my foot was upon the *Cannoo* to stop in, there was a sudden out-cry among them, and I must step back; and instead of going over the River, I must go four or five miles up the River farther Northward. Some of the *Indians* ran one way, and some another. The cause of this rout was, as I thought, their espying some *English Scouts*, who were thereabout. In this travel up the river, about noon the Company made a stop, and sat down; some to eat, and others to rest them. As I sate amongst them, musing of things past, my son *Joseph* unexpectedly came to me: we asked of each others welfare, bemoaning our dolefull condition, and the change that had come upon us. . . . I asked him whither he would read; he told me, he earnestly desired it. I gave him my Bible,[4] and he

---

[2]Whether or not Rowlandson got wet in making the crossings became extremely important to her because the cold was almost unendurable when she was soaked.

[3]Lot's wife was warned not to look back or she would be turned to a pillar of salt. See Genesis 19:26.

[4]Rowlandson had not been able to leave carrying anything except her child, but an Indian had later given her a Bible taken in the spoils of battle.

lighted upon that comfortable scripture, Psal. 118.17, 18. *I shall not dye but live, and declare the works of the Lord: the Lord hath chastened me sore, yet he hath not given me over to death.* Look here, Mother (sayes he), did you read this? . . . We traveled on till night; and in the morning, we must go over the River to *Philip's* crew. When I was in the Cannoo, I could not but be amazed at the numerous crew of Pagans that were on the Bank on the other side. When I came ashore, they gathered all about me, I sitting alone in the midst: I observed they asked one another questions, and laughed, and rejoyced over their Gains and Victories. Then my heart began to fail: and I fell a weeping which was the first time to my remembrance that I wept before them. Although I had met with so much Affliction, and my heart was many times ready to break, yet could I not shed one tear in their sight: but rather had been all this while in a maze [that is, amazed, stunned], like one astonished: but now I may say as Psal. 137.1 *By the rivers of Babylon, there we sat down: yea, we wept when we remembered Zion.* There one of them asked me, why I wept, I could hardly tell what to say: yet I answered, they would kill me: No, said he, none will hurt you. Then came one of them and gave me two spoon-fulls of Meal to comfort me, and another gave me half a pint of Pease; which was more worth than many Bushels at another time.[5] Then I went to see King *Philip*, he bade me come in and sit down, and asked me whether I would smoke . . .

Source: Mary Rowlandson, *The Sovereignty and Goodness of God, Together with the Faithfulness of His Promises Displayed* (Cambridge, MA: Samuel Green, 1682).

4.4 DECLARATION OF A PUEBLO INDIAN CAPTURED BY THE SPANIARDS (1680)

The Spanish had been a strong presence in New Mexico since 1598. In 1680, a rebellion broke out that was so successful for the Pueblo Indians that the surviving Spanish were forced to flee and were unable to retake the territory for a full 12 years. The leaders of the rebellion were well organized, orchestrating the timing across a wide region, and the movement had broad popular support. In the midst of the uprising, the Spanish sent out military parties in a desperate attempt to gather useful information and save Spanish sites. Their agenda essentially failed, but the Spanish did manage to capture some Indians for questioning.

In the place of El Alamillo, jurisdiction of El Socorro, on the 6th day of the month of September, 1680, for the prosecution of this case, and so that an Indian who was captured on the road as the camp was marching may be examined, in order to ascertain the plans, designs, and motives of the rebellious enemy, his lordship, the señor-gobernador and captain-general, caused the said Indian to appear before him. He received the oath from him in due legal form, in the name of God, our Lord, and on a sign of the cross, under charge of which he promised to tell the truth concerning what he might know and as he might be questioned. Having been asked his name and of what place he is a native, his condition, and age, he said that his name is Don Pedro Nanboa,[6] that he is a native of the pueblo of Alameda, a widower, and somewhat more than eighty years of age. Asked for what reason the Indians of this kingdom have rebelled, forsaking their obedience to his Majesty and failing in their obligation as Christians, he said that for a long time, because the Spaniards punished sorcerers and idolaters, the nations of the Teguas, Tao, Pecuríes, Pecos

---

[5]It was worth so much because the company was starving.

[6]The use of the title "don" by a native man in this period indicates that he was of high or noble status within his own community.

and Jemez had been plotting to rebel and kill the Spaniards and the religious [Franciscans], and that they had been planning constantly to carry it out, down to the present occasion. Asked what he learned, saw and heard in the juntas and parleys that the Indians have held, what they have plotted among themselves, and why the Indians have burned the church and profaned the images of the pueblo of Sandia, he said that he has not taken part in any junta, nor has he harmed any one; that what he has heard is that the Indians do not want religious [friars] or Spaniards. Because he is so old he was in the cornfield[7] when he learned from the Indian rebels who came from the sierra that they had killed the Spaniards of the jurisdiction and robbed all their haciendas, sacking their houses. Asked whether he knows about the Spaniards and religious who were gathered in the pueblo of La Isleta, he said that it is true that some days ago there assembled in the said pueblo of La Isleta the religious of Sandia, Jemez, and Zia, and that they set out to leave the kingdom with those of the said pueblo of La Isleta and the Spaniards—not one of whom remained—taking along their property. The Indians did not fight with them because all the men had gone with the other nations to fight at the villa [in the capital] and destroy the governor and captain-general and all the people who were with him. He declared that the resentment which all the Indians have in their hearts has been so strong, from the time this kingdom was discovered, because the religious and the Spaniards took away their idols and forbade their sorceries and idolatries; that they have inherited successively from their old men the things pertaining to their ancient customs; and that he has heard this resentment spoken of since he was of an age to understand. What he has said is the truth and what he knows, under the oath taken, and he signs and ratifies it, it being read and explained to him in his language through the interpretation of Captain Sebastián Montaño, who signed it with his lordship, as the said Indian does not know how, before me, the present secretary. Antonio de Otermín (rubric); Sebastián Montaño (rubric); Juan Lucero de Godoy (rubric); Luis de Quintana (rubric). Before me, Francisco Xavier, secretary of government and war (rubric).

Source: "Declaration of one of the rebellious Christian Indians who was captured on the road. El Alamillo, September 6, 1680." In Charles Wilson Hackett, ed., *Revolt of the Pueblo Indians of New Mexico and Otermín's Attempted Reconquest, 1680-1682* (Albuquerque: University of New Mexico Press, 1942), pp. 60–62.

4.5 ROBERT CALEF, EXCERPTS FROM *MORE WONDERS OF THE INVISIBLE WORLD* (1700)

As the witch hunts of 1692 unfolded in the colony of Massachusetts, many residents looked on in horror. Some colonists later wrote about the experience, while some collected other people's testimonies regarding the events that occurred in the ensuing months and years. Robert Calef, a Boston merchant, sent an extensive manuscript back to London in 1697. When it was published in 1700, Puritan minister Increase Mather had copies burned in Harvard Yard.

May 24, 1692. Mrs. Cary of Charlestown [Massachusetts], was examined and committed. Her husband Mr. Nathaniel Cary has given account thereof, as also of her escape, to this effect,

I having heard [for] some days, that my wife was accused of witchcraft, being much disturbed at it, by advice, we went to Salem Village, to see if the afflicted did know her; we arrived there, 24 May, it happened to be a day appointed for examination; accordingly soon after our arrival, Mr. Hathorne and Mr. Corwin, etc., went to the meeting house, which was the place appointed for that work, the minister began with prayer, and having taken care to get a convenient

---

[7]Don Pedro meant that because of his advanced age, he had been left to till the fields rather than invited to join the war party.

place, I observed, that the afflicted were two girls of about ten years old, and about two or three others, of about eighteen. One of the girls talked most, and could discern more than the rest. The prisoners were cavalled in one by one, and as they came in were cried out of,[8] etc. The prisoner was placed about 7 or 8 foot from the justices, and the accusers between the justices and them; the prisoner was ordered to stand right before the justices, with an officer appointed to hold each hand, lest they should therewith afflict them, and the prisoner's eyes must be constantly on the justices; for if they looked on the afflicted, they would either fall into their fits, or cry out of being hurt by them; after examination of the prisoners, who it was afflicted these girls, etc., they were put upon saying the Lord's prayer, as a trial of their guilt; after the afflicted seemed to be out of their fits, they would look steadfastly on some one person, and frequently not speak; and then the justices said they were struck dumb, and after a little time would speak again; then the justices said to the accusers, "which of you will go and touch the prisoner at the bar?" then the most courageous would adventure, but before they had made three steps would ordinarily fall down as in a fit; the justices ordered that they should be taken up and carried to the prisoner, that she might touch them; and as soon as they were touched by the accused, the justices would say, they are well, before I could discern any alteration; by which I observed that the justices understood the manner of it. Thus far I was only as a spectator, my wife also was there part of the time, but no notice taken of her by the afflicted, except once or twice they came to her and asked her name.

But I having an opportunity to discourse [with] Mr. Hale (with whom I had formerly an acquaintance) I took his advice, what I had best to do, and desired of him that I might have an opportunity to speak with her that accused my wife; which he promised should be, I acquainting him that I reposed my trust In him.

Accordingly he came to me after the examination was over, and told me I had now an opportunity to speak with the said accuser, viz. Abigail Williams, a girl of 11 or 12 years old; but that we could not be in private at Mr. Parris's house, as he had promised me; we went therefore into the alehouse, where an Indian man attended us, who it seems was one of the afflicted: to him we gave some cider, he showed several scars, that seemed as if they had been long there, and showed them as done by witchcraft, and acquainted us that his wife, who also was a slave, was imprisoned for witchcraft. And now Instead of one accuser, they all came in, who began to tumble down like swine, and then three women were called in to attend them. We in the room were all at a stand, to see who they would cry out of; but in a short time they cried out, Cary; and Immediately after a warrant was sent from the justices to bring my wife before them, who were sitting in a chamber nearby, waiting for this.

Being brought before the justices, her chief accusers were two girls; my wife declared to the justices, that she never had any knowledge of them before that day; she was forced to stand with her arms stretched out. I did request that I might hold one of her hands, but it was denied me; then she desired me to wipe the tears from her eyes, and the sweat from her face, which I did; then she desired she might lean herself on me, saying, she should faint.

Justice Hathorne replied, she had strength enough to torment those persons, and she should have strength enough to stand. I speaking something against their cruel proceedings, they commanded me to be silent, or else I should be turned out of the room. The Indian before mentioned, was also brought in, to be one of her accusers; being come In, he now (when before the justices) fell down and tumbled about like a hog, but said nothing. The justices asked the girls, who afflicted the Indian? They answered she (meaning my wife) and now lay upon him; the justices ordered her to touch him, In order to his cure, but her head must be turned another way, lest instead of curing, she should make him worse, by her looking on him, her hand being guided to take hold of his; but the Indian took hold on her hand, and pulled her down on the floor, In a barbarous manner; then his hand was taken off, and her hand put on his, and the cure was

---

[8]Those accused of witchcraft were jeered at, yelled at.

quickly wrought. I being extremely troubled at their inhumane dealings, uttered a hasty speech (that God would take vengeance on them, and desired that God would deliver us out of the hands of unmerciful men). Then her Mittimus was writ. I did with difficulty and charge obtain the liberty of a room, but no beds In It; if there had [been], [she] could have taken but little rest that night. She was committed to Boston prison; but I obtained a habeas corpus to remove her to Cambridge prison, which is in our County of Middlesex. Having been there one night, next morning the jailer put Irons on her legs (having received such command) the weight of them was about eight pounds; these irons and her other afflictions, soon brought her into convulsion fits, so that I thought she would have died that night. I sent to entreat that the irons might be taken off, but all entreaties were in vain, if it would have saved her life, so that in this condition she must continue. The trials at Salem coming on, I went thither, to see how things were there managed; and finding that the spectre evidence was there received, together with Idle if not malicious stories, against people's lives, I did easily perceive which way the rest would go; for the same evidence that served for one, would serve for all the rest. I acquainted her with her danger; and that if she were carried to Salem to be tried, I feared she would never return. I did my utmost that she might have her trial in our own county, I with several others petitioning the judge for it, and were put in hopes of it; but I soon saw so much, that I understood thereby it was not intended, which put me upon consulting the means of her escape; which through the goodness of God was effected, and she got to Rhode Island, but soon found herself not safe when there, by reason of the pursuit after her; from thence she went to New York, along with some others that had escaped their cruel hands; where we found his Excellency Benjamin Fletcher, Esqu., governor, who was very courteous to us. After this some of my goods were seized In a friend's hands, with whom I had left them, and myself Imprisoned by the sheriff, and kept in custody half a day, and then dismissed; but to speak of their usage of the prisoners, and their Inhumanity shown to them, at the time of their execution, no sober Christian could bear; they had also trials of cruel mockings; which is the more, considering what a people for religion, I mean the profession of it, we have been; those that suffered being many of them church members, and most of them unspotted In their conversation, till their adversary the devil took up this method for accusing them.

Source: Robert Calef, *More Wonders of the Invisible World* (London, 1700), as found in Frances Hill, ed., *The Salem Witch Trials Reader* (New York: Da Capo Press, 2000), pp. 68–71.

5

The Eighteenth-Century World

1700–1775

< **Library Company of Philadelphia**

AMERICAN PORTRAIT

Young Alexander Hamilton: One Immigrant's Story

In 1755, a woman named Rachel in the English Caribbean colony of Nevis gave birth to a child by a man who was not her husband. Her own father had been a French Huguenot doctor who had fled persecution in France and arrived in the Caribbean, and probably worked for slave dealers determining whether an ailing slave coming off the ships was likely to die. The doctor bought a small plantation with about seven slaves and married a local English woman, but they ended up separating. At his death, Rachel, then 16 years old, took her inheritance and her aging, impoverished mother and went to the town of Christiansted, in the Danish colony of St. Croix. There the girl was dazzled by a European gentleman, a Dane named Johann Lavien. They married immediately but got along so poorly that Lavien had his recalcitrant wife jailed. He thought it would teach her obedience, but instead he lost her entirely.

Once Rachel was released, she fled back to the English colony of Nevis. At age 21, she met James Hamilton, the fourth son of a Scottish lord. He was a ne'er-do-well whose family had sent him to the New World in hopes of improvement. He did not have the resources to marry a girl from an established family, and Rachel could not marry, so they set up household together, unbothered by the illegitimacy of their union. Both had benefited from the freedom afforded by the New World, where separate worlds existed in close proximity; but both had also suffered from the vulnerability that New World rootlessness bred. Not surrounded by extensive kin, they had no safety net to catch them when they made mistakes or had bad luck, and both experienced rapid downward social mobility as a result.

The couple named their first son James and their second Alexander. They had no money to send the boys to an elite school, but the island was home to many Sephardic Jews, some of whom ran informal schools in their homes. Alexander learned the English alphabet as well as the Decalogue in Hebrew. Eventually, money became so tight that the family returned to Christiansted, to be near Rachel's sister. Not long after, James Hamilton abandoned his family and Rachel opened a small grocery store to support herself. She and her sons lived in a room above the shop. In 1767, when she was 38 and Alexander was 12, they both contracted a fever; Rachel died. The boys' father did not reappear, so they went to live with a relative, but soon after, he also died. Thus, the colonial government put the boys into that era's version of foster care: their indentures were offered for sale. James was taken by a carpenter. Alexander had become good friends with a merchant's son, and his friend asked his father to take the clever boy on as a merchant's apprentice. Alexander went to work for the New York–based mercantile firm of Beekman and Cruger. He and his brother's life trajectories would thus be forever divergent.

As a merchant's apprentice, Alexander learned many things—about currencies, interest payments, and the need for insurance and stability. He also learned to hate slavery, for he was surrounded by its abuses without being cosseted by the wealth it generated. Most of all, he learned about migration and motion, about the possibility of going somewhere where the potential was richer. In his spare time, he wrote for the local paper. Without intending to, he wrote his ticket out of Nevis. After writing a particularly powerful piece about a hurricane that the town had experienced, his supporters took up a subscription to finance his education. Alexander was sent to New York to attend King's College (now Columbia University). In 1775, Alexander Hamilton packed his trunk and set off, hoping that the vagaries of life in the New World would be, for him, a blessing and not a curse.

The Population Explosion of the Eighteenth Century

As the colonies matured, they were tied in to the North Atlantic world and brought dramatic changes. One of the most important changes was the increase in population, from both immigration and natural increase. This population produced products for the world economy and provided a market for them as well, and its boom was both the product of American prosperity and the precondition for its further growth.

The Dimensions of Population Growth

The population in the American colonies grew at a rate unprecedented in human history, from just over 250,000 people in 1700 to more than 1 million by 1750. The rate of growth was highest in the free population in prosperous farming regions, but it was rapid everywhere, even among slaves.

Much of the colonies' population growth was caused by their unquenchable thirst for labor. They attracted an extraordinary number of immigrants, and when free labor did not meet the demand, unfree labor (slaves, indentured servants, and redemptioners) filled the gap. Increasingly, these immigrants reflected the broad reach of the North Atlantic political world. At the beginning of the eighteenth century, the population of the American colonies was primarily English in origin. By the beginning of the American Revolution, the population had changed significantly. There were small numbers of people with Finnish, Swedish, French, Swiss, and Jewish heritage, and large numbers of Welsh, Scotch-Irish, Germans, Dutch, and Africans. The foundation for American diversity had been laid.

Bound for America: European Immigrants

In the eighteenth century, about 425,000 Europeans migrated to the colonies, with large numbers from Scotland, Ireland, Wales, and Germany. The largest numbers of European immigrants were Scotch-Irish, that is, Scottish people who had moved to Northern Ireland to escape famine in their own country. As many as 250,000 came to seek a better life and to escape the religious persecution they experienced as Presbyterians in an Anglican society. At first, Massachusetts invited the Scotch-Irish to settle on its borders, as a buffer between the colony and the Indians. Once the impoverished Scotch-Irish began to arrive in large numbers, however, the English inhabitants worried that they would have to provide for them. In 1729, a Boston mob turned away a shipload of Scotch-Irish immigrants, and in 1738 the Puritans of Worcester burned down a Presbyterian church. Thereafter, the vast majority of Scotch-Irish immigrants headed for the more welcoming middle colonies and the South.

Going where land was the cheapest, the Scotch-Irish settled between the English sea-board settlements and the Indian communities to the west, from Pennsylvania to Georgia (see Map 5–1). As their numbers increased, the Scotch-Irish pressed against the Indians, seizing their lands. Like the Scotch-Irish, most German migrants settled in the backcountry from Pennsylvania to the Carolinas. Between 1700 and the start of the Revolution, more than 100,000 Germans arrived, and by 1775, a third of Pennsylvania's population was German.

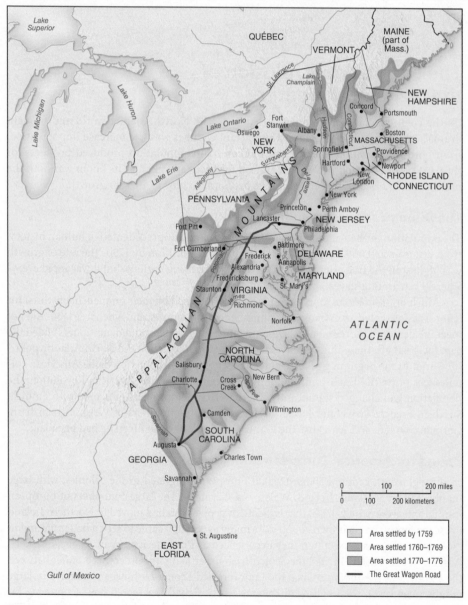

Map 5–1 Expansion of Settlement, 1720–1760 By 1760, the colonial population made up an almost continuous line of settlement from Maine to Florida and was pushing west over the Appalachian Mountains.

Including not only Lutherans and Catholics but also Quakers, Amish, and Mennonites, Germans established prosperous farming communities wherever they settled. Indeed, colonies such as Pennsylvania that welcomed the widest variety of immigrants became not only the most prosperous but also the ones in which prosperity was most widely shared. Unlike most seventeenth-century migrants, a large proportion of eighteenth-century migrants were artisans drawn to America by the demand for their labor. The majority of European migrants to the colonies were unfree—not only indentured servants and redemptioners but also the 50,000 British convicts whose sentences were commuted to a term of service in the colonies. Most English and Welsh migrants were single men between the ages of 19 and 23 who came as indentured servants. The Scotch-Irish migration included a larger number of families, and three-fourths of the Germans came in family groups. For all, the passage to America, which could take three months or more, was grueling and profoundly unhealthy. Once the migrants arrived, servants and convicts were sold for terms of service at auctions (see Figure 5–1).

Bound for America: African Slaves

The increase in the African population was even more dramatic than that of Europeans. In 1660, there were only 2,920 African or African-descended inhabitants of the mainland colonies. A century later there were more than 300,000. The proportion of Africans grew most rapidly in the southern colonies, to almost 40 percent on the eve of the Revolution.

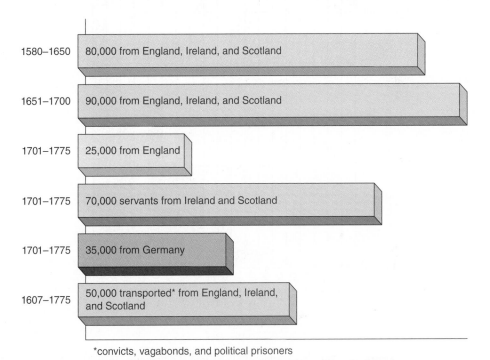

1580–1650 | 80,000 from England, Ireland, and Scotland

1651–1700 | 90,000 from England, Ireland, and Scotland

1701–1775 | 25,000 from England

1701–1775 | 70,000 servants from Ireland and Scotland

1701–1775 | 35,000 from Germany

1607–1775 | 50,000 transported* from England, Ireland, and Scotland

*convicts, vagabonds, and political prisoners

Figure 5-1   The Importation of Servants from Europe into British America, 1580–1775 By the time of the American Revolution, 350,000 servants had been imported into the colonies, most of whom came from the British Isles.
Source: Richard S. Dunn, "Servants and Slaves," in Jack P. Greene and J. R. Pole, *Colonial British America* (Baltimore: Johns Hopkins, 1984), p. 159.

By 1720, South Carolina had an African majority. Most of the increase in the African population came from the slave trade. By 1808, when Congress closed off the importation of slaves to the United States, about 523,000 African slaves had been imported into the nation (see Figure 5–2).

The African slave trade was a profitable and well-organized segment of the world economy. Until the eighteenth century, when demand from the New World increased, the transatlantic slave trade was controlled by Africans, in the sense that slaves were brought to the coast by other Africans for sale to Europeans. African nations had to participate in this activity because it was the only way they could purchase guns, and without guns, they were vulnerable to neighbors who had already bought them. Some nations supplied a steady stream of slaves, whereas others offered them intermittently, stopping when they had enough arms to defend themselves for a while. Most slaves were captives of war, and as the demand for slaves increased, the tempo of warfare in Africa intensified in response. The New World preferred male slaves, leaving most of the female captives to the African slave market, where they became domestic slaves or plural wives to wealthier Africans.

Because African slaves were unwilling and sometimes rebellious passengers on the ships that transported them across the Atlantic, European slave ships needed larger crews

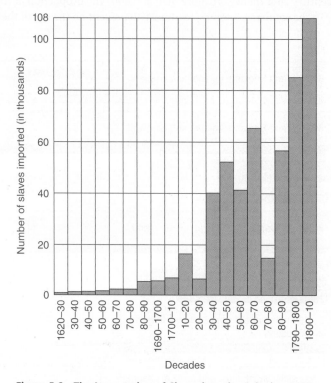

Figure 5-2 The Importation of Slaves into the Colonies, 1620–1810 The number of Africans imported into the colonies increased dramatically in the eighteenth century, and, except for an interruption during the American Revolution, continued until the African slave trade was made illegal in 1808.

Source: Helen Hornbeck Tanner, *The Settling of North America* (New York: Macmillan, 1995), p. 51.

Enslaved Africans Bound for the New World This group is being force-marched by an African slave trader from the interior of Africa to a European trading post on the coast.

and heavier weapons than usual. This resistance by slaves increased the cost of transporting them so much that the higher prices may have spared half a million Africans' enslavement.

As bad as the voyage to America was for indentured servants, the trip for enslaved Africans was worse. Perhaps 10 percent died before reaching the African coast. Many had never seen an ocean or a white man, and both sights terrified them. They were confined in pens or forts for as long as half a year while waiting for a ship.

The voyage, or "middle passage," proved lethal to many more. As the slave trade became more efficient in the eighteenth century, the mortality rate dropped, from perhaps 20 percent to half that amount. Those who survived were ready to begin their lives as New World slaves.

The Great Increase of Offspring

Most of the extraordinary increase in the colonies' population, European and African alike, came not from immigration or the slave trade but from natural increase.

For European Americans, population increase was mainly due to the lower age of marriage for women and the higher proportion of women who married. In England, for example, as many as 20 percent of women did not marry by age 45, compared with only 5 percent in the colonies. The age of marriage for women in the colonies was also considerably lower, with women marrying in their late teens or early 20s, compared to the late 20s in England. Because more women married, and married earlier, they bore more babies, on average seven or eight each, with six or seven surviving to adulthood. As a rule, the more economic opportunity, the earlier the age of marriage for women and men, and the more children. In the better climate, more children survived to adulthood, but child mortality rates were high. Thanks to rapid population growth, the American population was exceptionally young.

AMERICAN LANDSCAPE

The Slave Ship

We do not usually think of a ship as part of a landscape, but the slave ship was one of the most important places in the eighteenth century. It was at once a floating factory, prison, and fortress. It was there that Africans were transformed into slaves.

Any ship, small or large, could be made into a slave ship. Because the cost of transporting slaves across the Atlantic was so high, accounting for three-quarters of the price of a slave, slave merchants tried to crowd as many Africans as possible into each ship—300, 400, or even 600. The English were particularly efficient, carrying twice as many slaves as crew members and half again as many slaves per ship as the other nations, thereby increasing the profits.

To maximize the number of Africans on each ship, platforms were built between decks, thus doubling the surface area upon which the slaves could be placed. With perhaps only four and a half feet between the platform and the ceiling, the Africans could not stand up. They were packed so tightly that they could not move from side to side. Even the smallest spaces were filled with children.

Packing so many human beings into such tight quarters created the risk of suffocation. But if the hatches were kept open, the Africans might escape confinement and overpower the crew. Hence, grates were placed over the hatches, and small air openings were cut into the sides of the ship. Later, some ships used large funnel tubes to carry air below decks.

Men and women were kept separate, divided by partitions. Male slaves were shackled and confined below deck for most of each day. Chained together and without enough room to stand up, many were unable to reach the large buckets that served as latrines. Some captains let the slaves lie in their own filth until the voyage's end. Heat and disease compounded the misery. One ship's doctor reported that the slaves' deck "was so covered with the

In certain regards, the African American population resembled the European American population. Slaves born in the colonies married young and established families as stable as slavery permitted. By the time they were 18, most slave women had had their first child. They might not form a lasting union with the father, but within a few years many settled into long-lasting relationships with the men who would father the rest of their children. Slave women bore between six and eight children, on average. With child mortality even higher for African Americans than for European Americans, between 25 and 50 percent of slave children died before reaching adulthood. Even so, the slave population more than reproduced itself, and by the middle of the eighteenth century it was growing more from natural increase than from the importation of slaves. Only a tiny fraction of the Africans sold into slavery in the Americas ended up in mainland British colonies. Nonetheless, when slavery was abolished after the Civil War, the United States had the largest population of African descent in the New World.

blood and mucus which had proceeded from them in consequence of the flux, that it resembled a slaughterhouse." The women were left unshackled but were often prey to the sailors' lust. When slaves were brought above deck, some would jump overboard. Captains stretched netting around their ships to prevent such suicides.

To protect the crew in case of insurrection, slave ships often had thick, 10-foot-high walls—barricados—to separate the crew from the human cargo. Armed sailors patrolled atop the barricado. Ship captains gathered their human cargo from different regions, each with its own language, to make sure that the captives could not communicate with each other and foment rebellion. At the same time, the captains had to be careful not to bring together groups who might fight each other. With resistance from the enslaved the norm, ship captains used terror to maintain order. Flogging—a punishment for sailors as well—was common. Some captains used instruments of torture, such as the thumbscrew, "a dreadful engine, which, if the screw be turned by an unrelenting hand, can give intolerable anguish." The object was not only to punish the disobedient but also to frighten their shipmates. That was surely the result after some of the Africans aboard the *Brownlow* rebelled. The captain dismembered the rebels with an axe "till their bodies remained only like a trunk of a tree when all the branches are lopped away," and he threw the severed heads and limbs at the other slaves, chained together on the deck.

Such terror hardened captain and crew. Few sailors signed on to a slave ship if they had better options, and one captain described his crew as the "very dregs of the community." The life of a sailor was hard enough; service on a slave ship—a floating prison—was even harder. Yet even the lowest sailor was superior to the enslaved. Even though many sailors were dark-skinned men from Asia, the Caribbean, or India, at sea, they were all known as "white people." Over time, both captain and crew became practiced in the ways of cruelty. Silas Todd was apprenticed to a slave ship captain at the age of 14 and hoped to become a captain himself. Then, ashore in Boston in 1734, he was "saved" in the Great Awakening. Had he not been, he later reflected, he might have become "as eminent a savage" as the captains under whom he had served.

The Transatlantic Economy: Producing and Consuming

In the eighteenth century, as the colonies matured, they became capitalist societies in an Atlantic trade network. More and more, people produced for the market, so that they could buy the goods the market had to offer. Throughout the Atlantic world, ordinary people reshaped their lives so they could buy more goods. Historians talk about two economic revolutions in this period: a consumer revolution—a steady increase in the demand for and purchase of consumer goods—and an industrious revolution (not *industrial* but *industrious* revolution), in which people worked harder and organized their households (their families, servants, and slaves) to produce goods for sale so that they would have money to pay for items they wanted. Income went up only slightly in the eighteenth century, yet people were buying more. In the process, they created a consumer society, in which most people eagerly purchased consumer goods.

The Nature of Colonial Economic Growth

Throughout human history, population growth has usually led to a decline in the standard of living as more people compete for a finite supply of resources. In the American colonies, however, population growth led to an expansion of the economy, as more of the continent's abundant natural resources were brought under human control. The standard of living for most free Americans probably improved, although not dramatically. As the economy matured, a small segment—urban merchants and owners of large plantations—became wealthy. At the same time, the urban poor and tenant farmers began to slip toward poverty.

All of these changes took place, however, without any significant changes in technology (such as the power looms that would be invented later in the century). Most wealth was made from shipping and agriculture. Eighty percent of the colonies' population worked on farms or plantations, areas with no major technological innovations. Virtually all gains in productivity came instead from labor: more people were working, and they were working more efficiently.

The economy of colonial America was shaped by three factors: abundance of land and shortages of labor and of capital. The plantation regions of the South and the West Indies were best situated to take advantage of these circumstances, and the small-farm areas of New England were the least suitable. Tobacco planters in the Chesapeake and rice and indigo planters in South Carolina sold their products on a huge world market. Their large profits enabled them to purchase more land and more slaves to work it.

Because northern farmers raised crops and animals that were also produced in Europe, profits from agriculture alone were too low to permit them to acquire large tracts of land or additional labor (see Table 5–1). Northerners had to look to other opportunities for wealth. They found them in trade, exchanging their raw goods for European manufactured ones and selling them to American consumers.

The Transformation of the Family Economy

In colonial America, the family was the basic economic unit, and all family members contributed to it. Work was organized by gender. On farms, women were responsible for the preparation of food and clothing, child care, and care of the home. Women grew vegetables and herbs, provided dairy products, and transformed flax and wool into clothing. Daughters worked under their mothers' supervision, perhaps spinning extra yarn to be sold for a profit.

Men worked the rest of the farm. They raised grain and maintained the pastures. They cleared the land, chopped wood for fuel, and built and maintained the house, barn, and other structures. They took crops to market. Men's and women's work were complementary and necessary for survival. For example, men planted apple trees, children picked apples, and women pressed the apples into cider. When a husband was disabled, ill, or away from home, his wife could perform virtually all of his tasks as a sort of "deputy husband." Men almost never performed women's work, however, and men whose wives died remarried quickly to have someone to care for the household and children.

The eighteenth century's industrious revolution transformed the family economy: when people decided to produce goods to sell, they changed their family economies. Historians

Table 5-1 How Wealthy Were Colonial Americans?

Property-Owning Class	New England	Mid-Atlantic Colonies	Southern Colonies	Thirteen Colonies
Men	169	194	410	260
Women	42	103	215	132
Adults 45 and older	252	274	595	361
Adults 44 and younger	129	185	399	237
Urban	191	287	641	233
Rural	151	173	392	255
Esquires, gentlemen	313	1,223	1,281	572
Merchants	563	858	314	497
Professions, sea captains	271	241	512	341
Farmers only, planters	155	180	396	263
Farmer-artisans, ship owners, fishermen	144	257	801	410
Shop and tavern keepers	219	222	195	204
Artisans, chandlers	114	144	138	122
Miners, laborers	52	67	383	62

Source: Alice Hanson Jones, *Wealth of a Nation to Be: The American Colonies on the Eve of the Revolution* (New York: Columbia University Press, 1980), p. 224.

Note: Numbers given are in pounds sterling.

believe that increased production in this period came primarily from the labor of women and children, who worked harder and longer than they had before.

Sources of Regional Prosperity

The South, the most productive region, accounted for more than 60 percent of colonial exports (see Map 5–2). Tobacco was its chief cash crop. Next came cereals such as rice, wheat, corn, and flour, and then indigo, a plant used to dye fabric.

Slave labor accounted for most of the southern agricultural output and was organized to produce for the market. When tobacco profits began to slip because of falling prices and the depletion of the soil, planters worked their slaves harder and, in the Chesapeake, began to plant corn and wheat. By diversifying their crops, planters were able to make maximum use of their slave labor force by keeping slaves busy throughout the year.

The work routine of slaves depended on the crops they tended. On tobacco plantations, where careful attention to the plants was necessary to ensure high quality, planters or white overseers worked the slaves in small gangs carefully selected and arranged to maximize productivity.

In the rice-growing lower South, however, the enslaved were usually assigned specific tasks, which they would work at until the job was completed. Rice growing required far less supervision than did tobacco planting. Because many Africans had grown rice in

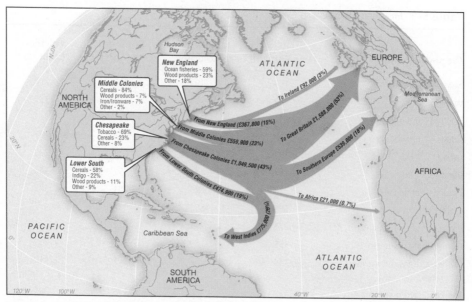

Map 5-2 Exports of the Thirteen Colonies, ca. 1770 Almost two-thirds of the exports from the colonies came from the South, and more than one-half went to Great Britain alone. Tobacco and grains were the most important exports of all.

Source: Jacob Cooke, ed., *Encyclopedia of North American Colonies* (New York: Scribner's, 1993), pp. 1, 514.

Africa and had likely taught Europeans how to grow it in America, rice planters let the slaves set their own pace. Once finished for the day, the enslaved people could use their time as they pleased. Many planted gardens to supplement their own diets or to earn a small income. Slaves trafficked in a wide range of products, from rice, corn, chickens, hogs, and catfish to canoes, baskets, and wax.

The inhabitants of the middle colonies grew prosperous by raising and selling wheat and other grains. The ports of Baltimore, Philadelphia, Wilmington, and New York became thriving commercial centers that collected grain from regional farms, milled it into flour, and shipped it to the West Indies, southern Europe, and other American colonies. Farmers relied on indentured servants, cottagers, and slaves to supplement the labor of family members. Cottagers were families who rented out part of a farmer's land, which they worked for wages.

As long as land was cheap and accessible, the middle colonies enjoyed the most evenly shared prosperity on the continent. Most inhabitants fell into the comfortable middle class, with the gap between the richest and the poorest relatively small. Pennsylvania, which offered both religious toleration and relatively simple ways to purchase land, was particularly prosperous. The energy that elsewhere went into religious conflict here fueled work and material accumulation. Gottlieb Mittelberger, who endured a horrendous journey to Pennsylvania, described his new home as a sort of paradise: "Our Americans live more quietly and peacefully than the Europeans; and all this is the result of the liberty which they enjoy and which makes them all equal."

When land became expensive or difficult to obtain, however, conflict might ensue. In the 1740s and 1750s, both New Jersey and New York experienced land riots when conflicting claims made land titles uncertain. In the Chesapeake and southeastern Pennsylvania, increasing land prices drove the poor into tenancy or to the urban centers. Widespread prosperity led Americans to expect that everyone who wished to would be able to own a farm. When land ownership was not fully possible, tension and anger grew.

New England was also primarily a farming region. Here, however, male family members, rather than indentured servants, cottagers, or slaves, provided most farm labor. Although farms in some regions, such as the Connecticut River valley, produced surpluses for the market, most farm families had to look for other sources of income to pay for consumer goods.

Town governments in New England encouraged enterprise, sometimes providing gristmills, sawmills, and fields on which cattle could graze. The region prospered, and New Englanders came to expect their governments to enhance the economy. Agricultural exports were relatively slight, although both grain and livestock were sold to the slave plantations of the West Indies, which received more than 25 percent of the American colonies' exports (and more than 70 percent of New England's).

The other major colonial exports in the eighteenth century were fur and hides. By the eve of the Revolution, 95 percent of the furs imported into England came from North America—most of them provided by Indians, who traded them to European middlemen.

Merchants and Dependent Laborers in the Transatlantic Economy

Almost all colonies participated in a transatlantic economy. In each region, those most involved in the market were those with the most resources: large planters in the southern colonies, owners of the biggest farms in the middle colonies, and urban merchants in the northern colonies. The wealthiest never made their fortunes from farming or planting alone but always added income from activities such as speculating in land, practicing law, or lending money.

If some economic development was spurred from above, by enterprising individuals or by governments, much was also created by ambitious ordinary men and women. New England's mixed economy of grain, grazing, fishing, and lumbering required substantial capital improvements such as gristmills, sawmills, and tanneries to be profitable. By the beginning of the eighteenth century, shipbuilding was a major activity, and by 1775, one-third of the English merchant fleet had been built in the colonies.

The shipbuilding industry, in turn, spurred further economic development, such as lumbering, sail making, and rope making. Linked economic development occurs when an enterprise is tied to a variety of other local businesses. Furthermore, the profits generated by shipbuilding and trade were reinvested in sawmills to produce more lumber, in gristmills to grind grain into flour, and, of course, in more trading voyages. The growth of shipping in port cities such as Boston, Newport, New York, Philadelphia, and Charleston created an affluent merchant class, but trading was a risky business, and few who tried it rose to the top. One ship lost to a storm could ruin a merchant, as could a sudden turn in the market. Insurance companies were born as a result.

The seafaring trades led capitalist development. A wealthy, risk-taking merchant class emerged, as well as another distinguishing mark of a capitalist economy, a wage-earning class. As long as there was a labor shortage in the colonies, workers had an advantage. By the beginning of the eighteenth century, however, rapid population increase led to

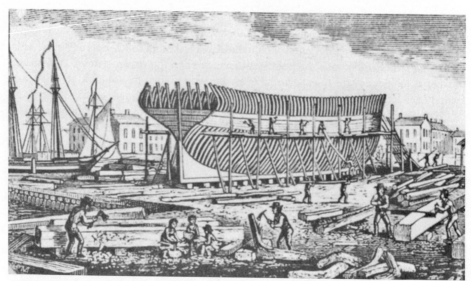

A Ship Being Built in New York Carpenters put together a ship for the growing trade out of colonial port cities.

a growing supply of labor. Although they were free to shop around for the best wages, workers became part of a wage-earning class, dependent on others for employment and income. Only a small portion of Americans were wage earners on the eve of the Revolution, but they were a sign of things to come.

Consumer Choices and the Creation of Gentility

Under the British mercantilist system (see Chapter 4), the colonies were supposed to export raw materials to the empire and import finished products back, sending West Indian sugar, tobacco, wheat, lumber, fish, and animal pelts to Britain in exchange for cloth and iron. Yet within this general pattern, individual men and women made choices about what to buy.

On both sides of the Atlantic, demand for plantation products and consumer goods was insatiable. At first only the wealthy could afford such luxuries as sugar and tobacco. But as more and more labor was organized to produce for the market, ordinary people had the added income needed to purchase luxury products. Tea, imported into both Britain and the colonies from Asia, became, like tobacco and sugar, a mass-consumed luxury. By the time of the Revolution, annual sugar consumption in England had skyrocketed to 23 pounds per person, and tobacco consumption was about 2 pounds per person. Demand for these plantation products led directly to the traffic in African slaves.

As plantation products flowed to England, so manufactured goods came back to the colonies. Consumer behavior on both sides of the Atlantic was similar: people smoked tobacco; sweetened their tea with sugar; and bought more clothing, household items, books, and every sort of manufactured goods.

This consumer revolution was not due to higher wages. Instead, people chose to work harder and chose work that brought in money. They decided what they would do with that money—they chose to buy particular items. Increasingly, people bought items that their friends and neighbors could see and that they could use in entertaining them. In seventeenth-century America, extra income was spent on items of lasting value, such as tablecloths and bed linens kept folded away in a chest, to pass on to one's children. In the eighteenth century, men and women bought more clothing made out of cheaper, less durable fabrics. Until this time, most people had only a few outfits. The wealthy, of course, always had large wardrobes made from fine fabrics. In the eighteenth century, however, fabric prices fell, and clothing made from cheaper fabrics satisfied growing consumer demand. Then people needed new pieces of furniture in which to store their new garments. Chests of drawers, or dressers, first available to the wealthy in the 1630s and 1640s, had, by 1760, become a standard item for the middle class.

People became increasingly interested in how they appeared to others. Ordinary people began to pay attention to the latest fashions, once a concern only of the wealthy. By 1700, two new items made it easier for those with the time and money to attend to their appearance: the dressing table and the full-length mirror. For the first time, people could see how they looked, head to toe. Washing oneself and styling one's hair or periwig became standard rituals for all who hoped to appear "genteel."

In the eighteenth century, the prosperous on both sides of the Atlantic created and tried to follow the standards of a new style of life, gentility. Gentility represented all that was polite, civilized, refined, and fashionable. It was everything that vulgarity, its opposite, was not. Gentility meant not only certain sorts of objects, such as a dressing table or a bone china teapot, but also the manners needed to use such objects properly. Standards of gentility established boundaries between the genteel and the vulgar. Those who considered themselves genteel looked down on those whose style of living seemed unrefined and became uncomfortable when required to associate with social inferiors.

Yet if the public display of gentility erected a barrier between people, it also showed the vulgar how to become genteel. All they needed to do was to acquire the right goods and learn how to use them. Throughout the colonies, ordinary people began to purchase goods that established their gentility. Even relatively poor people often owned a mirror, a few pieces of china, or a teapot. The slaves executed in New York City in 1741 (discussed subsequently) were probably conspiring not to burn the city down but to steal clothing and other fancy goods they could resell to poor people in the underground economy. This mass consumption and widespread distribution of consumer goods created and sustained the consumer revolution.

The consumer revolution had another egalitarian effect: it encouraged sociability. Throughout the Atlantic world, men and women, particularly those with a little leisure and money (perhaps half the white population), began to cultivate social life. Many believed that the purpose of life was the sort of society they created during an evening shared with friends and family in their parlors.

To put all of their guests on an equal footing, people began to purchase matching sets of dinner plates, silverware, glasses, and chairs. Until the eighteenth century, the most important people at the table—the man of the house, his wife, and high-ranking men—got the best chairs. Children, servants, and those of lower social standing sat on stools, benches, or boxes, or they stood. Dishes, utensils, and mugs rarely matched. Matched sets of tableware and chairs underscored the symbolic equality of all guests.

The New Gentility In 1750, in Charleston, South Carolina, Mr. Peter Manigault and his friends toasted each other, demonstrating their civility and their knowledge of the rules of polite behavior, including how to drink punch from a stem glass.

The newest and most popular consumer goods made their way quickly to America—forks, drinking glasses, and teapots, each with its own etiquette. Such rules were daunting for the uneducated, but once they were mastered, a person could enter polite society anywhere in the Atlantic world and be accepted. The eighteenth-century capitalist economy created a trade not only in goods and raw materials but in styles of life as well.

Historians debate the effects of the consumer revolution, but on balance it was a democratic force. Ordinary men and women and even slaves came to think it was their right to spend their money as they pleased. As one Bostonian put it in 1754, the poor should be allowed to buy "the Conveniencies, and Comforts, as well as Necessaries of Life . . . as freely as the Rich." After all, "I am sure we Work as hard as they do . . .; therefore, I cannot see why we have not as good a natural Right to them as they have."

The Varieties of Colonial Experience

Although the eighteenth-century industrious and consumer revolutions tied the peoples of the North Atlantic world together, climate, geography, immigration, patterns of economic development, and population density made for considerable variety. Although the vast majority of Americans lived in small communities or on farms, an increasing number lived in cities that played a critical role in shaping colonial life. At the same time, farming regions were maturing, changing the character of rural life, and the growing population continued to push at the frontiers, leading to the founding of Georgia, the last of the thirteen colonies.

Creating an Urban Public Sphere

At the end of the seventeenth century, Boston, with 7,000 people, was the only town that was much more than a rural village. By 1720, Boston's population had grown to 12,000, Philadelphia had 10,000 inhabitants, New York had 7,000, and Newport and Charleston almost 4,000 each. Forty years later, other urban centers had sprung up, each with populations around 3,000—Salem, Marblehead, and Newburyport in Massachusetts; Portsmouth, New Hampshire; Providence, Rhode Island; New Haven and Hartford, Connecticut; Albany, New York; Lancaster, Pennsylvania; Baltimore, Maryland; Norfolk, Virginia; and Savannah, Georgia. By the eve of the Revolution, Philadelphia had 30,000 residents, New York had 25,000, and Boston had 16,000 (see Map 5–3). All of these cities were either ports or centers for the fur trade. Colonial cities were centers of commerce; that was their reason for being.

Social life in colonial cities was characterized by two somewhat contradictory trends. On the one hand, nowhere in the colonies was social stratification among free people more pronounced. By the eve of the American Revolution, each city had an affluent elite, made up of merchants, professionals, and government officials, and each city also had a class of indigent poor. On the other hand, cities brought all classes of society together at theaters, in taverns, and at religious revivals. This civic life became one of the seedbeds of the Revolution because it provided a forum for the exchange of ideas.

Affluent city dwellers created a life as much like that of London as they could. They imported European finery and established English-style institutions, founding social clubs, dancing assemblies, and fishing and hunting clubs. Although many of these associations were for men only, some brought men and women together. Such organizations helped the elite function as a class.

Urban associations reflected the ideals of the Enlightenment (see "The Ideas of the Enlightenment," later in this chapter). Some, such as the Masons, a European fraternal order with branches in all the major colonial cities, espoused the ideal of universalism, that all people were by their nature fundamentally the same. Other institutions advocated self-improvement. Whereas some urban institutions separated out the elite and others challenged the ruling hierarchy, still others brought together all members of society in a "public sphere." City dwellers could see stage plays in Williamsburg by 1716, in Charleston and New York by the 1730s, and in Philadelphia and Boston by the 1740s. Taverns brought all ranks even closer. By 1737, Boston had 177 taverns, one for every 99 inhabitants. (Between 30 percent and 40 percent were owned by women, usually widows.) Taverns became true public institutions in which people could meet and discuss the issues of the day.

Newspapers also played a critical role in creating a public sphere and extending it beyond the cities. The first newspaper was the *Boston News-Letter*, which appeared in 1704. By the time of the Revolution, 39 newspapers were being published, and the chief town in each colony except Delaware had at least one newspaper.

Strict libel laws prohibited the printing of opinions critical of public officials, or even the truth if it cast them in a bad light. John Peter Zenger, editor of the *New-York Weekly Journal*, was tried in 1735 for criticizing the governor. Zenger's flamboyant attorney, Andrew Hamilton, persuaded the jury that they should rule not simply on the facts of the case (Zenger had criticized

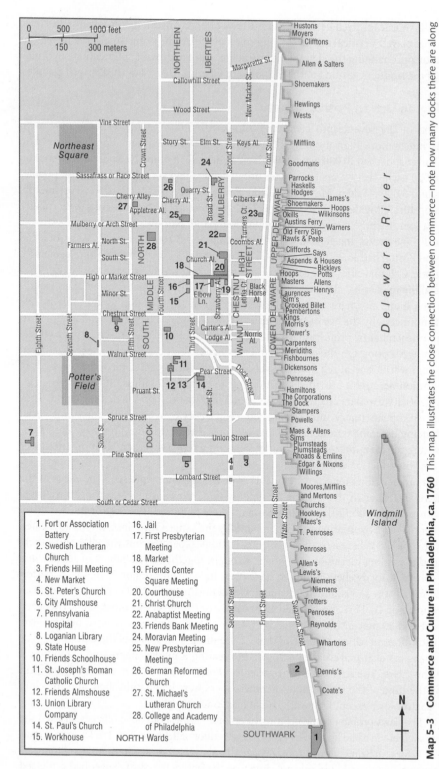

Map 5-3 Commerce and Culture in Philadelphia, ca. 1760 This map illustrates the close connection between commerce—note how many docks there are along the Delaware River—and culture. By 1760, Philadelphia was home to churches of many different denominations, as well as an array of enlightened institutions—a hospital, a college, and two libraries.

Source: Lester Cappon, ed., *The Atlas of Early American History* (Princeton, NJ: Princeton University Press, 1976), p. 10.

Key to map:

1. Fort or Association Battery
2. Swedish Lutheran Church
3. Friends Hill Meeting
4. New Market
5. St. Peter's Church
6. City Almshouse
7. Pennsylvania Hospital
8. Loganian Library
9. State House
10. Friends Schoolhouse
11. St. Joseph's Roman Catholic Church
12. Friends Almshouse
13. Union Library Company
14. St. Paul's Church
15. Workhouse
16. Jail
17. First Presbyterian Meeting
18. Market
19. Friends Center Square Meeting
20. Courthouse
21. Christ Church
22. Anabaptist Meeting
23. Friends Bank Meeting
24. Moravian Meeting
25. New Presbyterian Meeting
26. German Reformed Church
27. St. Michael's Lutheran Church
28. College and Academy of Philadelphia

NORTH Wards

the governor) but on whether the law itself was just. When the jury ruled in Zenger's favor, cheers went up in the courtroom. Although it would be many years before freedom of the press would be guaranteed by law, the Zenger case was a milestone in the developing relationship between the public and government officials. The verdict expressed the belief that in the contest between the two, the press spoke for the people, and hence it was the people themselves, not government, that would hold the press accountable.

City dwellers came to think of themselves as a "public" that had certain rights or liberties, such as making their views known and enjoying a fair price for their goods. At times, working people, acting as a public, and sometimes with support from the elite, used mob action to assert their political views. Mobs in both New York and Boston reacted violently to press gangs that scoured the waterfront for additional hands for the Royal Navy. By the time of the Revolution, city dwellers had a long history of asserting their rights in public.

The Diversity of Urban Life

Periodic downturns in the urban economy, especially after the middle of the century, led to increased activism by workers and the urban poor. Colonial politics had been premised on the deference of the less powerful to their social and economic "betters," but by the middle of the eighteenth century, the increasing wealth of those at the top and the appearance of a small class of permanently poor at the bottom of the economic hierarchy began to undermine the assumption of a common interest and that the wealthy and well educated could be trusted to govern for the benefit of everyone.

Although by today's standards the colonial population, even in the cities, was remarkably equal economically, in the eighteenth century it became more stratified. At the beginning of the eighteenth century, none of the cities had a substantial number of poor people. In New York, in 1700, there were only 35 paupers, almost all of whom were aged or disabled. Over the course of the century, however, colonial wars sent men home disabled and left many women widowed and children orphaned. Each city responded to the growth in poverty by building almshouses for the poor who could not support themselves and workhouses for those, including women and children, who could. In Philadelphia and New York about 25 percent of the population was at or below the poverty level, and in Boston perhaps as much as 40 percent of the population was living at or near subsistence. Many colonists feared that colonial cities were coming to resemble London, with its mass of impoverished and desperate poor.

All the major cities had slaves, and in some cities the black population was considerable. By 1746, 30 percent of New York City's working class consisted of enslaved people. After a serious slave revolt in 1712 and a rumored revolt in 1741, the white population responded with harsh punishments (but without halting the slave trade). In the wake of the 1712 revolt, which had left 9 white men dead, city officials executed 18 convicted rebels, burned 3 at the stake, let 1 starve to death in chains, and broke 1 on the wheel, a medieval instrument of torture. Six more committed suicide. The response to a rumored slave insurrection in 1741 resembled Salem's witchcraft trials: 18 slaves and 4 whites were hanged, and 13 slaves were burned at the stake.

New York enacted a stringent slave code after the 1712 revolt, and Boston and Pennsylvania imposed significant import duties on slaves. Nonetheless, the importation of slaves continued into all the port cities, where they were in demand as house servants and artisans. Almost all of Boston's elite owned at least one slave, as did many members of the middle class. Wealthy white artisans often purchased slaves instead of enlisting free whites as apprentices.

In Charleston, where more than half the population was enslaved, many masters let their slaves hire themselves out in return for a portion of their earnings. Such slaves set their own hours, chose their own recreational and religious activities, and participated in the consumer economy by selling their products and making purchases with the profits. Some whites complained about the fancy dresses of the black women at biracial dances attended by "many of the first gentlemen" of Charleston. Interracial sex in Charleston seems to have been common. Although white city dwellers were troubled by what they called the "impudence" of urban slaves, urban slavery flourished.

The Maturing of Rural Society

Population increases had a different impact in rural areas than in cities. During the eighteenth century, some long-settled regions became relatively overcrowded. Land that once seemed abundant had been carelessly farmed and had lost some of its fertility. This relative overcrowding, which historians call land pressure, led to a number of changes in colonial society, felt most acutely in New England. Population density increased, and with no additional farmland available, migration from farms to newly settled areas and cities increased. Both the concentration of wealth and social differentiation intensified, dividing the farm community into rich and poor.

Such broad economic changes had a direct impact on individual men and women. Families with numerous children were hard pressed if the original plot of land could not be divided into homesteads large enough for each son. (Daughters were given movable property such as farm animals, household equipment, and slaves.) Some sons migrated to cities, looking for employment. Others worked on other men's farms for wages or, in the South in particular, became tenant farmers. Daughters became servants in other women's households. In such older regions, the average age of marriage crept upward.

As young men and women in long-settled regions had to defer marriage, increasing numbers had sexual relations before marriage. In some towns, by the middle of the eighteenth century, between 30 percent and 50 percent of brides bore their first child within eight months of their wedding day. The growing belief that marriage should be based primarily on love probably encouraged some couples to become intimate before they married, especially if poverty required them to postpone marriage. Young women who engaged in sexual relations before marriage took a huge risk, however. If their lovers declined to marry them, they would be disgraced, and their futures would be bleak.

The World That Slavery Made

The rural economy of the South depended on slave labor. Whites and their black slaves formed two distinctive cultures, one in the black-majority lower South and the other in the Chesapeake region. In both regions, the most affluent slave masters sold their crops on the international market and used the profits to buy elegant furniture and the latest London fashions.

Chesapeake planters modeled themselves after English country gentlemen, whereas low-country planters imitated the elite of London. Chesapeake planters designed their plantations to be self-sufficient villages, like English country estates. Because slaves produced most of the goods and services the plantation needed, planters such as William Byrd II imagined themselves living "in a kind of independence on everyone but Providence." But unlike English country gentlemen, southern slave owners were wholly dependent on both slave labor and the vagaries of the market for their fortunes. South Carolina planters used their wealth to build elegant homes in Charleston and other coastal cities, where they spent much time and established a flourishing urban culture. By the eve of the Revolution, the area around Charleston was the most affluent in the mainland colonies. In spite of their affluence, the southern planter elite never achieved the secure political power enjoyed by their English counterparts. In England the social elite dominated the government: not only the hereditary positions but also the appointive and elective ones. With noble rank inherited and voting rights limited to male property owners, the English government was remarkably stable. The colonial elite, however (in the North as well as the South), were cut off from the top levels of political power, which remained in England. The colonists were at the mercy of whichever officials the Crown happened to appoint.

Unable to count on support from above, the colonial elite needed to guarantee the loyalty of those below them. In Virginia, the elite acted as middlemen for lesser planters, advancing them credit and marketing their tobacco. In general, they wielded their authority with a light hand, and punishments for crimes committed by whites were light.

Although members of the Virginia gentry tried to distance themselves from their slaves, whom they considered "vulgar," some whites crossed the color line in a dramatic way, despite eighteenth-century racial views. Sexual relations between whites and blacks were common. Several prominent Virginians acknowledged and supported their mixed-race children. Some interracial relationships were affectionate; most were coerced. All the resulting offspring were in a vulnerable position; like all slaves, they were dependent on the will of whites.

In the low country, the absenteeism of the planters combined with the task system to give plantation slaves an unusual degree of autonomy. As a majority, slaves in the low country were better able to retain their own religions, languages, and customs than were those in the Chesapeake. For example, the Gullah language, still spoken today on the Sea Islands off the coast of South Carolina and Georgia, combined English, Spanish, Portuguese, and African languages.

The mainland colonies' bloodiest slave revolt, the Stono Rebellion, took place in 1739 in South Carolina. The uprising was led by about 20 slaves born in Kongo (present-day Angola). The rebels were probably Catholics, for the king of Kongo, converted by the Portuguese, made Catholicism his nation's religion. Early in the morning of September 9, the rebels broke into a store near the Stono Bridge, taking weapons and ammunition and killing the storekeepers. The rebels moved south toward St. Augustine, killing whites and gathering blacks into their fold. Although the main body of the rebels was dispersed that evening and many were executed on the spot, skirmishes took place for another week, and the last of the ringleaders was not captured for three years.

The authorities reacted with predictable severity, putting dozens of slave rebels "to the most cruel Death" and revoking many liberties the slaves had enjoyed. A prohibitive duty was placed on the importation of slaves, and the immigration of white Europeans was encouraged. Although slave imports dropped significantly in the 1740s, by 1750 they rose to pre-Stono levels.

Georgia: From Frontier Outpost to Plantation Society

Nowhere was the white determination to create and maintain a slave society stronger than in the colony of Georgia. It is sometimes said that the introduction of slavery in North America was an unthinking decision, that the colonies became slave societies slowly, as individual planters purchased Africans already enslaved, and without society as a whole ever committing itself to slavery. Although there is some truth to this analysis, it is not accurate for Georgia, where the introduction of slavery was a purposeful decision.

The establishment of the English colony at South Carolina had, of course, made the Spanish nervous because of its proximity to their settlement at St. Augustine, Florida. With the French founding of New Orleans (1718) and Fort Toulouse (1717), Carolinians felt increasingly threatened. They were therefore eager for the English to establish a colony to the south, which would both serve as a buffer between Florida and South Carolina and, if extended far enough west, cut the French colonial empire in two.

The British Crown issued a 21-year charter to a group of trustees led by James Oglethorpe, who had achieved prominence by bringing about reforms in England's debtors' prisons. The colony, Georgia, was designed as a combination philanthropic venture and military-commercial outpost. Its colonists, who were to be drawn from Britain's "deserving poor," were supposed to protect South Carolina's borders and to make the new colony a sort of Italy on the Atlantic, producing wine, olives, and silk.

Unfortunately, Oglethorpe's humanitarianism was not matched by an understanding of the world economy. Because it was well known that excessive indulgence in alcohol was undermining the cohesion of many Indian tribes, Oglethorpe had banned liquor from the colony. However, without a product to sell, the colony could not prosper. South Carolina's wharves, merchants, and willingness to sell rum enabled it to dominate the trade with local Indians. Oglethorpe had also banned slavery for humanitarian reasons (making it the only colony expressly to prohibit slavery). As a result, Georgia farmers looked enviously across the Savannah River at South Carolinians growing rich off slave labor. The settlers were also angry that, contrary to colonial practice, women were not allowed to inherit property and that Georgia's trustees had made no provision for self-government. Georgia, despite its founders' noble intentions, lacked everything that the thriving colonies enjoyed: a cash crop or product, large plots of land, slaves to work the land, and laws of its own devising.

Never able to realize their dream of a colony of small and contented farmers, the trustees surrendered Georgia back to the Crown in 1752. With Oglethorpe's laws repealed and slavery introduced, the colony soon resembled the plantation society of South Carolina. Savannah became a little Charleston, with its robust civic and cultural life and its slave markets.

The Head and the Heart in America: The Enlightenment and Religious Awakening

American life in the eighteenth century was shaped by two movements, the Enlightenment and a series of religious revivals known as the Great Awakening. In many ways, these movements were separate, even opposite, appealing to different groups of people. The Enlightenment was a transatlantic intellectual movement that held that the universe could be understood and improved by the human mind. The Great Awakening was a transatlantic religious movement that held that all people were born sinners, that all could feel their own depravity without the assistance of ministers, and that all were equal in the eyes of God. Although the movements might seem fundamentally opposite, with one emphasizing the power of the human mind and the other disparaging it, both criticized established authority and valued the experience of the individual. Both contributed to the humanitarianism that emerged at the end of the century.

The Ideas of the Enlightenment

The roots of the Enlightenment can be traced to the Renaissance and its spirit of inquiry and faith in science that led explorers like Columbus halfway around the globe. Men and women of the Enlightenment, on both sides of the Atlantic, contrasted the ignorance, oppression, and suffering of the Middle or "Dark" Ages, as they called them, and their own enlightened time. Thomas Jefferson described the earlier period as "the times of Vandalism, when ignorance put everything in the hands of power and priestcraft." Enlightened thinkers believed fervently in the power of rational thinking and scoffed at superstition.

People of the Enlightenment believed that God and his world were knowable. Rejecting revelation as a guide, the Enlightenment looked instead to reason. Jefferson's "trinity of the three greatest men the world had ever produced" included not Jesus Christ but Isaac Newton, the scientist responsible for modern mathematics and physics; Francis Bacon, the philosopher who outlined the scientific method; and John Locke, the political philosopher of democracy. The Enlightenment was interested in knowledge not for its own sake but for the improvements it could make in human happiness.

Enlightenment thinkers were more interested in what all people had in common than in what differentiated them. No passage in the Bible was more important to them than Genesis 1:27: "So God created man in his own image." It was the basis not only for overcoming Calvinism's belief in humanity's innate depravity but also for asserting the principle of human equality. The Enlightenment encouraged a broad toleration of religion. Benjamin Franklin said that "if the Mufti of Constantinople were to send a missionary to preach Mahometanism to us, he would find a pulpit at his service."

Humanity's duties were clear and simple. Chief among them, according to Benjamin Franklin, was "doing good to [God's] other children." In fact, people served God best not by praying, which, as Thomas Paine put it, "can add nothing to eternity," but "by endeavouring to make his creatures happy." Scientific inquiry and experiments such as Franklin's with electricity all had as their object the improvement of human life.

Although there had been some improvements in the quality of life, life in the eighteenth century was still violent and filled with pain. The Enlightenment responded to the pain and violence of the world in two ways. First, it attempted to alleviate and curtail them. Scientists eagerly sought cures for diseases. The Reverend Cotton Mather of Boston learned about the procedure of inoculating against smallpox (using a small amount of the deadly virus) from a scientific article and from his African slave Onesimus, who knew of its practice in Africa. An epidemic gave him an opportunity to try out the technique. The revulsion against pain and suffering also encouraged humanitarian reform, such as James Oglethorpe's reform of English debtors' prisons and, eventually, the antislavery movement.

Men and women of the Enlightenment also cultivated a stoic resignation to the evils they could not change and a personal ideal of moderation, so that they would neither give nor receive pain. The gentility and politeness of the urban elite were expressions of this ideal of moderation. Both gentility and the Enlightenment were espoused by the same set of people, the urban elite: professionals, merchants, and prosperous planters tied in to the global economy.

STRUGGLES FOR DEMOCRACY

Books Become More Accessible

In the eighteenth century, very few people had ever held a book in their hands. Even fewer had had the experience of reading and recognizing a connection between themselves and someone who lived either long ago or far away, or of quickly and efficiently gaining access to desired knowledge or expertise. These forms of empowerment were reserved for the very wealthy.

In July 1731, Benjamin Franklin and some of his friends and colleagues met in Philadelphia to try to change that situation. They were members of a philosophical club called the Junto. Most were avid readers of the newspapers and leaflets that came off the ships coming in from England, and they had learned of an interesting recent development in London and other British towns. Libraries were relatively rare, even in Europe, and where they did exist in connection with certain institutions, they were not open to the public, and the books did not circulate. In the last few decades, however, that had begun to change, as collectives formed to buy books that all members of the group would then have access to. Inspired, fifty members of the Junto promised to contribute 40 shillings each to

start a circulating library. In addition, each man committed himself to giving 10 more shillings per annum to buy newly printed works and to maintain the collection. Their motto was a Latin phrase meaning "To support the common good is divine."

The master tradesmen, doctors, and small merchants who belonged to the Junto were certainly not poor, but they were not wealthy enough to buy large numbers of books, which were expensive at the time. By creating this institution, these men would have access to Enlightenment thinking in regards to law, science, and other subjects to an extent that they never could have managed on their own. Their ambitions of improving "the common good," however, extended beyond their own collectivity. They were also thinking of the improvement of the people of Philadelphia in general. The library was open to everyone on Saturday evenings from four to eight o'clock. Members could borrow books freely; visitors who were not members could also borrow a book, but they had to leave some sort of collateral, something of value that could be sold if the book was never returned.

The Economic and Social Foundations of Democracy

Enlightenment thinkers began to study the connections among society, politics, and the economy. John Locke, the English philosopher, was the first to link these in a theory. He argued that there was a systematic connection between social institutions (such as the family), political institutions, and property rights. He began with the claim that each person has the right to life and the right to preserve that life. To sustain their lives, people form families, and to support themselves and their families, they labor. The basic right

Library Company of Philadelphia
The founders of the Library Company were eager to bring ordinary people into contact with the world's intellectual currents.

The founding of "the Library Company," as the new institution was called, inspired the establishment of more libraries, both in Philadelphia and in other colonies. Circulating libraries grew increasingly common in America, and due to their presence, Enlightenment ideas spread far more rapidly than they otherwise would have. Only about 10 percent of the Library Company's books concerned theology, whereas in traditional institutional libraries—such as Harvard's—most of the titles were religious in nature. Instead, the Library Company offered books on history, geography, and science. Furthermore, the majority of the books were in English, rather than Latin, because the purpose in this case was not for readers to display their erudition but to gain access to what they viewed as practical knowledge. Eventually, circulating libraries helped to spread the patriots' ideas during the American Revolution. The Library Company, for example, loaned out its copy of Thomas Paine's *Common Sense*.

Of course, those who came to the library to read were generally middle-class citizens or even well-to-do. They were not the very poor, slaves, or former slaves, nor were they women. However, expanding access to knowledge from a tiny group to a substantially larger one was a necessary first step in democratizing access to education. Later, in the nineteenth century, the circulating library supported by subscription inspired the creation of the public libraries we know today.

to life thus gives people the right to the product of their labor: property. To protect their lives and their property, people create governments. They give up some of their liberty but receive protection of their lives and property in return.

Locke also developed a new economic theory. His idea that money has no intrinsic value was a departure from mercantilism, which said that the value of money was fixed. In the second half of the eighteenth century, Scottish philosophers such as Francis Hutcheson and Adam Smith carried Locke's ideas even further, arguing that human beings should be free to value the things that made them happy.

Using happiness as their standard for human life, the Scots argued that people should be free to produce. Adam Smith's influential *The Wealth of Nations* (1776) was both a critique of mercantilism and a defense of free markets and free labor. For Smith and other Enlightenment theorists, the best incentive to hard work was the increased wealth and comforts it would bring. Human beings were happiest, they said, when they lived under free governments, which protected private property but left the market largely unregulated. These ideas became increasingly popular around the time of the Revolution.

Enlightened Institutions

The Enlightenment spurred the creation of institutions that embodied its principles. Humanitarianism led to the building of the Pennsylvania Hospital in 1751 and the Eastern State Mental Hospital at Williamsburg in 1773. In 1743, Benjamin Franklin proposed a society of learned men, modeled after the Royal Society of London, to study and share information about science and technology. He also helped establish the Library Company of Philadelphia in 1731, the first lending library in the colonies. Philadelphia acquired a second library in 1751 when the Quaker James Logan bequeathed his library, books and building both, to the city. By the time of the Revolution, Newport, New York, Charleston, and Savannah all had libraries.

The Enlightenment had a significant effect on organized religion as well. The Anglicans, in particular, were receptive to its ideals of moderation and rationalism. In England, John Tillotson, the Archbishop of Canterbury, preached a comforting and simple Christianity: God was "good and just" and required nothing "that is either unsuitable to our reason or prejudicial to our interest . . . nothing but what is easy to be understood, and is as easy to be practiced by an honest and willing mind."

This message became popular in the colonies, even among Congregationalist ministers, who abandoned the Calvinism of their forefathers. John Wise, the minister of Ipswich, Massachusetts, insisted that "to follow God and to obey Reason is the same thing." Arminianism, the belief that salvation was partly a matter of individual effort rather than entirely God's will, enjoyed a new popularity. Harvard University became a hotbed of liberal theology, and, in response, religious conservatives founded Yale University in 1701 to guarantee ministers a proper Calvinist education.

Origins of the Great Awakening

The problem with rational religion was that it was not emotionally fulfilling. In addition, rapid population growth had left the colonies without enough churches and ministers. Popular demand for more and better religion led to a series of revivals known as the Great Awakening, which swept through the colonies between 1734 and 1745. At first, church leaders looked with pleasure on the stirrings of spiritual renewal. In the winter of 1734–1735, some of the rowdiest young people in Northampton, Massachusetts, who carried on parties for "the greater part of the night," began seeking religion at the church of a brilliant young minister, Jonathan Edwards. Everyone rejoiced at such signs of spiritual awakening.

The Grand Itinerant

When the English revivalist preacher George Whitefield arrived in Philadelphia in 1739, the local ministers, including those of his own Anglican church, welcomed him.

Whitefield drew audiences in the thousands everywhere he spoke. In the 15 months of his grand tour, he visited every colony from Maine to Georgia, met all the important ministers, and was heard at least once by most of the people of Massachusetts and Connecticut (see Map 5–4). He spoke to the entire community—rich, poor, slave, free, old, young, male, and female—acting out simple scripts based on biblical stories. The message was always the same: the sinfulness of man and the mercy of God.

Map 5-4   George Whitefield's Itinerary In the 15 months between October 30, 1739, and January 18, 1741, Whitefield covered thousands of miles, visiting every colony from New Hampshire to Georgia, and stopping in some states such as Pennsylvania, South Carolina, and Georgia several times.

In a calculated move, perhaps to increase his audiences, Whitefield began speaking out against some in the ministry, accusing them of being unconverted. He started with the deceased Archbishop of Canterbury, John Tillotson. Following his lead, Gilbert Tennent, on a preaching tour of New England, warned about "The Danger of an Unconverted Ministry." Tennent implied that some ministers were in it for the money and that true Christians should leave their churches for those of honest preachers.

Even sympathetic ministers were shocked by these accusations, which turned their congregations against them and split their churches. Some leading ministers, who already had reservations about the revivalists because of their emotional style, now condemned the revival. However, that only made the revivalists more popular and attracted larger crowds. Soon thousands were attending regularly.

Cultural Conflict and Challenges to Authority

The Great Awakening walked a fine line between challenging authority and supporting it, which may well explain its widespread appeal. It antagonized the most powerful and arrogant but did not challenge the fundamental structures of society. By attacking ministers but not government officials, the revivalists criticized authority without suffering any real consequences.

The Great Awakening appealed to all classes of people. Its greatest impact, however, was in areas facing the greatest change—in particular, cities (especially among the lower orders), the frontier, and older towns beginning to suffer from overcrowding. Here lived the people most disrupted by economic changes. Disturbed by an increasingly competitive society, men and women were attracted to the democratic fellowship of the revivalist congregation.

While criticizing the materialism and competitiveness of eighteenth-century society, the revival told people to look inside themselves for change, not to the structures of society. For example, a woman named Sarah Osborn blamed herself for her woes, which she saw as punishment for her sinful singing and dancing. After her spiritual rebirth, she

Time Line

▼**1701**
Yale founded

▼**1704**
First newspaper, *Boston News-Letter*, published in colonies

▼**1712**
Slave revolt in New York City

▼**1717**
French build Fort Toulouse

▼**1718**
French found New Orleans

▼**1731**
Library Company, first lending library in colonies, erected in Philadelphia

▼**1733**
Georgia founded

▼**1734**
Great Awakening begins

▼**1735**
John Peter Zenger acquitted of libeling New York's governor

trusted in God and accepted her poverty. Spiritual rebirth provided such people the joy and fulfillment that their world had been unable to supply.

The revival also walked a fine line in its treatment of slavery. Early in his travels, Whitefield spoke out against the cruelties of slavery and harangued slaveholders. At the same time, however, he maintained a slave plantation in South Carolina and pestered the trustees to permit slavery in Georgia. Like many slave owners after him, Whitefield argued that it was immoral to enslave Africans, but not to own them, provided that one treated them well and Christianized them. By linking humanitarianism, Christianity, and slavery, the Great Awakening anchored slavery in the South, at least for the time being.

Although it is doubtful that slaves were treated more humanely on the plantations of evangelicals, beginning in the 1740s large numbers of slaves were converted to Christianity, and by some point in the nineteenth century virtually all slaves had become Christians. Although some may have converted to please their masters and to get Sundays off, blacks were attracted to evangelical religion for the same reason that whites were, although their context was starker. It offered them a way to order and find meaning in their lives.

To a great extent, poor whites and slaves, especially in the South, had been left out of the society that more prosperous people had created. Evangelical religion placed the individual in a community of believers. It offered slaves the opportunity for church discipline and personal responsibility on almost the same terms as whites and gave some blacks the possibility of leadership in a biracial community. Africans grafted some of their religious practices, such as shouting and ecstatic visions, onto the revival, so that worship in southern Baptist and Methodist churches became a truly African American phenomenon.

What the Awakening Wrought

The opponents of the Great Awakening feared that it would turn the world upside down, but the leaders of the revival disciplined their own wildest members, such as New London's James Davenport. Davenport had led his flock through the streets late at night, singing at the tops of their lungs. They also made a bonfire to rid themselves of heresy,

▼**1739**
Stono Rebellion
George Whitefield begins his
   American tour

▼**1741**
Thirty-five people executed in
   New York City after slave-
   revolt scare

▼**1748**
College of New Jersey
   (Princeton) founded

▼**1751**
Pennsylvania Hospital built in
   Philadelphia

▼**1752**
Georgia becomes a Crown
   colony

▼**1754**
Columbia College founded

▼**1766**
Queens College (Rutgers)
   founded

▼**1773**
Eastern State Mental Hospital
   built in Williamsburg

by burning the books of their opponents, and idolatry, by burning the clothes they were wearing. The stripping party was stopped by evangelicals in the crowd, and Davenport was brought back to his senses by his fellow ministers. In general, the Great Awakening took colonial society in the direction in which it was already heading: toward individualism. Church after church split into evangelical and traditional factions, and new denominations appeared. Choosing a religion became a personal matter, and colonies with established churches tolerated dissenters. Religion, as a general force, was strengthened, making the colonies simultaneously the most Protestant and the most religiously diverse culture in the world.

The Great Awakening also spurred the establishment of educational institutions. Princeton, chartered in 1748 as the College of New Jersey, grew out of an evangelical seminary. Next came Brown in 1764, and Rutgers, chartered in 1766, to advance "true religion and useful knowledge." Dartmouth was established in 1769, building on a former school for Native Americans run by evangelicals. Columbia College, chartered in 1754, represented the Anglicans' response. The focus of higher education was slowly shifting from preparation for the ministry to the training of leaders more generally. The Great Awakening diminished the power of ministers while increasing the influence of personal religion.

At the height of the Awakening, religious enthusiasm was both attacked and defended. Yet the conflict was hardly a battle of the pious against the godless or the well-educated against the uninformed. Jonathan Edwards, one of the greatest minds of his age, drew from the Enlightenment, as well as from Calvinist ideas. For Edwards, however, reason and good habits were not enough, and reason had to be supplemented by emotion, in particular the emotion of God's grace. By insisting that religious salvation and virtue were more matters of the heart than of the head, Edwards opened the way for a popular religion that was democratic, intensely personal, and humanitarian.

Conclusion

Eighteenth-century America was part of an expanding world market and a capitalist political economy. A growing population sustained a vigorous economy, one that produced for and purchased from the world market. As participants in an "industrious revolution," white Americans worked themselves and their slaves harder to purchase consumer goods. These new goods enabled people to live more genteelly and to cultivate a social life. Especially in the cities, this new emphasis on social life spawned an array of institutions in which people could acquire and display learning and gentility. The benefits of the economy were not shared equally, however. Enslaved people produced for the market economy but were denied its rewards. The increasing stratification of urban society and land pressures in rural regions meant many were too poor to profit from the expanding economy.

The eighteenth-century world spawned two different but related intellectual responses, the Enlightenment and the Great Awakening. Both were critical in shaping the eighteenth-century colonial world, and both paved the way for the Revolution. The Enlightenment led some to believe that rational thought and the scientific method would conquer human ills. At the same time, the Great Awakening reminded men and women that life was short and ultimately beyond their control. In different ways, the Enlightenment and the Great Awakening both encouraged the individualism that would characterize American life.

Who, What, Where

Review Questions

1. What were the primary sources of population increase in the eighteenth century? Compare the patterns of population growth of Europeans and Africans in the colonies.

2. What was the "industrious revolution"? How did it shape the development of the colonial economy? What were the other key factors shaping the development of the colonial economy? What effect did this development have on the lives of ordinary men and women?

3. What were the primary changes in urban and rural life in the eighteenth century?

Critical-Thinking Questions

1. Was the development of the eighteenth-century consumer culture a democratizing force—or the opposite?

2. Why were some eighteenth-century men and women drawn to the ideas of the Enlightenment while others were drawn to the Great Awakening?

3. Analyze the relationship between humanitarianism and slavery, which developed at the same time.

Suggested Readings

Anderson, Jennifer. *Mahogany: The Costs of Luxury in Early America*. Cambridge, MA: Harvard University Press, 2012.

Butler, Jon. *Awash in a Sea of Faith*. Cambridge, MA: Harvard University Press, 1990.

Fischer, David Hackett. *Albion's Seed: Four British Folkways in America*. New York: Oxford University Press, 1989.

Jordon, Winthrop. *White over Black: American Attitudes Toward the Negro, 1550–1812*. New York: Norton, 1968.

For further review materials and resource information, please visit www.oup.com/us/oakes-mcgerr

CHAPTER 5: THE EIGHTEENTH-CENTURY WORLD, 1700–1775
Primary Sources

5.1 BENJAMIN FRANKLIN, *THE AUTOBIOGRAPHY OF BENJAMIN FRANKLIN* (1771–1790)

Benjamin Franklin began writing his autobiography in 1771 and returned to the task periodically until he died in 1790. In this selection from the first pages, he describes how he came to read and write with the flair that made him one of the eighteenth century's leading men of letters. The excerpt provides some insight into life in the first half of the eighteenth century in Boston, Massachusetts, despite the fact that it was written at a much later date.

From a child I was fond of reading, and all the little money that came into my hands was ever laid out in books. Pleased with the *Pilgrim's Progress*, my first collection was of John Bunyan's works in separate little volumes. I afterward sold them to enable me to buy R. Burton's Historical Collections; they were small chapmen's books, and cheap, 40 or 50 in all. My father's little library consisted chiefly of books in polemic divinity, most of which I read, and have since often regretted that, at a time when I had such a thirst for knowledge, more proper books had not fallen in my way since it was now resolved I should not be a clergyman. Plutarch's *Lives* there was in which I read abundantly, and I still think that time spent to great advantage. There was also a book of De Foe's, called an *Essay on Projects*, and another of Dr. Mather's, called *Essays to do Good*, which perhaps gave me a turn of thinking that had an influence on some of the principal future events of my life.

This bookish inclination at length determined my father to make me a printer, though he had already one son (James) of that profession. In 1717 my brother James returned from England with a press and letters to set up his business in Boston. I liked it much better than that of my father, but still had a hankering for the sea. To prevent the apprehended effect of such an inclination, my father was impatient to have me bound to my brother. I stood out some time, but at last was persuaded, and signed the indentures when I was yet but twelve years old. I was to serve as an apprentice till I was twenty-one years of age, only I was to be allowed journeyman's wages during the last year. In a little time I made great proficiency in the business, and became a useful hand to my brother. I now had access to better books. An acquaintance with the apprentices of booksellers enabled me sometimes to borrow a small one, which I was careful to return soon and clean. Often I sat up in my room reading the greatest part of the night, when the book was borrowed in the evening and to be returned early in the morning, lest it should be missed or wanted. . . .

There was another bookish lad in the town, John Collins by name, with whom I was intimately acquainted. We sometimes disputed, and very fond we were of argument, and very desirous of confuting one another, which disputatious turn, by the way, is apt to become a very bad habit, making people often extremely disagreeable in company by the contradiction that is necessary to bring it into practice; and thence, besides souring and spoiling the conversation, is productive of disgusts and, perhaps enmities where you may have occasion for friendship. I had caught it by reading my father's books of dispute about religion. Persons of good sense, I have since observed, seldom fall into it, except lawyers, university men, and men of all sorts that have been bred at Edinborough.

A question was once, somehow or other, started between Collins and me, of the propriety of educating the female sex in learning, and their abilities for study. He was of opinion that it was improper, and that they were naturally unequal to it. I took the contrary side, perhaps a little for dispute's sake. He was naturally more eloquent, had a ready plenty of words; and sometimes, as I thought, bore me down more by his fluency than by the strength of his reasons. As we parted without settling the point, and were not to see one another again for some time, I sat down to put my arguments in writing, which I copied fair and sent to him. He answered, and I replied. Three or four letters of a side had passed, when my father happened to find my papers and read them. Without entering into the discussion, he took occasion to talk to me about the manner of my writing; observed that, though I had the advantage of my antagonist in correct spelling and pointing (which I ow'd to the printing-house), I fell far short in elegance of expression, in method and in perspicuity, of which he convinced me by several instances. I saw the justice of his remark, and thence grew more attentive to the manner in writing, and determined to endeavor at improvement.

About this time I met with an odd volume of the *Spectator*.[1] It was the third. I had never before seen any of them. I bought it, read it over and over, and was much delighted with it. I thought the writing excellent, and wished, if possible, to imitate it. With this view I took some of the papers, and, making short hints of the sentiment in each sentence, laid them by a few days, and then, without looking at the book, try'd to compleat the papers again, by expressing each hinted sentiment at length, and as fully as it had been expressed before, in any suitable words that should come to hand. Then I compared my *Spectator* with the original, discovered some of my faults, and corrected them.

Source: Benjamin Franklin, *The Autobiography of Benjamin Franklin* (Rockville, MD: Arc Manor, 2008), pp. 15–17.

5.2 SAMSON OCCOM, EXCERPTS FROM *A SHORT NARRATIVE OF MY LIFE* (1768)

Samson Occom was a Mohegan Indian from Connecticut. By the eighteenth century, the Mohegans had lost their land and with it their way of life. In the 1740s, Occom was educated at the school that would later become Dartmouth College and became a minister to Indians on Long Island. In 1768, he penned a brief autobiography, revealing that in his experience, hard work did not pay off as well as it had for Benjamin Franklin: when a white friend and ally advocated for him with the society for missionaries, asking for more reasonable pay, he was rebuffed.

The Reverend Mr. Buell was so kind as to write in my behalf to the gentlemen of Boston; and he told me they were much Displeased with him, and heard also once again that they blamed me for being Extravagant; I Can't Conceive how these gentlemen would have me Live. I am ready to forgive their Ignorance, and I would wish they had Changed Circumstances with me but one month, that they may know, by experience what my Case really was; but I am now fully convinced, that it was not Ignorance, For I believe it can be proved to the world that these Same

---

[1]This was a popular daily published in London from 1711 to 1712.

Gentlemen gave a young Missionary a Single man, *One Hundred Pounds* for one year; and fifty Pounds for an Interpreter, and thirty Pounds for an Introducer, so it Cost them One Hundred & Eighty Pounds in one Single Year, and they Sent too where there was no Need of a Missionary.

Now you See what difference they made between me and other missionaries; they gave me 180 pounds for 12 Years Service, which they gave for one years Services in another Mission.—In my Service (I speak like a fool, but I am Constrained) I was my own Interpreter. I was both a School master and Minister to the Indians, yea I was their Ear, Eye & Hand, as well as Mouth. I leave it with the World, as wicked as it is, to Judge, whether I ought not to have had half as much, they gave a young man Just mentioned which would have been but 50 pounds a year; and if they ought to have given me that, I am not under obligations to them, I owe them nothing at all; what can be the Reason that they used me after this manner? I can't think of anything, but this as a Poor Indian Boy said, Who was Bound out to an English Family, and he used to Drive Plow for a young man, and he whipt and beat him almost every Day, and the young man found fault with him, and Complained of him to his master and the poor Boy was Called to answer for himself before his master, and he was asked, what it was he did, that he was So Complained of and beat almost every Day. He Said, he did not know, but he Supposed it was because he could not drive any better; but says he, I Drive as well as I know how; and at other Times he Beats me, because he is of a mind to beat me; but says he believes he Beats me for the most of the Time "because I am an Indian."

Source: Colin Calloway, ed., *The World Turned Upside Down: Indian Voices from Early America* (New York: Bedford), p. 61.

5.3 OLAUDAH EQUIANO, EXCERPTS FROM *THE INTERESTING NARRATIVE AND OTHER WRITINGS* (1789)

The late eighteenth-century autobiography of Gustavus Vassa, or Olaudah Equiano, is probably the most famous slave narrative ever published. He claimed to have been born in Africa and brought to America, but scholars have recently demonstrated that it is far more likely that Equiano was American-born and made this claim about himself so as to be able to speak about—and criticize—the slave trade with "authenticity." In any case, having been at sea during the French and Indian War, acting first as a naval officer's personal servant and then as a fighter, he assumed he was to be freed by his master but was disappointed instead.

Our ship having arrived at Portsmouth, we went into the harbour and remained there till the latter end of November, when we heard great talk about peace, and to our very great joy in the beginning of December we had orders to go up to London with our ship to be paid off. We received this news with loud huzzas and every other demonstration of gladness, and nothing but mirth was to be seen throughout every part of the ship. I too was not without my share of the general joy on this occasion. I thought now of nothing but being freed and working for myself, and thereby getting money to enable me to get a good education: for I always had a great desire to be able at least to read and write, and while I was on ship-board I had endeavoured to improve myself in both. While I was in the *Ætna* particularly, the captain's clerk taught me to write, and gave me a smattering of arithmetic as far as the rule of three. There was also one Daniel Queen, about forty years of age, a man very well educated, who messed [that is, ate] with me on board this ship, and he likewise dressed and attended the captain. Fortunately this man soon became very much attached to me and took very great pains to instruct me in many things. He taught me to shave and dress hair a little and also to read in the Bible, explaining many passages to me which I did not comprehend. I was wonderfully surprised to see the laws and rules of my country written almost exactly here, a circumstance which I believe tended to impress our manners and customs more deeply on my memory. I used to tell him of this resemblance, and many a time we have sat up the whole night together at this employment. In short, he was like a father to me, and some even used to call me after his name; they also styled me the black Christian. Indeed I almost loved him with the affection of a son. Many things I have denied myself that he might have them, and when I used to play at marbles or any other game and won a few halfpence, or got any little money, which I sometimes did, for shaving anyone, I used to buy him a little sugar or tobacco, as far as my stock of money would go. He used to say that he and I never should part, and that when our ship was paid off, as I was as free as himself or any other man on board, he would instruct me in his business by which I might gain a good livelihood. This gave me new life and spirits, and my heart burned within me while I thought the time long till I obtained my freedom. For though my master had not promised it to me, yet besides the assurances I had received that he had no right to detain me, he always treated me with the greatest kindness and reposed in me an unbounded confidence; he even paid attention to my morals, and would never suffer me to deceive him or tell lies, of which he used to tell me the consequences; and that if I did so God would not love me; so that from all this tenderness, I had never once supposed, in all my dreams of freedom, that he would think of detaining me any longer than I wished.

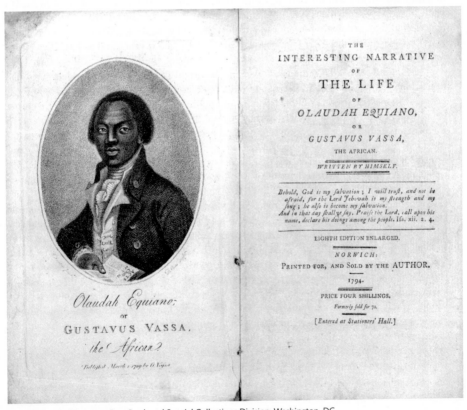

Source: Library of Congress Rare Book and Special Collections Division, Washington, DC.

In pursuance of our orders we sailed from Portsmouth for the Thames and arrived at Deptford 10 December, where we cast anchor just as it was high water. The ship was up about half an hour, when my master ordered the barge to be manned, and all in an instant, without having before given me the least reason to suspect anything of the matter, he forced me into the barge, saying I was going to leave him, but he would take care I should not. I was so struck with the unexpectedness of this proceeding that for some time I did not make a reply, only I made an offer to go for my books and chest of clothes, but he swore I should not move out of his sight, and if I did he would cut my throat, at the same time taking his hanger [a short sword]. I began, however, to collect myself, and plucking up courage, I told him I was free and he could not by law serve me so. But this only enraged him the more, and he continued to swear, and said he would soon let me know whether he would or not, and at that instant sprung himself into the barge from the ship to the astonishment and sorrow of all on board. The tide, rather unluckily for me, had just turned downward, so that we quickly fell down the river along with it till we came among some outward-bound West Indiamen, for he was resolved to put me on board the first vessel he could get to receive me. The boat's crew, who pulled against their will, became quite faint, different times, and would have gone ashore, but he would not let them. Some of them strove then to cheer me and told me he could not sell me, which revived me a little, and I still entertained hopes, for as they pulled along he asked some vessels to receive me, but they could not. But just as we had got a little below Gravesend, we came alongside of a ship which was going away the next tide for the West Indies; her name was the *Charming Sally*, Captain James Doran, and my master went on board and agreed with him for me, and in a little time I was sent for into the cabin. When I came there Captain Doran asked me if I knew him; I answered that I did not; "Then," said he, "you are now my slave." I told him my master could not sell me to him, nor to anyone else. "Why," said he, "did not your master buy you?" I confessed he did. "But I have served him," said I, "many years, and he has taken all my wages and prize-money, for I only got one sixpence during the war; besides this I have been baptized, and by the laws of the land no man has a right to sell me." And I added that I had heard a lawyer and others at different times tell my master so. They both then said that those people who told me so were not my friends, but I replied, "It was very extraordinary that other people did not know the law as well as they." Upon this Captain Doran said I talked too much English, and if I did not behave myself well and be quiet he had a method on board to make me. I was too well convinced of his power over me to doubt what he said, and my former sufferings in the slave-ship presenting themselves to my mind, the recollection of them made me shudder. However, before I retired I told them that as I could not get any right among men here I hoped I should hereafter in Heaven, and I immediately left the cabin, filled with resentment and sorrow. The only coat I had with me my master took away with him, and said if my prize-money had been £10,000 he had a right to it all and would have taken it. I had about nine guineas which, during my long seafaring life, I had scraped together from trifling perquisites and little ventures, and I hid it that instant lest my master should take that from me likewise, still hoping that by some means or other I should make my escape to the shore; and indeed some of my old shipmates told me not to despair for they would get me back again, and that as soon as they could get their pay, they would immediately come to Portsmouth to me, where this ship was going: but, alas! all my hopes were baffled and the hour of my deliverance was yet far off. My master, having soon concluded his bargain with the captain, came out of the cabin, and he and his people got into the boat and put off; I followed them with aching eyes as long as I could, and when they were out of sight I threw myself on the deck, while my heart was ready to burst with sorrow and anguish.

Source: Olaudah Equiano, *The Interesting Narrative and Other Writings,* edited by Vincent Carretta (New York: Penguin Books, 1995), pp. 91–94.

5.4 GEORGE WHITEFIELD, ACCOUNT OF A VISIT TO GEORGIA (1738)

George Whitefield, the leading preacher of the Great Awakening, maintained a diary in which he recorded his travels to spread the word of the Lord. He edited and published these journals in regular installments so as to reach a wider audience. Though an Englishman by birth, he visited America seven times. This 1738 selection, detailing his visit to the relatively young colony of Georgia, comes from his first trip to the thirteen colonies, which was very successful, in that he drew large crowds and made many converts.

Tuesday, August 8 [1738]

After a pleasant passage of five or six days, I arrived at Frederica, a town situated southwardly above a hundred miles from Savannah, and consisting of about a hundred-and-twenty inhabitants. The people received me most gladly, having had a famine of the Word for a long season. May God give a blessing to my coming amongst them.

In the evening we had public prayers, and expounding of the Second Lesson under a large tree, and many more [were] present than could be expected.

Wednesday, August 9. Began to day visiting from house to house and found the people in appearance desirous of being fed with the sincere milk of the Word, and solicitous for my continuance amongst them. Poor creatures! My heart ached for them, because I saw them and their children scattered abroad as sheep having no shepherd. Lord, in Thy due time send forth some labourer into this part of Thy vineyard.

This evening, had prayers in a house which Mr. Horton hired for us during my stay, and most of the [town's] inhabitants, I believe, were present. Blessed be God, timber is sawing for the erecting a more commodious place for public worship, till a church can be built. God grant we may always worship Him in spirit and in truth, and then we may be assured that at all times and in all places He will hear us.

Friday, August 11. Went in the morning to, and returned in the evening from, the Darien, a settlement about twenty miles off from Frederica, whither I went to see Mr. MacLeod, a worthy minister of the Scotch Church; and God gave me a most pleasant passage.

Saturday, Aug. 12 . . . In the evening, because I was to go about midnight, I gave notice I would preach as well as expound, at which almost all the inhabitants were present; for many were oblig'd to stand without the door. The Lesson was very applicable to my circumstances. It was the First of St. James wherein the Apostle bids us rejoice when we fall into divers temptations. God enabled me to enlarge on it pretty much. I told the people that God called me and I must away, at which some wept. Oh God, how does Thou follow me with Thy blessings wherever Thou sendest me! I looked for persecution, but lo! I am received as an angel of God.

Sunday, August 13. Being disappointed of going by the boat last night, I read prayers and preached to my dear little flock twice, which caused great joy among them. Mr. Horton was extremely civil, and did everything he could to oblige me. This afternoon another sermon, I intended to go with him to preach to the soldiers at the Fort of St. Simon's and then the next day to go to St. Andrew's, but Lord Thou callest me elsewhere. O grant I may have no will of my own, but whenever or wherever Thou shalt be pleased to call me, may I without the least reluctance say, Lo I come! Had an alarm brought to Frederica that the Spaniards had taken possession of Fort St. George and fired at one of our boats; but this was quickly found to be entirely groundless.

About two in the afternoon, having first read prayers, and preached, most of the inhabitants recompanied [sic] me to the Bluff and took their leaves of me in an affectionate manner and laded me with things convenient for my journey. The good Lord reward them ten thousand fold, and make me thankful for His unmerited mercies!

Source: William Wale, ed., *Whitefield's Journals* (London: Henry Drane, 1905), pp. 155–157.

5.5 PHILLIS WHEATLEY, "TO THE UNIVERSITY OF CAMBRIDGE, IN NEW ENGLAND" (1773)

Phillis Wheatley was brought as a slave from Africa to America in 1761, when she was about eight years old. She was purchased by the wealthy Boston merchant John Wheatley to be a companion to his wife. Wheatley proved to be an excellent student, and they tutored her in English, Latin, history, and Christianity. During this time, the students at Harvard University were becoming increasingly known for their wild and destructive behavior. Here, Wheatley reminds them what people of African descent would do with the education they were being offered if it was given to them. Years later, she would receive her freedom from the Wheatley family.

To the University of Cambridge, in New England

While an intrinsic ardor prompts to write,
The muses promise to assist my pen;
'Twas not long since I left my native shore
The land of errors, and *Egyptian* gloom:
Father of mercy, 'twas thy gracious hand
Brought me in safety from those dark abodes.
        Students, to you 'tis giv'n to scan the heights
Above, to traverse the ethereal space,
And mark the systems of revolving worlds.
Still more, ye sons of science ye receive
The blissful news by messengers from heav'n,
How *Jesus'* blood for your redemption flows.
See him with hands out-stretcht upon the cross;
Immense compassion in his bosom glows;
He hears revilers, nor resents their scorn:
What matchless mercy in the Son of God!
When the whole human race by sin had fall'n,
He deign'd to die that they might rise again,
And share with him in the sublimest skies,
Life without death, and glory without end.

Source: Library of Congress Rare Book and Special Collections Division,
Washington, DC.

> Improve your privileges while they stay,
> Ye pupils, and each hour redeem, that bears
> Or good or bad report of you to heav'n.
> Let sin, that baneful evil to the soul,
> By you be shunn'd, nor once remit your guard;
> Suppress the deadly serpent in its egg.
> Ye blooming plants of human race devine,
> An *Ethiop* tells you 'tis your greatest foe;
> Its transient sweetness turns to endless pain,
> And in immense perdition sinks the soul.

Source: Julian D. Mason, ed., *The Poems of Phillis Wheatley* (Chapel Hill: University of North Carolina Press, 1989 [1966]),
p. 52.

Conflict in the Empire

1713-1774

< Benjamin West, *The Death of General Wolfe*

AMERICAN PORTRAIT

Susannah Willard Johnson Experiences the Empire

Today the town is Charlestown, New Hampshire, but then it was "No. 4," a small farming village on the northern frontier of Massachusetts. In 1754, Susannah Willard Johnson and her husband, James, lived there, having moved to the frontier during a break in the struggle between Britain and France for North America. At 24, Susannah had been married for seven years and had three children, with another due any day. James, a native of Ireland, had started his life in America as a servant indentured to Susannah's uncle. After working for him for 10 years, James purchased the remainder of his time, married Susannah, and made his way by farming and shopkeeping. He also became a lieutenant in the militia.

The region's Abenaki Indians—Algonquians who were allied with the French and had their own grievances against the encroaching settlers—presented both danger and opportunity. At first the settlers at No. 4 were so frightened that they stayed in the fort. However, Susannah later reported that "hostility at length vanished—the Indians expressed a wish to traffic, the inhabitants laid by their fears. . . ." James Johnson was part of the consumer revolution, selling goods to his fellow settlers and to the Abenakis, who gave him furs in return.

Susannah Johnson described her family's life as "harmony and safety" and "boasted with exultation that I should, with husband, friends, and luxuries, live happy in spite of the fear of savages." By the summer of 1754, however, the rumors of impending warfare with France would make the frontier village a target of France's Abenaki allies.

On August 30, 1754, just before daybreak, a neighbor coming to work for the Johnsons appeared at the door. As the Johnsons opened the door, the neighbor rushed in, followed by 11 Abenaki men. Soon, Susannah said, they were "all over the house, some upstairs, some hauling my sister out of bed, another had hold of me, and one was approaching Mr. Johnson, who stood in the middle of the floor to deliver himself up."

The Abenakis tied up the men, gathered the women and children, and marched the party to the north. On the second day of her captivity, Susannah went into labor. Attended by her sister and husband, she gave birth to a daughter, whom she named Captive. Before they returned home five years later, Susannah and her family were held captive in Canada and sent to England as part of a prisoner exchange.

The French and Indian War had begun on the northern frontier, and the Indians were manipulating it to their advantage. In peacetime they traded furs for manufactured goods, but in wartime they seized British settlers, took them to Canada, and sold them to the French, who either ransomed them back to the British or traded them for prisoners of war. What to others might seem an imperial struggle was to Susannah Johnson a terrifying assault that took her from her home and family. The consumer revolution that gave settlers such as the Johnsons the opportunity to live a good life on the frontier was rooted in a struggle between

France and England, two empires competing over both the markets the consumer revolution was creating and the lands it was populating. As families such as the Johnsons pushed at the frontiers, they became actors on a global stage.

The Victory of the British Empire

From 1689 to 1763, Britain and France were at war more than half of the time. These wars gave shape to the eighteenth century and created the international context for the American Revolution in several ways. First, the Revolution grew out of Britain's ineffective efforts to govern the enlarged empire it won from France in 1763. Second, France's support for the colonies in their war against Britain helped secure the colonies' victory. Third, once the colonies secured their independence, they entered a world still torn by conflict between Britain and France.

All of these wars were rooted in a struggle for world dominance between two powerful empires. To a great extent, colonial and imperial objectives coincided. Both Britain and the colonies would benefit from securing the empire's borders and from expanding British markets. Yet the imperial wars also exposed the growing divergence between the political economy of the colonies and that of the mother country. When the growing empire and its wars threatened to increase Britain's power over the colonists, raise their taxes to pay for the empire, and station among them a permanent army, the colonists resisted and finally rebelled.

New War, Old Pattern

England and France were at peace from the end of Queen Anne's War in 1713 (see Chapter 4) until 1739. It was an uneasy peace in the British North American colonies, however. In what is now Maine, New Englanders continued to fight the Abenakis, forcing them into a closer alliance with the French, who were attempting to stabilize relations with the Algonquians. The most common method was by providing "gifts" of trade goods.

France and Spain had also arrived at an uneasy peace in North America. Each had come to an arrangement with the increasingly powerful Comanche empire in the Southwest. When France built its forts along the lower Mississippi valley (see Chapter 4), Spain responded, in 1716, with an outpost in Texas. Both had hoped to expand their empires across the plains but were thwarted by the Comanches, who, like the Iroquois to the east, played the European powers off against each other. By the 1740s, the Comanches had forced both France and Spain to trade with them on advantageous terms, while blocking both from further expansion.

Another round of international warfare broke out in 1739 and lasted nine years. In the War of Jenkins's Ear (1739–1744), Britain attempted to expand into Spanish territories and markets in the Americas. Urged on by merchants, and with the approval of colonists who wanted to eliminate Spain as a rival, Britain found an excuse for declaring war: a ship's captain, Robert Jenkins, turned up in Parliament in 1738 holding in his hand what he claimed was his ear, severed by the Spanish seven years earlier in the Caribbean. Once again, colonists joined in what they hoped would be a glorious international endeavor, only to be disillusioned. In 1741, 3,600 colonists, mostly poor young men lured by the promise of Spanish plunder, joined 5,000 Britons in a failed attack on Cartagena, Colombia. More than half the colonial contingent died.

Another ambitious move against the Spanish empire failed in 1740. James Oglethorpe and settlers hired by South Carolina, accompanied by Cherokee and Creek allies, failed to seize the Spanish outpost at St. Augustine and left the southern border vulnerable. When Oglethorpe's troops repulsed a Spanish attack in 1742, however, Spain's plan to demolish Georgia and South Carolina and arm their slaves was thwarted.

Just as the War of Jenkins's Ear ended in stalemate, so did King George's War (1744–1748), a conflict between Britain and Austria on one side and France and Prussia on the other over succession to the Austrian throne. A French raid on a fishing village in Nova Scotia met with a huge retaliation by the British. Troops from Massachusetts, supported by the British navy, captured the French fort at Louisbourg. Finally, a joint British-colonial venture had succeeded. But a planned attack on Québec was called off when the British fleet failed to arrive. At war's end, Britain returned Louisbourg to France and warned the colonists that they had to maintain the peace. The British blockade of French ports cut off trade to Canada, including the all-important presents to Indian allies and trade partners. Without these gifts, the French-Indian empire began to crumble.

The Local Impact of Global War

Successive rounds of warfare had a significant impact on politics and society in British North America. Although the colonists identified strongly with the British cause, decades of warfare were a constant drain on the colonial treasury and population.

Wars are expensive. Generally, rates of taxation in colonial America were low, except when wars had to be financed. In a rehearsal for the conflicts that would lead to the American Revolution, the British government complained that the colonists were unwilling to contribute their fair share to the imperial wars. As a rule, colonial legislatures were willing to go only so far in raising taxes to pay for imperial wars or expeditions against Indians. Then they simply issued paper money. Inevitably, the currency depreciated, making even worse the boom-and-bust cycles that war economies always produce.

No colony did more to support the imperial war efforts than Massachusetts, but the result was heightened political conflict at home. Royal governors, eager to please officials in London, pushed the colony to contribute to the imperial wars. As many as one-fifth of the colony's men may have served in the military in the middle of the eighteenth century. In 1747, Boston mobs rioted for three days to resist the Royal Navy's attempt to "impress" (force) men into service, and the local militia refused to restore order. For the first time, Bostonians began to speak about a right to resist tyranny.

Much more than in Europe, civilians in America became victims of war. By the eighteenth century, conventions of "civilized" warfare that held that civilians should be spared broke down in America for two reasons. First, without a transportation system to supply the army, troops often relied on plunder. Second, frontier Indians, adapting their traditional practices of war, routinely attacked villages, seizing captives to replenish their populations and to ransom to the French. Between 1675 and 1763, when frontier settlers such as Susannah Johnson were at risk, Indians took more than 1,600 New England settlers as captives, more than 90 percent during times of war (see Figure 6–1).

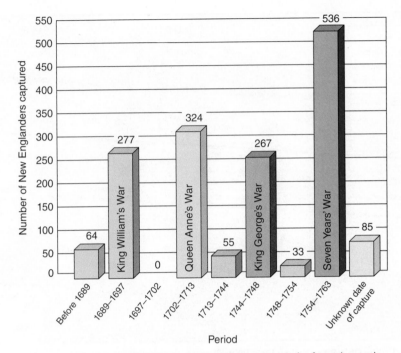

Figure 6-1   New England Captives, 1675–1763 During periods of war, the number of New Englanders taken captive by northern Indians and the French increased dramatically; more than 90 percent of captives were taken during wartime.
Source: Alden Vaughan, *Roots of American Racism* (New York: Oxford University Press, 1990), p. 31.

Almost half the colonists seized eventually returned home, but, as with Susannah Johnson's son Sylvanus, who had forgotten English entirely, Indian customs "wore off" only "by degree." Other captives died during the arduous march to Canada, sometimes killed by Indians who thought them too weak to survive the journey. Many died of disease, and a few, typically girls between 7 and 15, remained with their captors voluntarily. Historians debate why this was so. Perhaps it was because Puritan culture trained girls to respond without question to those in authority. Or perhaps it was because, after the rigors of a Puritan upbringing, the relative freedom of Indian culture was inviting.

The French Empire Crumbles from Within

In the years after King George's War, a change in French policy offered a small band of Miami Indians the chance to gain an advantage over rivals. In the process, they started a chain of events that led to the French and Indian War.

Although King George's War had ended in a stalemate, it weakened the French position in North America. The costs of war had forced the French to cut back on their presents to allied Algonquian tribes, especially in the Ohio River valley. To raise revenue, the French sharply increased their charges for the lease of trading posts; in turn, traders raised the prices that they charged the Indians for trade goods. These changes significantly

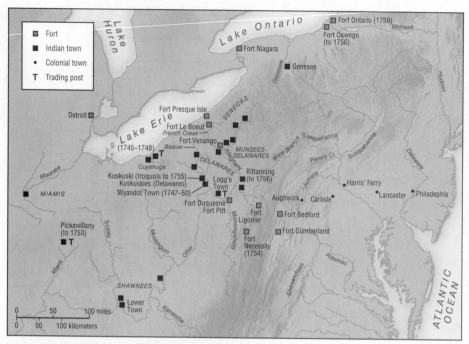

Map 6-1 The Ohio River Valley, 1747-1758 This territory, inhabited by a number of small bands of Indians, was coveted by both the French and the British, not to mention several competing groups of colonial land speculators. The rivalries between the imperial powers, among the Indian bands, and between rival groups of speculators made this region a powder keg.
Source: Adapted from Michael McConnell, *A Country Between* (Lincoln: University of Nebraska, 1992), pp. 116-117.

weakened the French hold over their Indian allies, creating political instability that was the underlying North American cause of the French and Indian War.

The Ohio River valley was home to small, refugee tribes (see Map 6–1). As long as the French provided liberal presents and cheap trade goods, they maintained a loose control. Once that control ended, however, each tribe sought to increase its advantage over the others, at a time when the British recognized the strategic and economic importance of the region.

The temporary power vacuum afforded a small group of Miamis, led by a chieftain called Memeskia, an opportunity to play one group of colonists off another. The chain of events that led to the French and Indian War began in 1748 when Memeskia's group established a new village, Pickawillany, near the head of the Miami River. Memeskia welcomed English traders from Pennsylvania, because their goods were better and cheaper than those of the French. He hoped to trade with the British free of political or military obligations.

Memeskia's move threatened not only the balance of power between Britain and France but also that between Pennsylvania and Virginia. The Pennsylvanians welcomed trade with the Miamis, for it gave them a claim to the western lands that Virginians sought. At the same time, Memeskia used his access to British traders to attract many small bands of followers to his village. Alarmed, the French shifted away from trade to force. In 1749, they sent a small expedition to cow their former Indian allies back into submission. When it failed, they began to raid dissident Indian encampments and planned to establish a fort in the Ohio River valley. With this change in French policy, Indians faced two options: to gather Indian allies (Memeskia's tactic) or to make alliances with the British (the strategy of an Iroquois chieftain named Tanacharison). Neither route promised real security, but the chaos these bids for advantage created drew the French and British into war.

In 1752, Tanacharison agreed to give Virginia not only the 200,000 acres claimed by the Ohio Company, a group of Virginia speculators, but also all the land between the Susquehanna and Allegheny Rivers (today's Kentucky, West Virginia, and western Pennsylvania). In return, Virginia promised Tanacharison's people trade and protection from their enemies. Memeskia was isolated. With no European or Indian power dominant in the region, conflicts broke out, and the French pried off some of Memeskia's allies and conquered the rest. In a raid on Pickawillany, 250 pro-French Ottawas and Chippewas killed Memeskia. Their village destroyed, the demoralized Miamis returned to the French for protection. For the moment, the French regained power, but by shifting their policy from trade to force, they set a course that would lead to the loss of their North American empire.

The Virginians Ignite a War

Both France and Virginia now claimed the Ohio River valley, and they raced to establish forts to secure their claims. Virginia entrusted the job to a well-connected 21-year-old with almost no qualifications for the post: George Washington. Washington was tied to the powerful Fairfax clan, a British family that owned 5 million acres in Virginia and held a share in the Ohio Company. In the Anglo-American world, advancement came through such linked ties of family and patronage.

In the spring of 1754, the French and Virginians scrambled to see who could build a fort first at the Forks of the Ohio (present-day Pittsburgh). The force that Virginia sent to the region, with Washington second in command, was pathetically small. Although the French army—numbering 1,000—was only 50 miles away, a combined Virginia-Indian band led by Washington attacked and defeated a small French reconnaissance party. The French and Indian War (known in Europe as the Seven Years' War) had begun.

The Virginians had bitten off more than they could chew. Washington's small fort was reinforced by British regulars but was quickly deserted by Indian allies, who recognized it as indefensible. The French overwhelmed the fort, driving Washington and his troops back to Virginia. Although war was not officially declared in Europe until May 1756, fighting soon spread throughout the frontier.

From Local to Imperial War

At the beginning of the war, the advantage was with the French. Although the population in the British colonies greatly outnumbered that of New France, France's population was three times larger than Britain's and its army 10 times the size. More important, the more centralized French state was better prepared to coordinate the massive effort an international war required. The British government, aware that lack of coordination among its colonies could cripple the war effort, in summer 1754 instructed all the colonies north of Virginia to plan for a collective defense and to shore up the alliance with the Six (Iroquois) Nations. Pennsylvania's Benjamin Franklin offered the delegates, who met in Albany, a plan, known as the Albany Plan of Union, which every colony rejected.

The localism of the American colonies made cooperation difficult if not impossible. A deeply ingrained value, localism was suspicious of the centralized European state and its army of professionals.

Britain was now in its fourth war with France in less than a century. It had authorized Virginia's foray into the Ohio River valley and sent two regiments, under the command of General Edward Braddock, to Virginia in late 1754, hoping that the colonists could fight with only a little British assistance. But the disarray continued: colonial soldiers were reluctant to obey an officer from another colony, let alone one from the British army.

With four times as many troops as the British had in North America, superior leadership, and no intercolonial rivalries, the French dominated the first phase of the war, from 1754 through 1757. The British and colonial armies planned to besiege four French forts: Fort Duquesne (Pittsburgh), Fort Niagara (Niagara Falls), Fort St. Frédéric (Crown Point, at the southern end of Lake Champlain), and Fort Beauséjour (Nova Scotia).

DEFEAT *and* DEATH *of*
GENERAL BRADDOCK
in North America ?

Braddock was to attack Fort Duquesne with a combined force of British regulars and colonial troops, but without Indians. He had alienated the regional Indians, who rejoined the French alliance. After a grueling two-month march, on July 9, 1755, Braddock's forces were surprised close to their objective by a French and Indian force. Almost 1,000 British and colonial troops were killed or wounded; Braddock himself died from wounds suffered in the ambush. One of the survivors was George Washington, who had been serving as an unsalaried adjutant to Braddock to learn the art of war.

Two of the other three planned assaults ended in disappointment as well. William Shirley, who became the British commander in chief, led the attack on Fort Niagara himself and assigned Fort St. Frédéric to William Johnson, a Mohawk

Braddock's Defeat This detail depicting Braddock's defeat is from a drawing by an engineer with the British army.

Valley Indian trader who was soon made superintendent of Indian affairs for the northern colonies. Well suited for leading Iroquois forays against the French, Johnson led a force of about 3,500, including 300 Iroquois. Their advance was stopped by the French and their Native American allies, but with equal casualties on both sides and the capture of the French commander, the British declared victory and elevated Johnson to the nobility. In the winter of 1755–1756, the British built Fort William Henry, and the French, Fort Carillon (which the British renamed Ticonderoga).

Hampered by rough terrain and intercolonial wrangling, Shirley's force never made it to Fort Niagara. The only outright success was at Fort Beauséjour, near the British colony at Nova Scotia. A British-financed expedition of New England volunteers easily seized the fort, and the British evicted 10,000 Acadians (French residents of Nova Scotia) who would not take an oath of loyalty. About 300 ended up in French Louisiana, where their name was abbreviated to "Cajuns."

Both the British and the French expected their colonists to carry most of the load of the war. Their defeats and continued intercolonial rivalries left the British vulnerable and the frontier exposed. The French began a cautious but successful offensive. First, they encouraged Indian raids along the frontier from Maine to South Carolina. Indians swung back to the French because the French appeared less dangerous than the land-hungry British. The price for French friendship, however, was participation in the war against the British. By the fall of 1756, some 3,000 settlers had been killed, and the line of settlement had been pushed back 150 miles in some places.

The French and their Indian allies seized Fort Bull in March 1756 and Fort Oswego several months later. A little over a year later, a massive French force attacked Fort William Henry. This loosely organized army of 8,000 included 1,000 Indian warriors and another 800 converted Algonquians accompanied by their Catholic priests. After a seven-day siege and heavy bombardment, the British commander surrendered on August 9, 1757. Louis-Joseph de Montcalm, the French commander, offered European-style terms: the British were to return their French and Indian prisoners, keep their personal weapons, and march back to Fort Edward, on the lower Hudson River, promising not to fight the French for 18 months. Historians still debate whether Montcalm knew what was about to take place. The Indians had expected, as was their custom, to be allowed to take plunder and captives. Denied this opportunity, they fell on the British, including the sick, women, and children, as they were evacuating the fort the next morning.

The massacre at Fort William Henry had significant repercussions. Still angry at being denied the spoils of war, Montcalm's Indian allies returned home, taking smallpox with them. The French would never again have the assistance of such a significant number of Indian allies. The British were outraged. The new British commander, Lord Jeffrey Amherst, declared the surrender terms null and void. Later, under his order, Delaware Indians who had been invited to a peace talk were given, ostensibly as presents, blankets that had been infected with smallpox. Historians are not certain whether these blankets were responsible for the outbreak of the disease among local Indians, but that was certainly Amherst's intent.

Problems with British-Colonial Cooperation

The British and the colonists blamed each other for their defeats. There was some truth in their accusations: unwillingness to sacrifice and disastrous infighting among the colonists, and arrogance among the British. These recriminations, more than any side's failing, created problems. The colonists and the British had different expectations about their roles in the war. The colonists were not prepared for the high taxes or sacrifice of liberty that waging an international war required.

The British were dismayed by what they perceived as the colonists' selfishness, as they engaged in profiteering and trading with the enemy. Colonial governments were no more generous. Braddock's expedition to Fort Duquesne was delayed by the colonies' unwillingness to provision his army.

After Braddock's defeat, colonials deserted in droves. The British began recruiting servants and apprentices, angering their masters. Another serious problem was that of quartering soldiers over the winter. Under English law, which did not extend specifically to the colonies, troops in England could be lodged in public buildings rather than private homes. In the colonies, however, there weren't enough buildings in which to house soldiers without resorting to private homes. The residents of Albany took in soldiers only under threat of force. Philadelphians were rescued by the ever-resourceful Franklin, who opened a newly built hospital to the troops. In Charleston, soldiers had to camp outdoors, where they fell victim to disease.

Other problems arose from joint operations. The British army was a disciplined professional fighting force, led by members of the upper classes; service in it was a career. In contrast, colonial soldiers were primarily civilian amateurs, led by members of the middle class from their hometowns. Colonial soldiers believed that they were fighting by contract for a set period of time, for a specific objective, for a set rate of pay, and under a particular officer. If any of the terms were violated, the soldier considered himself free to go home.

The British, however, expected the same discipline from the colonists as they did from their own army. All colonial soldiers operating with regular forces were subject to British martial law, which was cruel and uncompromising. One regular soldier, for example, was sentenced to 1,000 lashes for stealing a keg of beer, which a merciful officer reduced to a mere 900! The British officers were almost unanimous in their condemnation of colonial soldiers. According to Brigadier General James Wolfe, "The Americans are in general the dirtiest most contemptible cowardly dogs that you can conceive."

Yet the colonists certainly believed that they were doing their share. Tax rates were raised sharply, tripling in Virginia in three years, for example. The human contribution was even more impressive. At the height of the war, Massachusetts was raising 7,000 soldiers a year, from a colony of only 50,000 men. Perhaps as many as 3 out of 10 adult men served in the military during the war, and only the Civil War and the Revolution had higher casualty rates.

The British Gain the Advantage

Montcalm's victory at Fort William Henry marked the French high-water mark. After a change of government in 1757, Britain resolved to win the war, as William Pitt became head of the cabinet. His rise to power represented the triumph of the commercial classes and their vision of the empire. Pitt was the first British leader who was as committed to a victory in the Americas as in Europe, believing that the future of the British Empire lay in the extended empire and its trade. Britain's aim in North America now shifted from simply regaining territory to seizing New France itself. Pitt sent 2,000 additional troops, promised 6,000 more, and asked the colonies to raise 20,000 of their own. To support so large an army, Pitt raised taxes on the already heavily taxed British and borrowed heavily, doubling the size of the British debt. He won the cooperation of the colonies by promising that Britain would pay up to half of their costs for fighting the war. As all of this money poured into the colonies, it improved their economies dramatically.

Now the British could take the offensive (see Map 6–2). In a series of great victories, they won Louisbourg on Cape Breton Island in July 1758; then Fort Frontenac in August; and finally, in November, Fort Duquesne, which the British renamed Fort Pitt. The only defeat was at Fort Carillon (called Ticonderoga by the British). There, Susannah Johnson's husband, James, was one of the casualties. The British seized Fort Frontenac, disrupting the supply lines from the French to the Ohio Valley Indians, who shifted their allegiance. The British also moved from a policy of confrontation to one of accommodation. In the Treaty of Easton (1758), 13 Ohio Valley tribes agreed to remain neutral in return for a promise to keep the territory west of the Alleghenies free of settlers. Also, gifts to the Iroquois brought them back into the fold.

The British were now ready for the final offensive. Historians always argue about when and why a war is "lost": unless an army has been annihilated and the population entirely subjugated, which is rare, when to surrender is always a subjective decision. Political and military leaders must decide when the loss in lives and resources can no longer be justified, and the population must agree that further fighting is pointless. By 1759, some of the French believed that the war was essentially over. Casualties were extremely high, food was in short supply, and inflation was rampant. Most of the Indian allies had deserted the cause, and the French government was unable to match Pitt's spending on the war.

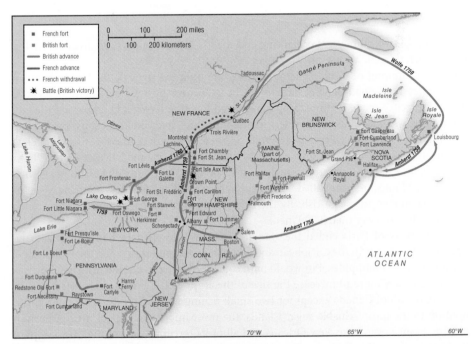

Map 6-2 The Second Phase of the French and Indian War, 1758-1763 This map shows British advances in Pennsylvania, New York, and Canada.

Benjamin West, *The Death of General Wolfe* Both the French commander, Louis-Joseph de Montcalm, and his British counterpart, James Wolfe, met their deaths on the Plains of Abraham, in Québec. Casualties were high on both sides.

It would take two more years of fighting and the loss of thousands more lives before the French surrendered, however.

In the summer of 1759, General James Wolfe took the struggle for North America into the heart of Canada, laying siege to Québec. Québec's position on a bluff high above the St. Lawrence made it almost impregnable, so for months Wolfe bombarded the city and tried to wear down its citizens, terrorizing those who lived on its outskirts by burning crops and houses. In mid-September, Wolfe ordered an assault up the 175-foot cliff below the city. In a battle that lasted only half an hour, his soldiers claimed victory on the Plains of Abraham. Each side suffered casualties of 15 percent, and both Wolfe and his French opponent, Montcalm, were killed. Four days later, New France's oldest permanent settlement surrendered to the British. By the time the British reached Montréal, the French army numbered fewer than 3,000 men.

The Treaty of Paris ended the war in 1763. By then, Britain had also seized the French sugar islands in the Caribbean and, after Spain entered the war on the French side, Havana and the Philippines. Pitt would have continued to fight, but the British public was unwilling to pay more to increase the size of the empire. The French, exhausted by war, surrendered all of Canada except for two small fishing islands in return for the right to hold on to the most valuable sugar islands, the most important part of their American empire. France even gave New Orleans and all of its territory west of the Mississippi to Spain as compensation for losing Florida, which the British claimed (see Map 6–3). (Britain let Spain keep Havana and the Philippines.) Britain staked its future on the mainland of

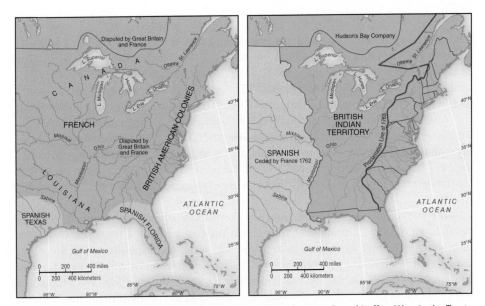

Map 6-3   The North American Colonies Before and After the French and Indian War In the Treaty of Paris in 1763, more American territory was transferred than at any time before or since.
Source: Helen Hornbeck Tanner, *Atlas of Great Lakes Indian History* (Norman: University of Oklahoma Press, 1987), p. 54.

North America, believing correctly that it would ultimately be more valuable than the sugar islands of the Caribbean.

Enforcing the Empire

Even before the French and Indian War, some in the British government urged tighter control over the American colonies. Colonists smuggled and even traded with the enemy throughout the war, and colonial assemblies sometimes impeded the war effort. Pitt had increased Britain's debt to pay for the war, rather than waiting for the colonial assemblies. Now, with the war over, Britain faced a staggering debt of £122,603,336. Moreover, there was a huge new territory to govern, one coveted by speculators and settlers and inhabited by Indian tribes determined to resist encroachment.

The American Revolution grew out of Britain's attempts to draw its American colonies more closely into the imperial system. Although various master plans for reorganizing the empire had been circulated, there had never been an overarching design or a clear set of guidelines. By 1763, there was a new resolve to enforce a vision of the empire and the role of colonies in it. In 1760, a new king, the 22-year-old George III, ascended to the throne upon the death of his grandfather. Reasonably well educated, the young king was determined to play a role in government. He changed ministers so frequently that chaos ensued. It is not clear, however, that more enlightened leadership would have prevented the war, for George's ministers pursued a fairly consistent policy toward the colonies. In resisting that policy, the American colonists developed a new and different idea of the purpose of government, one that propelled them to revolution.

Pontiac's Rebellion and Its Aftermath

Because the British had defeated the French and had entered into alliances with the Iroquois and the Ohio Valley Indians, peace in the West should have come easily. The British, however, soon made the same mistake that the French had made when they discontinued presents to their Indian allies 15 years earlier. Thinking they could impose their will on the Indians, the British instead found themselves embroiled in another war.

At the end of the French and Indian War, the western Algonquian tribes hoped the British would follow the practices of the middle ground by mediating their disputes, trading with them at good prices, and giving them presents. Lord Jeffrey Amherst, commanding British forces in North America, cut off the presents, believing them too expensive. He thought that threats of an Indian revolt were exaggerated and was willing to take the risk of war.

The war of 1763 is commonly known as Pontiac's Rebellion, named after the Ottawa chieftain who played a prominent role. It was the first battle in a long, and ultimately unsuccessful, attempt by Indians to keep the region between the Mississippi River and the Alleghenies free of European settlers. The Indians seized every fort except for Pitt, Niagara, and Detroit, and Detroit was under siege for six months (see Map 6–4). Casualties were high: about 2,000 civilians, 400 soldiers, and an unknown number of Indians. Tortures by both sides were horrific, and American colonists took out their aggressions on peaceful or defenseless Indians. In December 1763, a party of 50 armed men from the Pennsylvania village of Paxton descended on a tiny community of Christian Indians living at Conestoga Manor, eight miles west of Lancaster. They killed and scalped the six people they found— two men, three women, and a child—and burned their houses. Two weeks later, another

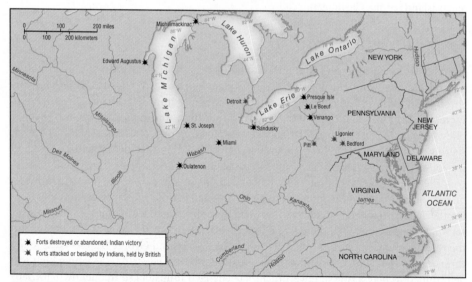

Map 6–4   Pontiac's Rebellion, 1763 The war began when the British abandoned the policy of the middle ground and cut off presents to the western Indians. In their uprising, the Indians destroyed nine British forts and attacked another four before the war ended in a draw.
Source: Helen Hornbeck Tanner, *Atlas of Great Lakes Indian History* (Norman: University of Oklahoma Press, 1987), p. 49.

group of these "Paxton Boys" broke into the county workhouse, where the remainder of the small tribe had been put for their own protection, and killed them, too.

Although colonial leaders decried acts of violence, they did little to prevent or punish them. British officials saw the failure of the colonists to maintain order on the frontier and protect innocent Indians as further proof of the incompetence of colonial governments. Even before Pontiac's Rebellion ended in a draw, the British had decided that peace with the western Indians could be preserved only by keeping colonial settlers and speculators away. The Proclamation of 1763 attempted to confine the colonists to the east of an imaginary line running down the spine of the Alleghenies. George Washington called the proclamation "a temporary expedient to quiet the minds of the Indians" and ignored it. Other Virginia speculators sought to take the territory by force. A pretext came in 1774 when several settlers killed several Indians, and John Logan, a Mingo Indian, sought vengeance for his slain relatives. Rather than resolving this conflict in the ways of the middle ground, Virginia's royal governor sent a force of 2,000 to vanquish the Indians. Although the Virginians' success in Lord Dunmore's War ended Indian claims to Kentucky, Britain was still not ready to permit speculators or settlers to claim the land.

Paying for the Empire: Sugar and Stamps

On the edge of the British Empire, the colonies were important, but not nearly as important as Britain's domestic concerns. One of George III's highest priorities was to maintain the size of the army. During the French and Indian War, it had doubled, and it was filled with officers loyal to the king. Parliament in 1763 agreed to maintain a huge peacetime army, part of which would be posted in the colonies and West Indies. Colonists feared that the army would enforce customs regulations rather than police the Indians.

This large army, of course, would strain a budget already burdened by a huge war debt. George Grenville, the new prime minister, believed that the colonists should pay a portion of the £225,000 a year that the standing army would cost.

Under Grenville's leadership, Parliament passed four pieces of legislation to force the colonies to contribute to their own upkeep. The Molasses Act of 1733 had established a duty of six cents per gallon, but smugglers paid off customs officials at the rate of one and a half cents a gallon. At Grenville's urging, Parliament passed the Sugar Act (1764), which dropped the duty to three cents but established procedures to make certain it was collected. To discourage smuggling, shippers were required to file elaborate papers each time an item was loaded onto a ship. In addition, accused violators were to be tried in admiralty courts in Nova Scotia, where the burden of proof would be on the defendant and the judgment would be rendered by judges rather than a jury.

To regulate colonial economies in the interest of British creditors, the Currency Act (1764) forbade the issuing of any colonial currency. British merchants had complained that colonists were discharging their debts in depreciated paper money. Moreover, the Sugar Act and the Stamp Act (passed the following year) required that duties and taxes both be paid in specie (silver and gold). The colonists complained that there was not anywhere near as much specie in the colonies as they needed.

The third and most important piece of imperial legislation was the Stamp Act (1765). The first direct tax on the American people, the Stamp Act sought to raise revenue by taxing documents used in court proceedings; papers used in clearing ships from harbors; college diplomas; appointments to public office; bonds, grants, and deeds for mortgages;

AMERICA AND THE WORLD

Paying for War

For most of human history, the costs of war have worked as a check on war making: a country could not spend any more on warfare than it could pay for. Some countries plundered their neighbors. Others taxed their own people, but there are always absolute limits to how much money can be extracted in this way. Other countries borrowed from foreigners, which put them at the mercy of foreign creditors.

In the seventeenth century, the Dutch figured out a new method of financing government: borrowing money from its own citizens by selling them interest-paying bonds. The government then taxed its people to pay off the bonds and the interest, which enabled it to spread out the costs of war over a long period. The result was higher taxes in peacetime—but no excessive burden during times of war. Those who bought government bonds were literally making an investment in their nation and profiting from its success.

This was the method that Britain used to pay for its rise to power beginning in the eighteenth century. It raised astronomical sums of money: £31 million for King William's War, £51 million for Queen Anne's War, £73 million for the Seven Years' War. And with each war, the government borrowed an increasing portion of the costs.

As Britain's war debt increased (see Figure 6-2)—it was up to £122,603,336 at the end of the Seven Years' War—the country had to raise taxes to pay for it. The English were paying higher taxes than any other nation in the world except for the Dutch. In fact, at the time of the French Revolution—caused in part by unacceptably high taxes—the British were taxed at a higher rate than the French. Yet the political mechanisms of taxation were so efficient that the government was able to collect tax revenues with relatively little resistance.

This achievement is remarkable when one considers the relative unfairness of the English tax system. The burden fell on the middle classes, whereas both the poor and the affluent were relatively lightly taxed. There was widespread agreement that the wages and necessities of the poor should be taxed lightly or not at all. Instead, the burden should fall, in theory, on the wealthy. Indeed, in 1690, 47 percent of England's revenues came from taxes on land and other property of the rich, but the powerful landowners refused to pay higher rates. As the need for revenue increased, the proportion of taxes paid by the wealthy fell. By 1763, it was down to 23 percent.

In search of revenue, the English government levied excise and stamp taxes, which fell most heavily on the middle classes. By the end of the Seven Years' War, the public had come close to reaching its

indentures, leases, contracts, and bills of sale; liquor licenses; playing cards and dice; and pamphlets, newspapers (and the ads in them), and almanacs.

The final piece of legislation, the Quartering Act (1765), required the colonies to house troops in public buildings and provide them with firewood, candles, and drink.

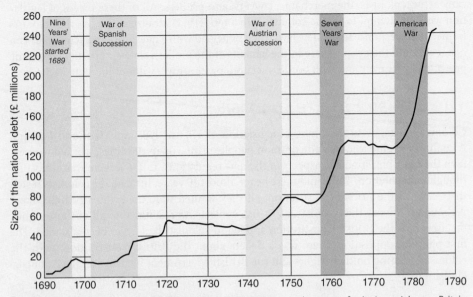

Figure 6-2 Britain's Growing National Debt, 1691–1785 In order to pay for its imperial wars, Britain took on ever-mounting debt. The burden for paying it fell to the middle class.
Source: B. R. Mitchell and Phyllis Deane, *Abstract of British Historical Statistics* (Cambridge: Cambridge University Press, 1962), pp. 401–402.

limit. Already unhappy with the tax on beer, it objected to one on cider to help finance the last year of war.

Parliament worried that it could not increase taxes on its own people any further, and so it looked for other sources of revenue in other parts of its empire. At just the time that Parliament tried to tax the American colonies to pay for the troops stationed there, it was also stationing more forces in Ireland—and trying, unsuccessfully, to get the Irish parliament to pay for them. When the East India Company conquered the huge Indian state of Bengal, King George III

imagined that India's wealth was "the only safe method of extracting this country out of its . . . load of debt." In return for letting the East India Company govern Bengal, the government extracted a fee of £400,000 a year, which the Company demanded from the Bengalis. This crushing tax burden, which coincided with a serious drought, plunged Bengal into a famine that killed 10 million people, a third of the population. With strong traditions of local government, the American colonists and the Irish were better able to resist England's attempts to tax them.

Although the colonists objected to all of these pieces of legislation, the Stamp Act was the most troubling. By taxing newspapers and pamphlets, it foolishly angered printers and editors at a time when newspapers were taking the lead in criticizing the government and were perhaps the most significant public institution in the colonies. The Stamp Act also angered lawyers, for every time a lawyer performed the simplest task of his trade, he would have to buy a stamp. These laws fell hardest on the most affluent and politically active colonists, the merchants, lawyers, and printers. All of these pieces of legislation were an attempt to tie the colonies into a modern, centralized state. As the colonists framed their response to the new laws, they struggled with a question central to American history: Could the people share in the benefits of the modern state—in particular a trade protected by its navy and with borders secured by its army—without the state itself?

The British Empire in Crisis

Colonial resistance to the imperial legislation of 1763 to 1765 was swift and forceful. A coalition of elite leaders and common people, primarily in the cities, worked to overturn the most objectionable aspects of the new regulations. In 1765, there was almost no thought of revolution, nor would there be for almost 10 years. Instead, the colonists rested their case on the British Constitution: all they wanted were the rights of Englishmen. Although in theory the colonists, as British subjects, were entitled to all of those rights, precisely how the British Constitution applied to colonists had never been clarified. The first phase of opposition, then, was a debate about the British Constitution, with the colonists insisting on their rights and the British government focusing on the colonists' obligations.

An Argument About Constitutional Government

All along, Britain had maintained its right to regulate the colonies. Precisely what this meant became a matter of dispute after 1763. Did it mean regulation of trade? Taxation? Legislation? When Parliament passed these pieces of legislation, it acknowledged that the empire was a whole, that the parts existed for the benefit of the whole, and that Parliament had the authority to govern for the whole.

Britons were justifiably proud of their Parliament, one of the premier institutions of self-government in the world at the time. In principle, Parliament represented all the elements in society: the king, the aristocrats (in the House of Lords), and the common people (in the House of Commons). It mixed and balanced these three elements of society, which also represented the three possible forms of government—monarchy, rule by the king; aristocracy, rule by hereditary aristocrats; and democracy, rule by the people—thus preventing both tyranny and anarchy and preserving liberty.

The British believed, and American colonists agreed, that their superb government was the product of centuries of struggle. First, the aristocrats struggled with the king for more freedom, gaining it in the Magna Carta of 1215, and then the people struggled and won liberty, most recently in the Glorious Revolution of 1688. In this view, liberty was a collective right held by the people against the rulers and a limitation on the power of the monarch. A chief example of public or civil liberty was the right to be taxed only by one's own representatives. Taxes were a free gift of the people that no monarch could demand.

These ideas about the British government can be described as *constitutionalism*. Constitutionalism comprised two elements: the rule of law and the principle of consent, that one could not be subjected to laws or taxation except by duly elected representatives. Both were rights that had been won through struggle with the monarch. In the decade between 1765 and the outbreak of the American Revolution, the colonists worked out their own theory of the place of the colonies in the empire. A consensus formed on the importance of the rule of law and the principle of consent. Those colonists who became revolutionaries never wavered on these two points. In the decade between the Stamp Act and the beginning of the American Revolution, what colonists debated was whether particular pieces of legislation violated these principles and how far colonists should go in resisting those that did.

British officials never denied that the colonists should enjoy the rights of Englishmen. They merely asserted that the colonists were as well represented in Parliament as the majority of Britons. In fact, only 1 out of 10 British men could vote, compared with about 70 percent of American white men. Yet British officials said that all Britons were represented in Parliament, if not "actually," by choosing their own representatives, then by virtual representation, because each member of Parliament was supposed to act on behalf of the entire empire. In Britons' minds, Parliament was supreme, and it had full authority over the colonists. In the decade between the Stamp Act and the beginning of the American Revolution, the controversy turned on only two questions: How forcefully would the British government insist on the supremacy of Parliament? And could colonial radicals put together a broad enough coalition to resist Britain's force when it came?

The Theory and Practice of Resistance

While newspapers and pamphlets were filled with denunciations of the new imperial legislation, Americans were taking their protests to the streets and to the colonial legislatures. Everywhere, a remarkable cross-class alliance of prosperous merchants and planters and poor people joined to protect what they perceived as their rights from encroachment by British officials.

By the day that the Stamp Act was to go into effect, November 1, 1765, every colony except Georgia had taken steps to ensure that the tax could not be collected. In Virginia, the House of Burgesses took the lead. A young and barely literate lawyer, Patrick Henry, played a key role in the debate on the Virginia Resolves, the four resolutions protesting the Stamp Act that were passed by the burgesses. They asserted that the inhabitants of Virginia brought with them the rights of Englishmen, that Virginia's royal charters confirmed these rights, that taxation by one's own representatives was the only constitutional policy, and that the people of Virginia had never relinquished these rights. In Boston, too, the protest united the elite with poorer colonists. Massachusetts was still reeling from the loss of life and extraordinary expense of the French and Indian War. Imperialists such as Lieutenant Governor Thomas Hutchinson wanted to tie Massachusetts more tightly to the empire. He advocated a consolidation of power, a diminution of popular government (e.g., by reducing the power of the town meeting), making offices that were elective appointive instead, and limiting the freedom of the press.

Boston's public, with its history of radicalism, was ready for a much stronger response to the Stamp Act than the Massachusetts House of Representatives seemed prepared to make. The *Boston Gazette* criticized the House's resolution as a "tame, pusillanimous, daubed, insipid thing." Once word of the more radical Virginia Resolves arrived, the *Gazette* rebuked the weak political leadership again. A group of artisans and printers who called themselves the Sons of Liberty began organizing the opposition, probably in concert with more prominent men who would emerge as leaders of the revolutionary movement, such as James Otis, John Adams, and his cousin Samuel Adams, the Harvard-educated son of a brewer.

In a carefully orchestrated series of mob actions, Bostonians made certain that the Stamp Act would not be enforced. When the militia refused to protect royal officials, including the collector of the stamp tax, the officials took refuge in Castle William in the harbor. Over several days, the mob systematically vandalized the homes of several wealthy government loyalists, including Hutchinson. Although the mob consisted mostly of artisans and poor people, it had the support of Boston's merchant elite, for no one was ever punished. The protest succeeded, and the Stamp Act was never enforced.

Not only did each colony protest against the Stamp Act, but a majority were now ready to act together. In October 1765, delegates from nine colonies met in New York in the Stamp Act Congress to ratify a series of 14 resolutions protesting the Stamp Act on constitutional grounds. At the same time, activists shut down colonial courts so that no stamps could be used, and merchants agreed not to import any British goods until the act was repealed. With 37 percent of British exports then going to the colonies, this was no idle threat (see Figure 6–3).

Facing this opposition, the British partly backed down. George Grenville was replaced by the 35-year-old Marquess of Rockingham, who preferred racehorses to politics. Parliament repealed the Stamp Act but was not prepared to concede the constitutional

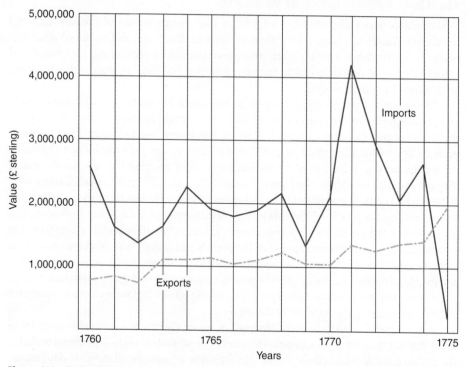

Figure 6-3   Trade Between England and the Colonies In the years between 1760 and 1775, colonial exports to England grew slowly but steadily, dropping off only after the beginning of the Revolution. On the other hand, imports from England—which always exceeded exports—rose and fell in response to political conditions. Colonial nonimportation agreements forced drops in imports after the imposition of the Stamp Act and Townshend Duties. But in both cases, imports increased after repeal, and the growth of imports after repeal of the Townshend Duties was dramatic and unprecedented.

point, asserting in the Declaratory Act of 1766 that Parliament "had, hath, and of right ought to have, full power and authority to make laws and statutes . . . to bind the colonies and people of America, subjects of the Crown of Great Britain, in all cases whatsoever."

Contesting the Townshend Duties

Britain gave up on trying to tax the colonies directly, for even some prominent Britons such as William Pitt sided with the colonists on that point. But between 1767 and 1774, those in power still tried to force their vision of empire on the colonies. In response, radical activists and thinkers formed a national opposition and took constitutionalism in new directions. By the time of the American Revolution, they had turned it into a new theory of government.

After a brief return to power by William Pitt, Charles Townshend, a brilliant but erratic man nicknamed "Champagne Charlie," became the third prime minister in as

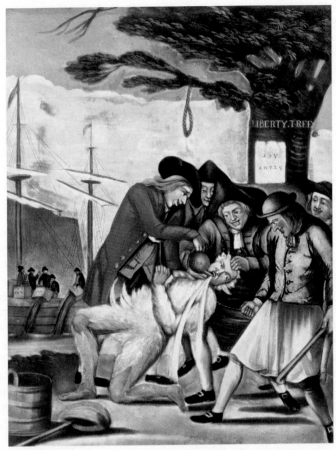

Tarring and Feathering the Customs Officer, 1774 Two Bostonians dress British customs officer John Malcolm in tar and feathers and force him to drink tea, turning him into a "macarony," an effete man who affected the latest fashion.

many years. His first act was to punish New York's assembly, which intentionally violated the Quartering Act. The assembly, denied the right to pass any legislation until it complied with the Quartering Act, quickly backed down.

The colonies refused, however, to comply with the next piece of legislation, the Townshend Revenue Act of 1767, which levied import duties on lead, paint, glass, paper, and tea. Townshend believed that the colonists objected only to taxes within the colonies, "internal taxes," but that they would accept an "external tax," such as an import duty. The revenue would be used to support colonial officials, making them independent of the colonial assemblies that had paid their salaries.

Resistance to the Townshend Act built slowly, as it was hard for colonists to make a case against all duties. Merchants were now complying with the new Revenue Act of 1766, which reduced the duty on molasses. Those colonists most troubled by the first round of imperial legislation, however, were convinced that the Townshend Duties were part of a design for tyranny.

A body of thought known as *republicanism* helped the colonists make sense of British actions. Republicanism was a set of doctrines rooted in the Renaissance that held that power is always dangerous, because "it is natural for Power to be striving to enlarge itself, and to be encroaching upon those that have none." Republicanism supplied constitutionalism with a motive. It explained how a balanced constitution could be transformed into tyranny. Would-be tyrants had access to a variety of tools, including a standing army, whose ultimate purpose was not the protection of the people but their subjection. Tyrants also engaged in corruption, in particular by dispensing patronage positions. So inexorable was the course of power that it took extraordinary virtue for an individual to resist its corruption. Consequently, republican citizens, it was thought, had to be economically independent; the poor were dangerous because they could easily be bought off by would-be tyrants. A secular theory with connections to Puritanism, republicanism asserted that people were naturally weak and that exceptional human effort was required to protect liberty and virtue.

Not only did people have to keep a close eye on power-hungry tyrants, but they also had to look inside themselves. According to republican thought, history demonstrated that republics fell from within when their citizens lost their virtue. The greatest threat to virtue was luxury, an excessive attachment to the fruits of the consumer revolution. When colonists worried that they saw luxury and corruption everywhere, they were criticizing the world that the consumer revolution had created. Although it is understandable why poor people embraced republicanism, it might seem perplexing that wealthy merchants and planters would also strongly denounce "malice, covetousness, and other lusts of man." Yet the legacy of Puritanism was powerful, and even those profiting most from the new order felt ambivalent about its effects on their society. Joining with poorer people in criticizing British officials and accusing them of attempting to undermine colonial liberties helped forge a cross-class alliance.

The colonial legislatures slowly began to protest the duties. Massachusetts's House of Representatives, led by Sam Adams, asked each of the other lower houses in the colonies to join in resisting "infringements of their natural & constitutional Rights because they are not represented in the British Parliament. . . ." When Lord Hillsborough, a hardline secretary of state for the colonies, saw the request, he instructed the colonial governors to dissolve any colonial assembly that received the petition from Massachusetts. Massachusetts refused to rescind it, so Governor Francis Bernard dissolved the legislature.

With representative government threatened, those colonial legislatures that had not already approved the Massachusetts petition did so now—and were then dissolved. In response, many legislatures met on their own, as extralegal bodies.

Not only did legislators assert their own authority, but ordinary people did so as well. In each colony, the radicals who called themselves Sons of Liberty organized a nonimportation movement using both coercion and patriotic appeal. Women were actively recruited into the movement, both to encourage household manufacture (an economic activity redefined as a political one) and to refuse British imports. In 1769, women in little Middletown, Massachusetts, wove 20,522 yards of cloth, and throughout the colonies women signed the nonimportation agreements. This politicization of ordinary people horrified conservative British observers. Although there were pockets of defiance, the movement succeeded in cutting imports dramatically. By the time that the Townshend Duties were repealed in 1770, Britain had collected only £21,000 and lost £786,000 in trade.

A Revolution in the Empire

The resistance to the Townshend Duties established a pattern that would be repeated again and again in the years before the Revolution. Each attempt to enforce the empire met with organized colonial opposition, to which the British government responded with a punitive measure. Ostensibly economic regulations such as the Sugar Act, the Townshend Duties, and the subsequent Tea Act, when rejected by the colonies, led to clearly political responses from Britain. Economics and politics became inseparable, as two visions of the empire came into conflict. Britain saw the colonies as a small but integral part of a large empire held together by an increasingly centralized and powerful government. The goal of the empire was to enhance its collective wealth and power, albeit under a system of constitutional government. Although they did not reject the notion of a larger empire outright, the colonists increasingly equated representative government with prosperity, not just for the empire as a whole but for its citizens in the colonies as well. Each round of colonial protest mobilized a larger segment of the population.

"Massacre" in Boston

Years of conflict with royal officials, combined with a growing population of poor and underemployed, had made Boston the most radical and united spot in the colonies. The political leadership had learned how to win popular favor in their ongoing strife with the governor and those who were loyal to him. The repeated attempts of the British government to enforce its legislation increased pressure on Boston and led finally to revolution.

In an attempt to tighten up the collection of customs duties, the British government, now led by Lord North, decided to make an example of John Hancock, Boston's wealthiest merchant and not yet a confirmed radical. In June 1768, customs commissioners seized Hancock's sloop, the *Liberty*, on a technical violation of the Sugar Act and threatened fines totaling £54,000 (most of which would go to the governor and the informer). All charges were dropped, however, after a riot of 2,000 "sturdy boys and men" sent the customs officials once again fleeing to Castle William for protection. Now Hancock was a radical.

After the *Liberty* riot, Governor Bernard called for troops to support the customs commissioners. Rather than restoring order, the arrival of the troops led to further conflict and a year and a half of tension. The Boston Massacre grew out of these tensions.

STRUGGLES FOR DEMOCRACY

The Boston Massacre

On the evening of March 5, 1770, shots rang out in front of the Boston custom house on King Street. The British soldiers who had fired were stunned, and three Bostonians lay dead in the snow. Two others would prove to be mortally injured. The image of the politicized populace of Boston standing up to representatives of the British army and being fired on at point-blank range is a familiar one to all American students; to this day we call the event the Boston Massacre. In this narrative, the people were united in their anger at the arrogance of the British Empire, and the tragic incident only strengthened their determination to make their voices heard.

Boston Massacre Paul Revere's iconic image of the Boston Massacre (based on Henry Pelham's design) is less an accurate representation of the event than a political statement, depicting the British soldiers as more resolute (and less frightened) and the Bostonians, who had been pelting them with snowballs, as more innocent than they in fact were.

Recent research has made it clear that the Boston "Massacre" is a misnomer. On the preceding Friday evening, some off-duty British soldiers had come to blows with some local apprentices, and tensions remained high on Monday, March 5. Locals began to taunt and torment a lone British sentry standing guard in front of the custom house. His commanding officer, Captain Thomas Preston, could see what was happening from the main guard station and came to his defense with a relief party, forming a semicircle in front of the building. A larger crowd gathered, with men shouting and daring the soldiers to fire. At length a gun did go off, and in the panic that ensued, the soldiers fired into the crowd.

Whichever element of the story one chooses to emphasize, the moment nevertheless remains an important one in the ongoing creation of American democracy. On one hand, it remains unequivocally true that the British soldiers were an unwelcome presence, a veritable army of occupation. First the Stamp Act and then the Townshend duties had genuinely aroused the ire of a colonial population long accustomed to managing without much assistance from the mother country, and who did not want to be called upon to pay the parent nation's bills. The colonists certainly did not want to host the British army. The young men who demonstrated such belligerence on March 5 were hard-working people who had been hurt by the partial strangulation of the shipyards and port caused by the British presence. Those who died included Crispus Attucks, a former slave who had run away and was supporting himself as a laborer in the city until he could join a ship's crew; Samuel Maverick,

an ivory tuner's apprentice; Samuel Grey, a laborer at a rope-making business; James Caldwell, a sailor; and Patrick Carr, a recent Irish immigrant. They and their peers all wanted a provincial point of view to be taken as seriously as the perspective of a Londoner. And as they would have wished, the incident became a rallying point in the build-up to the Revolution.

If, on the other hand, we focus on the lone sentry and the crowd that instigated the violence, we feel far less moved by the political sentiments of the angry Bostonians. Even in this regard, however, the story is an important one, in that it allowed the American political activists to demonstrate that they really were fighting for a more equitable rule of law, not a period of massive upheaval. Thanks to the efforts not only of the British army but also of the American patriots, the violence did not escalate after that evening. Two well-known lawyers, Josiah Quincy and John Adams, agreed to defend the much maligned British soldiers, despite real risk to their careers. They were successful and Captain Thomas Preston and six of the eight soldiers were acquitted. The two remaining soldiers, whom witnesses were convinced had fired at Attucks and one of the others, were found guilty of manslaughter rather than murder and they were released. It was more than they could have hoped for on the night of March 5. An important precedent had been set.

However one looks at the event dubbed "the Boston Massacre," the conflict and the anger from which it stemmed were both real. The continued suppression of the colonists' voices, through direct or indirect means, would not prove to be possible.

What angry colonists called a "massacre" was the culmination of months of scuffling between young men and adolescents and soldiers, perhaps inevitable in a town with so many men competing for work. On March 5, 1770, a fracas between a young apprentice and an army officer escalated as a crowd surrounded the officer, insulting him and pelting him with snowballs. Someone shouted, "Fire!" and the crowd grew. Seven soldiers came to rescue their terrified colleague, and they too were hit with snowballs and taunts of "Kill them." When one was knocked down, he screamed, "Damn you, fire!" and the soldiers fired on the crowd. Eleven men were wounded, and five were killed. One victim was Crispus Attucks, a 47-year-old free black sailor. The soldiers were later tried, but the only two convicted were later pardoned. The British withdrew their troops from Boston.

As long as the British were willing to back down, more serious conflicts could be avoided. The Boston Massacre was followed by a three-year period of peace. The Townshend Duties had been repealed—except the one on tea, which the colonists could not manufacture themselves—and the nonimportation movement had collapsed. Colonial trade resumed its previous pace, and in 1772, imports from England and Scotland doubled. Colonists were not prepared to deny themselves consumer goods for long. The Quartering Act had expired, and the Currency Act was repealed. As long as Britain allowed the colonists to trade relatively unimpeded, permitted them to govern themselves, and kept the army out of their cities, all could be, if not forgotten, at least silenced.

The Empire Comes Apart

Although the British government was controlled by conservatives who believed the colonists would eventually need to acknowledge Parliament's supremacy, the move that led to revolution was more accidental than calculated. The North American colonies were only part of Britain's empire. There were powerful British interests in India, where the British East India Company was on the verge of bankruptcy. Parliament decided to bail out the company, both to rescue its empire in India and to help out influential stockholders. The duty for importing tea into Britain—but not America—was canceled, and Parliament allowed the company to sell directly to Americans through a small number of agents. As a result, the price of tea would drop below that of smuggled Dutch tea. Also, only five men in Massachusetts would be allowed to sell British tea—relatives and friends of the despised Governor Hutchinson. Agents in the other colonies were also well-connected loyalists.

Radicals faced a real challenge, for they realized that once the cheap tea was available, colonists would be unable to resist it. In each port city, activists warned that the Tea Act (1773) was a trick to con colonists into accepting the principle of taxation without representation. In Philadelphia, a mass meeting pronounced anyone who imported the tea "an enemy to his country."

As might be expected, the most spirited resistance came in Boston, where Hutchinson decided the tea would be unloaded and sold—and the duty paid. Sam Adams led extralegal town meetings attended by 5,000 people each (almost one-third of the population of Boston) to pressure Hutchinson to turn the ships away. When Hutchinson refused, Adams reported back to the town meeting, on December 16, 1773: "This meeting can do nothing more to save the country!" Almost as if it were a prearranged signal, the crowd let out a whoop and poured out of the meetinghouse for the wharf. There, about 50 men, their faces darkened and their bodies draped in Indian blankets, boarded three tea-bearing ships, escorted the customs officials ashore, and opened and dumped 340 chests of tea into Boston Harbor: 90,000 pounds, worth £9,000. Perhaps as many as 8,000 Bostonians observed the "tea party." John Adams, never much for riots, was in awe. "There is," he said, "a Dignity, a Majesty, a Sublimity in this last Effort of the Patriots that I greatly admire."

The British government saw only defiance of the law and wanton destruction of property. Parliament passed five bills in the spring of 1774 to punish Boston and Massachusetts. First, the Boston Port Bill closed the port to all trade until the East India Company was repaid for the dumped tea. Second, the Massachusetts Government Act changed the Charter of 1691. The Council (upper house) would now be appointed by the king, rather than elected by the House; town meetings were forbidden without approval of the governor; the governor would appoint all the provincial judges and sheriffs; and the sheriffs would select juries, who had until then been elected by the voters. Third, the Administration of Justice Act empowered the governor to send to Britain or another colony for trial any official or soldier accused of a capital crime who appeared unlikely to get a fair trial in Massachusetts. Fourth, a new Quartering Act permitted the quartering of troops in private homes. Fifth was the Quebec Act. It assigned to Québec the Ohio River region, which the colonists coveted. In Québec, there was to be no representative government, civil cases would be tried without juries, and the Roman Catholic religion would be tolerated. Together, these acts were known in Britain as the Coercive Acts and in the colonies as the Intolerable Acts (see Table 6–1).

Table 6-1 Major Events Leading to the Revolutionary War, 1763–1774

1763	Proclamation of 1763	Confines colonists to the east of an imaginary line running down the spine of the Allegheny Mountains.
1764	Sugar Act	Drops duty on molasses to 3 cents/gallon, but institutes procedures to make sure it is collected, such as trial at Admiralty Court (closest is in Nova Scotia), where burden of proof is on defendant and verdict is rendered by judge rather than jury.
1764	Currency Act	Forbids issuing of any colonial currency.
1765	Stamp Act	Places a tax on 15 classes of documents, including newspapers and legal documents; clear objective is to raise revenue.
1765	Quartering Act	Requires colonies to provide housing in public buildings and certain provisions for troops.
1766	Declaratory Act	Repeals Stamp Act, but insists that Parliament retains the right to legislate for the colonies "in all cases whatsoever."
1767	Townshend Revenue Act	Places import duty on lead, paint, glass, paper, and tea; objective is to raise money from the colonies.
1770	Boston Massacre	Several citizens killed by British soldiers whom they had pelted with snowballs; grew out of tensions caused by quartering of four army regiments in Boston to enforce customs regulations.
1773	Tea Act	After Townshend Duties on all items other than tea are removed, British East India Company is given a monopoly on the sale of tea, enabling it to drop price—and cut out middlemen.

continued

Table 6-1 Major Events Leading to the Revolutionary War, 1763–1774 (*continued*)

1773	Boston Tea Party	To protest Tea Act, Bostonians dump 90,000 pounds of tea into Boston Harbor.
1774	Intolerable Acts	To punish Massachusetts in general and Boston in particular for the "Tea Party":
		1. Port of Boston closed until East India Company repaid for dumped tea.
		2. King to appoint Massachusetts's Council; town meetings to require written permission of governor; governor will appoint judges and sheriffs, and sheriffs will now select juries.
		3. Governor can send officials and soldiers accused of capital crimes out of Massachusetts for their trials.
		4. Troops may be quartered in private homes.
1774	Quebec Act	Gives Ohio River valley to Québec; Britain allows Québec to be governed by French tradition and tolerates Catholic religion there.
1774	First Continental Congress	Representatives of 12 colonies meet in Philadelphia and call for a boycott of trade with Britain, adopt a Declaration of Rights, and agree to meet again in a year.

At the same time, General Thomas Gage was appointed governor of Massachusetts and authorized to bring as many troops to Boston as he needed. Boston soon became an armed camp. The Port Act was easily enforced as Gage deployed troops to close the ports of Boston and Charlestown. The Government Act was another matter.

Time Line

▼**1718**
French build New Orleans

▼**1720**
French build Louisbourg and Fort Niagara

▼**1731**
French build Fort St. Frédéric

▼**1733**
Molasses Act

▼**1739–1744**
War of Jenkins's Ear

▼**1741**
Attack upon Cartagena fails

▼**1744–1748**
King George's War

▼**1748**
Village of Pickawillany established by Memeskia and his band of Miamis

▼**1749**
French military expedition fails to win back dissident Indians in Ohio Valley

▼**1752**
Tanacharison cedes huge chunk of Ohio Valley to Virginia

▼**1753**
French build small forts near forks of Ohio River

▼**1754**
Albany Plan of Union

▼**1754–1763**
French and Indian War

▼**1755**
Braddock's forces defeated

▼**1757**
British defeated at Fort William Henry, survivors massacred
William Pitt accedes to power in Britain

Citizens summoned by the sheriff simply refused to serve on juries, and some judges even refused to preside. When Gage called for an election to the legislature, only some towns elected delegates, and a shadow "Massachusetts Provincial Congress" met in Concord in October 1774. The citizens of Massachusetts had taken government into their own hands.

The British had thought that Massachusetts could be isolated, but they underestimated the colonists' attachment to their liberties. The threat to representative government presented by the Intolerable Acts was so clear that the other colonies soon rallied around Massachusetts. In June 1774, the Virginia Burgesses sent out a letter suggesting a meeting of all the colonies. At about the same time, Massachusetts had issued a similar call for a meeting in Philadelphia. These two most radical colonies spurred the others to meet in early September.

The First Continental Congress

Every colony except Georgia sent delegates to the First Continental Congress, which convened on September 5, 1774. Only a few of the delegates had ever met any of their counterparts from the other colonies, so provincial were the colonies. For seven weeks these strangers met in formal sessions and social occasions. Together they laid the foundation for the first national government.

With Massachusetts and Virginia almost ready to take up arms, and the middle colonies favoring conciliation, the greatest challenge was how to achieve unity. Since Massachusetts needed the support of the other colonies, it was ready to abandon any discussion of offensive measures against the British. In return, the Congress ratified the Suffolk Resolves, a set of Massachusetts resolutions that recommended passive resistance to the Intolerable Acts.

▼**1758**
Treaty of Easton secures neutrality of Ohio Valley tribes in return for territory west of Alleghenies

▼**1759**
British seize Québec

▼**1763**
Treaty of Paris, ending French and Indian War, signed
Pontiac's Rebellion
Proclamation of 1763
Parliament increases size of peacetime army to 20 regiments

▼**1764**
Sugar Act
Currency Act

▼**1765**
Stamp Act
Quartering Act
Stamp Act Congress

▼**1766**
Declaratory Act

▼**1767**
Townshend Revenue Act

▼**1768**
John Hancock's sloop *Liberty* seized

▼**1770**
Boston Massacre

▼**1773**
Tea Act
Boston Tea Party

▼**1774**
Intolerable Acts (known as Coercive Acts in Britain)
Lord Dunmore's War

▼**1775**
First Continental Congress

The delegates could now consider national action. Hoping to exert economic pressure on Britain, Congress issued a call for a boycott of all imports and exports between the colonies, Britain, and the West Indies. Then the delegates adopted a Declaration of Rights that for the first time expressed as the collective determination of every colony (except Georgia) what had become standard constitutional arguments. The colonists were entitled to all the "rights, liberties, and immunities of free and natural-born subjects" of England. Parliament could regulate trade for the colonies only by the "consent" of the colonies. Parliament could neither tax nor legislate for the colonies. Again and again, the Declaration reiterated the twin principles on which resistance to imperial legislation had been based: consent and the rule of law.

Finally, Congress agreed to reconvene in half a year, on March 10, 1775, unless the Intolerable Acts were repealed. The delegates had achieved consensus on the principles that would shortly form the basis for a new and independent national government.

Conclusion

Within a decade, the British Empire had come apart on its westernmost edge. The stage had been set decades earlier when Britain unintentionally allowed the colonies to develop more self-government and personal freedom than in Britain itself, without requiring them to pay a proportionate share of the costs of empire. As a result, the colonies created their own vision, one that linked democratic government and prosperity. Once Britain decided to knit the colonies more tightly into the empire and impose on them the controls of the centralized state, conflict was inevitable. At the same time, both Britons and Americans revered the same constitution, whose values and protections Americans invoked in their protests. That those protests would end in revolution was by no means a foregone conclusion. Revolution would require two key elements: Britain's unwillingness to compromise on issues of governance, and the ability of colonial radicals to convince moderates that there was no other way. By the end of 1774 that point had almost been reached.

Who, What, Where

Adams, Sam 178

Albany Plan of Union 163

Boston 160

Constitutionalism 174

Hutchinson, Thomas 175

Memeskia 162

Ohio River valley 161

Pitt, William 166

Pontiac's Rebellion 170

Proclamation of 1763 171

Republicanism 178

Washington, George 163

Review Questions

1. What were the reasons for the conflicts among the British, French, Spanish, and the various Indian tribes on the North American continent?

2. How and why did Britain attempt to reorganize its North American colonial empire?

3. Why did the colonies resist Britain's attempts to reorganize its North American colonial empire?

Critical-Thinking Questions

1. For much of the eighteenth century, Britain and France were at war, involving the American colonies. How did this warfare affect the colonies and their people?

2. What was the series of events that brought Britain and the colonies to the brink of war by 1774? To what extent were they the product of poor leadership? Differing theories of government? Different social experiences?

3. At what point did the American Revolution become unavoidable? Until that point, how might it have been avoided?

Suggested Readings

Demos, John. *The Unredeemed Captive: A Family Story from Early America.* New York: Alfred Knopf, 1994.

Morgan, Edmund S., and Helen M. Morgan. *The Stamp Act Crisis: Prologue to Revolution.* Chapel Hill: Published for the Institute of Early American History and Culture at Williamsburg, Virginia, by the University of North Carolina Press, 1953.

White, Richard. *The Middle Ground: Indians, Empires, and Republics in the Great Lakes Region, 1650–1815 (Studies in North American Indian History).* New York: Cambridge University Press, 1992.

For further review materials and resource information, please visit www.oup.com/us/oakes-mcgerr

CHAPTER 6: CONFLICT IN THE EMPIRE, 1713–1774

Primary Sources

6.1 LETTER FROM GEORGE WASHINGTON TO ROBERT DINWIDDE, GOVERNOR OF VIRGINIA (1755)

In 1755, an exhausted and ill George Washington wrote Virginia Governor Robert Dinwiddie describing General Edward Braddock's disastrous attempt to take the French fort at the Forks of the Ohio (the site of modern-day Pittsburgh). Washington describes the chaos of a battle that left the commander and 300 of his soldiers dead and Washington himself with four bullet holes in his coat. The letter also defended the conduct of the Virginia militia, whom the British blamed for the defeat.

Fort Cumberland, July 18, 1755.

. . . We continued our March from Fort Cumberland to Frazier's (which is within 7 Miles of Duquisne) with't meet'g with any extraordinary event, hav'g only a stragler or two picked up by the French Indians. When we came to this place, we were attack'd (very unexpectedly I must own) by abt. 300 French and Ind'ns; Our numbers consisted of abt. 1300 well arm'd Men, chiefly Regular's, who were immediately struck with such a deadly Panick, that nothing but confusion and disobedience of order's prevail'd amongst them: The Officer's in gen'l behav'd with incomparable bravery, for which they greatly suffer'd, there being near 60 kill'd and wound'd. A large proportion, out of the number we had! The Virginian Companies behav'd like Men and died like Soldiers; for I believe out of the 3 Companys that were there that day, scarce 30 were left alive: Captn. Peyrouny and all his Officer's, down to a Corporal, were kill'd; Captn. Polson shar'd almost as hard a Fate, for only one of his Escap'd: In short the dastardly behaviour of the English Soldier's expos'd all those who were inclin'd to do their duty to almost certain Death; and at length, in despight of every effort to the contrary, broke and run as Sheep before the Hounds, leav'g the Artillery, Ammunition, Provisions, and, every individual thing we had with us a prey to the Enemy; and when we endeavour'd to rally them in hopes of regaining our invaluable loss, it was with as much success as if we had attempted to have stop'd the wild Bears of the Mountains. The Genl. was wounded behind in the shoulder, and into the Breast, of w'ch he died three days after; his two Aids de Camp were both wounded, but are in a fair way of Recovery; Colo. Burton and Sir Jno. St. Clair are also wounded, and I hope will get over it; Sir Peter Halket, with many other brave Officers were kill'd in the Field. I luckily escap'd with't a wound tho' I had four Bullets through my Coat and two Horses shot under me. It is suppose that we left 300 or more dead in the Field; about that number we brought of wounded; and it is imagin'd (I believe with great justice too) that two thirds of both [those numbers?] received their shott from our own cowardly English Soldier's who gather'd themselves into a body contrary to orders 10 or 12 deep, wou'd then level, Fire and shoot down the Men before them.

I tremble at the consequences that this defeat may have upon our back settlers, who I suppose will all leave their habitations unless there are proper measures taken for their security.

Source: The Writings of George Washington from the Original Manuscript Sources, 1745–1799. Edited by John C. Fitzpatrick. Vol. 1.

6.2 PONTIAC'S SPEECH TO THE OTTAWA, POTAWATOMI, AND HURONS (1763)

Pontiac's Rebellion was a military campaign to drive British settlers out of the Ohio Valley and restore the Native way of life in what is known as a religious revitalization movement. Leaders promoted pan-Indian unity and the rejection of European ways of life. In this speech, given to the assembled representatives of the Ottawa, Potawatomi, and Hurons in April 1763, Pontiac tells the story of Neolin ("The Indian"), a prophet from the Delaware tribe who journeyed to the home of the Master of Life to seek his advice. This version of the speech comes from an anonymous French transcription.

After the Indian was seated the Lord said to him: "I am the Master of Life, and since I know what thou desirest to know, and to whom thou wishest to speak, listen well to what I am going to say to thee and to all the Indians: I am He who hath created the heavens and the earth, the trees, lakes, rivers, all man, and all that thou seest and hast seen upon the earth. Because I love you, ye must do what I say and love, and not do what I hate. I do not love that ye should drink to the point of madness, as ye do; and I do not like that ye should fight one another. Ye take two wives, or run after the wives of others; ye do not well, and I hate that. Ye ought to have but one wife, and keep her till death. When ye wish to go to war, ye conjure and resort to the medicine dance, believing that ye speak to me; ye are mistaken—it is to Manitou that ye speak, an evil spirit who prompts you to nothing but wrong, and who listens to you out of ignorance of me.

"This land where ye dwell I have made for you and not for others. Whence comes it that ye permit the Whites upon your lands? Can ye not live without them? I know that those whom ye call the children of your Great Father supply your needs, but if ye were not evil, as ye are, ye could surely do without them. Ye could live as ye did live before knowing them—before those whom ye call your brothers had come upon your lands. Did ye not live by the bow and arrow? Ye had no need of gun or powder, or anything else, and nevertheless ye caught animals to live upon and to dress yourselves up with their skins. But when I saw that ye were given up to evil, I led the wild animals to the depths of the forests so that ye had to depend upon your brothers to feed and shelter you. Ye have only to become good again and do what I wish, and I will send back the animals for your food. I do not forbid you to permit among you the children of your Father; I love them. They know me and pray to me, and I supply their wants and all they give you. But as to those who come to trouble your lands—drive them out, make war upon them. I do not love them at all; they know me not, and are my enemies, and the enemies of your brothers. Send them back to the lands which I have created for them and let them stay there. . . . Tell all the Indians for and in the name of the Master of Life: Do not drink more than once, or at most twice in a day; have only one wife and do not run after the wives of others nor after the girls; do not fight among yourselves; do not 'make medicine' but pray, because in 'making medicine' one talks with the evil spirit; drive off your lands those dogs clothed in red who will do you nothing but harm."

Source: Mary Agnes Burton, ed., *Journal of Pontiac's Conspiracy 1763* (Detroit: Clarence Monroe Burton under the Auspices of the Michigan Society of the Colonial Wars, 1912), pp. 28–32. http://www.americanjourneys.org/aj-135/print/

6.3 BENJAMIN FRANKLIN, EXCERPTS FROM "A NARRATIVE OF THE LATE MASSACRES" (1764)

The fullest account we have of the Paxton Boys' attacks on the Conestoga Indians comes from Benjamin Franklin, who joined with other civic leaders to persuade a force of 250 men to turn back when they began marching on Philadelphia. Franklin's sympathy for the Natives, who were Christian converts, is evident, as is his contempt for the men who attacked them. Shehaes, mentioned in the excerpt that follows, was an elderly Conestoga who had been present in 1701 when William Penn entered into a treaty with the Indians "and ever since continued a faithful and affectionate Friend to the English."

These Indians were the Remains of a Tribe of the Six Nations, settled at Conestogoe [Conestoga], and thence called Conestogoe Indians. On the first Arrival of the English in Pennsylvania, Messengers from this Tribe came to welcome them, with Presents of Venison, Corn and Skins; and the whole Tribe entered into a Treaty of Friendship with the first Proprietor, William Penn, which was to last "as long as the Sun should shine, or the Waters run in the Rivers." This Treaty has been since frequently renewed, and the Chain brightened, as they express it, from time to time. It has never been violated, on their Part or ours, till now. It has always been observed, that Indians, settled in the Neighbourhood of White People, do not increase, but diminish continually. This Tribe accordingly went on diminishing, till there remained in their Town on the Manor, but 20 Persons, viz. 7 Men, 5 Women, and 8 Children, Boys and Girls . . .

On Wednesday, the 14th of December, 1763, Fifty-seven Men, from some of our Frontier Townships, who had projected the Destruction of this little Common-wealth, came, all well-mounted, and armed with Firelocks, Hangers and Hatchets, having travelled through the Country in the Night, to Conestogoe Manor. There they surrounded the small Village of Indian Huts, and just at Break of Day broke into them all at once. Only three Men, two Women, and a young Boy, were found at home, the rest being out among the neighbouring White People, some to sell the Baskets, Brooms and Bowls they manufactured, and others on other Occasions. These poor defenceless Creatures were immediately fired upon, stabbed and hatcheted to Death! The good Shehaes, among the rest, cut to Pieces in his Bed. All of them were scalped, and otherwise horribly mangled. Then their Huts were set on Fire, and most of them burnt down. When the Troop, pleased with their own Conduct and Bravery, but enraged that any of the poor Indians had escaped the Massacre, rode off, and in small Parties, by different Roads, went home. . . .

The Magistrates of Lancaster sent out to collect the remaining Indians, brought them into the Town for their better Security against any further Attempt, and it is said condoled with them on the Misfortune that had happened, took them by the Hand, comforted and promised them Protection. They were all put into the Workhouse, a strong Building, as the Place of greatest Safety.

When the shocking News arrived in Town, a Proclamation was issued by the Governor, in the following Terms:

"Whereas I have received Information, That on Wednesday, the Fourteenth Day of this Month, a Number of People, armed, and mounted on Horseback, unlawfully assembled together, and went to the Indian Town in the Conestogoe Manor, in Lancaster County, and without the least Reason or Provocation, in cool Blood, barbarously killed six of the Indians settled there, and burnt and destroyed all their Houses and Effects: And whereas so cruel and inhuman an Act, committed in the Heart of this Province on the said Indians, who have lived peaceably and inoffensively among us, during all our late Troubles, and for many Years before, and were justly considered as under the Protection of this Government and its Laws, calls loudly for the vigorous Exertion of the civil Authority, to detect the Offenders, and bring them to condign Punishment."

. . . Notwithstanding this Proclamation, those cruel Men again assembled themselves, and hearing that the remaining fourteen Indians were in the Work-house at Lancaster, they suddenly appeared in that Town, on the 27th of December. Fifty of them, armed as before, dismounting, went directly to the Work-house, and by Violence broke open the Door, and entered with the utmost Fury in their Countenances. When the poor Wretches saw they had no Protection nigh, nor could possibly escape, and being without the least Weapon for Defence, they divided into their little Families, the Children clinging to the Parents; they fell on their Knees, protested their Innocence, declared their Love to the English, and that, in their whole Lives, they had never done them Injury; and in this Posture they all received the Hatchet! Men, Women and little Children—were every one inhumanly murdered!—in cold Blood!

The barbarous Men who committed the atrocious Fact, in Defiance of Government, of all Laws human and divine, and to the eternal Disgrace of their Country and Colour, then mounted their Horses, huzza'd in Triumph, as if they had gained a Victory, and rode off—unmolested!

The Bodies of the Murdered were then brought out and exposed in the Street, till a Hole could be made in the Earth, to receive and cover them.

But the Wickedness cannot be covered, the Guilt will lie on the whole Land, till Justice is done on the Murderers. The Blood of the Innocent will cry to Heaven for Vengeance. . . .

There are some (I am ashamed to hear it) who would extenuate the enormous Wickedness of these Actions, by saying, "The Inhabitants of the Frontiers are exasperated with the Murder of their Relations, by the Enemy Indians, in the present War." It is possible; but though this might justify their going out into the Woods, to seek for those Enemies, and avenge upon them those Murders; it can never justify their turning in to the Heart of the Country, to murder their Friends.

If an Indian injures me, does it follow that I may revenge that Injury on all Indians? It is well known that Indians are of different Tribes, Nations and Languages, as well as the White People. In Europe, if the French, who are White People, should injure the Dutch, are they to revenge it on the English, because they too are White People? The only Crime of these poor Wretches seems to have been, that they had a reddish brown Skin, and black Hair; and some People of that Sort, it seems, had murdered some of our Relations.

Source: "A Narrative of the Late Massacres [January 30, 1764]," Founders Online, National Archives (http://founders.archives.gov/documents/Franklin/01-11-02-0012, ver. 2014-05-09). *Source: The Papers of Benjamin Franklin,* vol. 11, *January 1, through December 31, 1764,* ed. Leonard W. Labaree (New Haven, CT: Yale University Press, 1967), p. 42ff.

6.4 A VISITING FRENCHMAN'S ACCOUNT OF PATRICK HENRY'S CAESAR–BRUTUS SPEECH (1765)

Patrick Henry may be best known as the man who said, "Give me liberty or give me death!" His radicalism, however, appeared much earlier than that 1775 speech. As the Virginia House of Burgesses was about to conclude its business in May 1765, Henry introduced a series of resolutions protesting the Stamp Act. He came close to committing treason when he named historic dictators who had been assassinated and suggested King George III might deserve the same fate, but he quickly backed away, pleading "the heat of passion." This description of his speech comes from the travel diary of a Frenchman who was visiting Virginia at the time.

May the 30th. Set out early from half-way house in the chair and broke fast at York[town], arived at Williamsburg at 12, where I saw three negroes hanging at the galous for having robbed Mr. Waltho[w] of 300 pounds. I went immediately to the Assembly which was seting, where I was entertained with very strong debates concerning dutys that the Parlement wants to lay on the America colonys, which they call or stile stamp dutys. Shortly after I came in, one of the members stood up and said he had read that in former time Tarquin and Julius had their Brutus, Charles had his Cromwell, and he did not doubt but some good American would stand up in favour of his Country; but (says he) in a more moderate manner, and was going to continue, when the Speaker of the House rose and, said he, the last that stood up had spoke traison, and [he] was sorey to see that not one of the members of the House was loyal enough to stop him before he had gone so far. Upon which the same member stood up again (his name is Henery) and said that if he had afronted the Speaker or the House, he was ready to ask pardon, and he would shew his loyalty to His Majesty King George the third at the expence of the last drop of his blood; but what he had said must be attributed to the interest of his country's dying liberty which he had at heart, and the heat of passion might have lead him to have said something more than he intended; but, again, if he said anything wrong, he begged the Speaker and the House's pardon. Some other members stood up and backed him, on which that afaire was droped.

May the 31st. I returned to the Assembly to-day, and heard very hot debates stil about the stamp dutys. The whole House was for entering resolves on the records but they differed much with regard [to] the contents or purport thereof. Some were for shewing their resentment to the highest. One of the resolves that these proposed, was that any person that would offer to sustain that the Parlement of England had a right to impose or lay any tax or dutys whatsoever on the American colonys, without the consent of the inhabitants therof, should be looked upon as a traitor, and deemed an enemy to his country: there were some others to the same purpose, and the majority was for entring these resolves; upon which the Governor disolved the Assembly, which hinderd their proceeding.

Source: A visiting Frenchman's account of Patrick Henry's Caesar-Brutus Speech. http://www.redhill.org/life/1765_2.html

6.5 THE STAMP ACT RIOTS: THE DESTRUCTION OF THOMAS HUTCHINSON'S HOUSE (1765)

As Lieutenant Governor of Massachusetts, a royal appointment, Thomas Hutchinson was required to enforce the Stamp Act and widely (if incorrectly) believed to support it. On the evening of August 26, 1765, a well-organized mob protesting the Act drove Hutchinson and his family from their home, looted it, and left the house in shambles. Four days later, Hutchinson described the events to a British official.

Boston Aug. 30 1765
My Dear Sir, I came from my house at Milton the 26 in the morning. After dinner it was whispered in town there would be a mob at night ans that Paxton, Hallowell, and the custom-house, and admiralty officers' houses would be attacked; but my friends assured me the rabble were satisfied with the insult I had received and that I was become rather popular. In the evening whilst I was at supper and my children round me, somebody ran in & said the mob were coming. I directed my children to fly to a secure place and shut up my house as I had done before, intending not to quit it; but my eldest daughter repented her leaving me and hastened back and protested she would not quit the house unless I did. I could n't stand against this, and withdrew with her to a neighbouring house where I had been but a few minutes before the hellish crew fell upon my house with the rage of devils, and in a moment with axes split down the door & entered. My son being in the great entry heard them cry: 'Damn him, he is upstairs we'll have him.' Some ran immediately as high as the top of the house, others filled the rooms below and cellars, and others remained without the house to be employed there. Messages soon came one after another to the

house where I was, to inform me the mob were coming in pursuit of me, and I was obliged to retire through yards and gardens to a house more remote, where I remained until 4 o'clock, by which time one of the best finished houses in the Province had nothing remaining but the bare walls and floors. Not contented with tearing off all the wainscot and hangings, and splitting the doors to pieces, they beat down the partition walls; and altho that alone cost them near two hours they cut down the cupola or lanthorn, and they began to take the slate and boards from the roof and were prevented only by the approaching daylight from a total demolition of the building. The garden-house was laid flat, and all my trees, etc., broke down to the ground. Such ruins were never seen in America. Besides my plate and family pictures, household furniture of every kind, my own, my children's, and servants' apparel they carried off about £900 sterling in money and emptied the house of everything whatsoever except a part of the kitchen furniture, not leaving a single book or paper in it, and have scattered or destroyed all the manuscripts and other papers I had been collecting for 30 years together, besides a great number of publick papers in my custody.

The evening being warm I had undressed me and put on a thin camlet surtout over my waistcoat. The next morning the weather being changed, I had not cloathes enough in my possession to defend me from the cold and was obliged to borrow from my friends. Many articles of clothing and a good part of my plate have since been picked up in different quarters of the town, but the furniture in general was cut to pieces before it was thrown out of the house, and most of the beds cut open and the feathers thrown out of the windows. The next evening, I intended with my children to Milton, but meeting two or three small parties of the ruffians, who I suppose had concealed themselves in the country, and my coachman hearing one of them say, "There he is!" my daughters were terrified and said they should never be safe, and I was forced to shelter them that night at the Castle.

The encouragers of the first mob never intended matters should go this length, and the people in general express the utmost detestation of this unparalleled outrage, and I wish they could be convinced what infinite hazard there is of the most terrible consequences from such demons when they are let loose in a government where there is not constant authority at hand sufficient to suppress them. I am told the government here will make me a compensation for my own and my family's loss, which I think cannot be much less than £3000 sterling. I am not sure that they will. If they should not, it will be too heavy for me and I must humbly apply to his Majesty in whose service I am a sufferer; but this and a much greater sum would be an insufficient compensation for the constant distress and anxiety of mind I have felt for some time past, and must feel for months to come. You cannot conceive the wretched state we are in. Such is the resentment of the people against the Stamp-Duty, that there can be no dependence upon the General Court to take any steps to enforce, or rather advise, to the payment of it. On the other hand, such will be the effects of not submitting to it, that all trade must cease, all courts fall, and all authority be at an end. Must not the ministry be extremely embarrassed.? On the one hand, it will be said, if concessions be made, the Parliament endanger the loss of their authority over the Colony: on the other hand, if external force should be used there seems to be danger of a total lasting alienation of affection. Is there no alternative? May the infinitely wise God direct you.

Source: James K. Hosmer, *The Life of Thomas Hutchinson, Royal Governor of the Province of Massachusetts Bay* (1896), 91–94.

6.6 THE INTOLERABLE ACTS (1774)

In response to the 1774 Boston Tea Party, Parliament passed a series of acts to try to bring Massachusetts back under the authority of the British Crown. The acts, which American patriots called the "Intolerable Acts," closed the Boston Harbor, allowed for trials to take place in Great Britain rather than Massachusetts, suspended local elections, and allowed for the quartering of troops on private property. Although the Quebec Act did not directly affect Boston, many patriots were angry that the British government seemed to grant more freedom to the French Catholics living in recently conquered Quebec while simultaneously curtailing political liberty in Massachusetts.

Boston Port Act:

AN ACT to discontinue . . . shipping, of goods, wares, and merchandise, at the town, and within the harbour, of Boston, in the province of Massachuset's Bay, in North America

Whereas dangerous commotions and insurrections have been fomented and raised in the town of Boston, *in the province of* Massachuset's Bay, *in New England, by divers ill affected persons, to the subversion of his Majesty's government, and to the utter destruction of the publick peace, and good order of the said town; in which commotions and insurrections certain valuable cargoes of teas, being the property of the* East India Company, *and on board certain' vessels lying within the bay or harbour of* Boston, *were seized and destroyed: And whereas, in the present condition of the said town and harbour, the commerce of his Majesty's subjects cannot be safely carried on there, nor the customs payable to his Majesty duly collected; and it is therefore expedient that the officers of his Majesty's customs should be forthwith removed from the said town: . . .* be it enacted . . ., That from and after June 1, 1774, it shall not be lawful for any person or persons whatsoever to lade, put, or cause to procure to be laden or put, off or from any quay, wharf, or other place, within the said town of *Boston,* or in or upon any part of the shore of the bay, commonly called *The Harbour of Boston.*

Administration of Justice Act:

AN ACT for or the impartial administration of justice in . . . Massachuset's Bay, in New England

Whereas in his Majesty's province of Massachuset's Bay, in New England, *an attempt hath lately been made to throw off the authority of the parliament of Great Britain over the said province, and an actual and avowed resistance, by open force, to the execution of certain acts of parliament, hath been suffered to take place, uncontrouled and unpunished, . . .: and whereas, in the present disordered state of the said province, it is of the utmost importance . . . to the reestablishment of lawful authority throughout the same;* be it enacted . . ., That if any inquisition or indictment shall be found, or if any appeal shall be sued or preferred against any person, for murther, or other capital offense, in the province of the Massachuset's Bay, and it shall appear, by information given upon oath to the governor . . . that an indifferent trial cannot be had within the said province, in that case, it shall and may be lawful for the governor . . ., to direct, with the advice and consent of the council, that the inquisition, indictment, or appeal, shall be tried in some other of his Majesty's colonies, or in Great Britain.

Massachusetts Government Act:

AN ACT for the better regulating the government of the province of the Massachuset's Bay, in New England

Whereas the method of electing such counsellors or assistants, to be vested with the several powers, authorities, and privileges, therein mentioned, . . . hath been found to be extremely ill adapted to the plan of government established in the province of the Massachuset's Bay . . ., *and hath . . . for or some time past, been such as had the most manifest tendency to obstruct, and, in great measure, defeat, the execution of the laws; to weaken the attachment of his Majesty's well disposed subjects in the said province to his Majesty's government, and to encourage the ill disposed among them to proceed even to acts of direct resistance to, and defiance of, his Majesty's authority: And it hath accordingly happened, that an open resistance to the execution of the laws hath actually taken place in the town of* Boston, *and the neighbourhood thereof, within the said Province: And whereas it is, under these circumstances, become absolutely necessary, . . . that the said method of annually electing the counsellors or assistants of the said Province should no longer be suffered to continue, . . .* Be it therefore enacted . . . that the council, or court of assistants of the said province for the time being, shall be composed of such of the inhabitants or proprietors of lands within the same as shall be thereunto nominated and appointed by his Majesty.

Quartering Act of 1765:

Whereas doubts have been entertained whether troops can be quartered otherwise than in barracks . . . in such cases, it shall and may be lawful for . . . the officer . . . in command of His Majesty's forces in *North America,* to cause any officers or soldiers in His Majesty's service to be quartered and billeted in such manner as is now directed by law where no barracks are provided by the colonies.

And be it further enacted by the authority aforesaid that, if it shall happen at any time that any officers or soldiers in His Majesty's service shall remain within any of the said colonies without quarters for the space of twenty four hours after such quarters shall have been demanded, it shall and may be lawful for the governor of the province to order and direct such and so many uninhabited houses, outhouses, barns, or other buildings as he shall think necessary to be taken (making a reasonable allowance for the same) and make fit for the reception of such officers and soldiers, and to put and quarter such officers and soldiers therein for such time as he shall think proper.

Quebec Act:

AN ACT for making effectual Provision for the Government of the Province of Quebec, in North America

It is hereby declared, That His Majesty's Subjects professing the Religion of the Church of Rome, of, and in the said Province of *Quebec,* may have, hold, and enjoy, the free Exercise of the Religion of the Church of Rome . . . and that the Clergy of the said Church may hold, receive, and enjoy their accustomed Dues and Rights, with respect to such Persons only as shall profess the said Religion.

Source: http://www.ushistory.org/declaration/related/intolerable.html

Photo Credits

Chapter 1: Photo by DeAgostini/Getty Images, 2-3; Gianni Dagli Orti/National History Museum, Mexico City/The Art Archive/Art Resource, NY, 4; 100 B.C.-A.D. 200 Mexico, Nayarit Culture Ceramic 30.5 × 25.4 × 17.1 cm. Gift of Joanne P. Pearson, in memory of Andrall E. Pearson, 2015. Metropolitan Museum of Art Accession Number: 2015.306, 7; Cahokia Mounds State Historic Site. Photo by Art Grossman, 9; Bettmann/Getty Images, 15; Photo by DeAgostini/Getty Images, 20; Granger–All rights reserved, 24; Benson Latin American Collection, University of Texas, Austin, 28; Photo by DeAgostini/Getty Images, S1-1; DEA/SIOEN/Getty Images, S1-1.

Chapter 2: Indians Fishing (colour litho), White, John (fl. 1570–93) (after)/Private Collection/Bridgeman Images, 32–33, 55; Indian in Body Paint (litho) White, John (fl. 1570–92) (after). Private Collection/Bridgeman Images, 34; Granger–All rights reserved, 42; Governor Peter Stuyvesant (1592–. . .) Couturier, Hendrick (fl. 1648-d.c . . .). Collection of the New York Historical Society, USA/Bridgeman Images, 54; © The Trustees of the British Museum/Art Resource, NY, 56.

Chapter 3: Granger–All rights reserved, 60–61; National Portrait Gallery, Washington, D.C. (Photo by VCG Wilson/Corbis via Getty Images), 62; Granger–All rights reserved, 64; Marilyn Angel Wynn/Nativestock.com, 67; Ira Block/Getty Images, 67; Pilgrim Hall Museum, Plymouth, MA, 78.

Chapter 4: An American Indian Man and his M . . . Mexican School, (18th century). Museo de America, Madrid, Spain/Bridgeman Images, 88–89, 119; Photo by Briggs Co./George Eastman House/Getty Images, 90; NYC Department of Records & Information Services, 94; Plan et Scituation des Villages Tchikachas Plan and Situation of the Chicksaw Villages, Alexandre de Batz, 1737. French copy of a map made by a visitor to the Chicksaw, 97; Plymouth County Commissioners, Plymouth Court House, Plymouth, MA/Dublin Seminar for New England Folklife, Concord, MA, 105; Courtesy of The Newberry Library, Chicago. Call # Ayer MS map 30, Sheet 77, 115; Kevin Fleming/Corbis/VCG/Getty, 117.

Chapter 5: Granger–All rights reserved, 124–125, 149; Courtesy of the Library of Congress, 126; Granger–All rights reserved, 131; Granger–All rights reserved, 138; Mr. Peter Manigault and his

Friends, 1854, By Louis Manigault (American, 1828–1899) after George Boone Roupell (1726–1794), Wash and ink on paper, Gift of Mr. Joseph e. Jenkins, 1968.005.0001, Image courtesy of the Gibbes Museum of Art/Carolina Art Association, 140; Courtesy of the Library of Congress, S5-3; GraphicaArtis/Getty Images, S5-7.

Chapter 6: Benjamin West, 1738–1820 The Death of General Wolfe, 1770 oil on canvas 152.6 × 214.5 cm National Gallery of Canada Gift of the 2nd Duke of Westminster to the Canadian War Memorials, 1918, Transfer from the Canadian War Memorials, 1921, 156–157, 168; Frontispiece from *A Narrative of the Captivity of Mrs. Johnson* (Bowie, MD: Heritage Books, Inc. 1990), p. v, 181, 158; Granger–All rights reserved, 164; Granger–All rights reserved, 177; Granger–All rights reserved, 180.

Chapter 7: Yale University Art Gallery, 188–189, 201; Abigail Smith Adams, c 1766 (pastel on paper), Blyth, Benjamin (c. 1746-c. 1786)/Massachusetts Historical Society, Boston, MA, USA/Bridgeman Images, 190; Granger–All rights reserved, 194; Courtesy of the Library of Congress, 195; Anonymous, 18th century English, after J.F. Renault: The British surrendering their arms to General Washington after their defeat at Yorktown in Virginia, October 1781. Colored engraving, Inv.: CFAc 295. © RMN-Grand Palais/Art Resource, NY, 204; Granger–All rights reserved, 211.

Chapter 8: Henry Francis Du Pont Winterthur Museum, 24–225, 233; Courtesy Independence National Historical Park, 226; Henry Francis Du Pont Winterthur Museum, 233; Residence of Washington in High . . . Breton, William L. (fl. 1830). Library Company of Philadelphia, PA, USA/Bridgeman Images, 235; Map located in the Military Journal of Major Ebenezer Denny, an officer in the Revolutionary and Indian Wars (J.B. Lippincott & Co., for the Historical Society of Pennsylvania, 1859), available via the Boston Public Library (E83.79.D4 1859 ×), 244; Granger–All rights reserved, S8-4.

Chapter 9: Courtesy of the Library of Congress, 256–257, 267; Anna Claypoole Peale, American, 1791–1878. Andrew Jackson (1767–1845) 1819 Watercolor on ivory 3 1/8 × 2 7/16 in. (7.9 × 6.2 cm) Mabel Brady Garvan Collection 1936.302. Yale University Art Gallery, 258; American

Antiquarian Society copy the gift of Armstrong Hunter, 1991, 265; Kean Collection/Getty Images, 273; Catlin, George (1796–1872) Ten-squát-a-way, The Open Door, Known as The Prophet, Brother of Tecumseh. Shawnee. 1830. Oil on canvas. 29 × 24 in. (73.7 × 60.9 cm) Location: Smithsonian American Art Museum, Washington, DC, U. Photo Credit: Smithsonian American Art Museum, Washington, DC/Art Resource, NY, 280; Image located in Robert Stuart Sanders, Presbyterianism in Paris and Bourbon County, Kentucky, 1786–1961 (First Presbyterian Church, 1961), p. 209, 282.

Chapter 10: Granger–All rights reserved, 288–289, 308; McKenney and Hall (19th CE) John Ross, A Cherokee Chief. From History of the Indian Tribes of North America. ca. 1843. Hand-colored lithograph on paper. 19 5/8 × 13 3/8 in. (49.9 × 34 cm). Smithsonian American Art Museum, Washington, DC/Art Resource, NY National Portrait Gallery, Smithsonian Institution, gift of Betty A. and Lloyd G. Schermer, 290; Granger–All rights reserved, 292; Granger–All rights reserved, 299; Page 041, in the Manigault Family Papers #484, Southern Historical Collection, Wilson Library, University of North Carolina at Chapel Hill, 305; Courtesy of the Library of Congress, 320; Gilcrease Museum, Tulsa, OK, 322; Courtesy of the Library of Congress, S10-4.

Chapter 11: Geoffrey Clements/Getty Images, 330–331, 345; Courtesy of the Library of Congress, 332; Courtesy of the Library of Congress, 333; Granger–All rights reserved, 335; Photo by: Universal History Archive/UIG via Getty Images, 339; Granger–All rights reserved, 350; Granger–All rights reserved, 354.

Chapter 12: Photo by Herbert Orth/The LIFE Images Collection/Getty Images, 360-361, 381; Granger–All rights reserved, 362; Courtesy of the Library of Congress, 365; Apic/RETIRED/Getty Images, 373; George Catlin (1796–1872) [Buffalo Hunt, with Wolf-Skin Mask.], 1844. Toned lithograph with applied watercolor. Amon Carter Museum of American Art, Fort Worth, Texas, 376; Los Angeles Public Library, 386; Thomas Cole, Landscape, 1825 oil on canvas 23 ¾ × 31 ½ in. Minneapolis Institute of Art 15.299 Bequest of Mrs. Kate L. Dunwoody, S12-3; Granger–All rights reserved, S12-4; Louis Rémy Mignot Landscape in Ecuador, 1859 24 × 39 ½ in. (61.0 × 100.3 cm) Oil on canvas. Purchased with funds from gifts by the American Credit Corporation in memory of Guy T. Carswell, and various donors, by exchange 91.2, S12-4.

Chapter 13: Granger–All rights reserved, 388–389, 415; Frederick Douglass. ca. 1855.

Daguerreotype, 7.0 × 5.6 cm (2 ¾ × 2 3/16 in.). The Rubel Collection, Partial and Promised Gift of William Rubel, 2001 (2001.756). Image copyright © The Metropolitan Museum of Art. Image source: Art Resource, NY, 390; Outward Bound, The Quay of Dubli . . . Nicol, J (19th century) (after). Collection of the New York Historical Society, USA/Bridgeman Images, 393; Granger–All rights reserved, 399; Granger–All rights reserved, 407; Courtesy of the Library of Congress, 411.

Chapter 14: Granger–All rights reserved, 420–421, 446; Penn School Papers, Southern Historical Collection, University of North Carolina at Chapel Hill, 422; Granger–All rights reserved, 431; Granger–All rights reserved, 441; Courtesy of the Library of Congress, 445; David Gilmour Blythe (American, 1815–1865), Lincoln Crushing the Dragon of Rebellion, 1862 oil on canvas 45.72 × 55.88 cm. Museum of Fine Arts Boston 48.413 Bequest of Martha C. Karolik for the M. and M. Karolik Collection of American Paintings, 1815–1865. Photograph © 2018 Museum of Fine Arts, Boston, 451; Culver Pictures/The Art Archive/Art Resource, NY, 453.

Chapter 15: Photo by MPI/Getty Images, 458–459, 489; Courtesy of the Library of Congress, 460; Courtesy of the Library of Congress, 468; Courtesy of the Library of Congress, 473; Bettmann/Getty Images, 480; Granger–All rights reserved, 482; Courtesy of the Library of Congress, 486.

Chapter 16: The Granger Collection, 496–497, 510; The Granger Collection, 498; The Granger Collection, 505; Curt Teich Postcard Archives Collection (Newberry Library) DPC79785, 507; California History, Vol. 64, No. 3, Summer 1985, page 174 (University of California Press and California Historical Society), 515; The Granger Collection, 522; Courtesy of the Library of Congress, S16-2.

Chapter 17: Courtesy of the Ohio History Connection, 524–525, 541; Nebraska State Historical Society, 526; Photo by PhotoQuest/Getty Images, 529; The Granger Collection, 534; Bettmann/Getty Images, 535; Weir, John Ferguson (1841–1926) Forging the Shaft. 1874–77. Oil on canvas, 52 × 73 ¼ in. (132.1 × 186.1 cm). Purchase, Lyman G. Bloomingdale Gift, 1901 (01.7.1). Location: The Metropolitan Museum of Art, New York, NY, USA Photo Credit: Image copyright © The Metropolitan Museum of Art. Image source: Art Resource, NY, 550; Kansas State Historical Society, 553; The Granger Collection, S17-5; Courtesy of the Library of Congress, S17-7; Courtesy of the Library of Congress, S17-7.